# Advance Praise for
## *Put Y'all Back in Chains*

"Whether you agree or disagree, Horace Cooper's latest book tackles the question of how Joe Biden's policies affect Americans, especially those in minority and underserved communities. His research shows that the injuries are calamitous. Instead of a rising tide lifting all boats, the Biden policies are having a reverse effect, one that devastates bank accounts, crushes entrepreneurship, and steals the promise of the American Dream.

"Horace painstakingly combs through the harsh results of these efforts, especially on lower income and working class people, who are hit hardest by the woke-policies of Joe Biden. If you want to see the real story the media isn't telling, this book is a must read!"

— SEAN HANNITY, Fox News Host

"Horace Cooper 'breaks every chain' while shining the light on racist, divisive politics from President 47. Read this eye opener today."

— ALVEDA KING, PhD

"It's always been one of life's great mysteries: why is it that 90 percent of blacks vote for Democrats year after year when the Dems have done so much to hold blacks down? Horace Cooper shows the folly of blacks voting for the policies that deter advancement and attainment of the American Dream."

— STEPHEN MOORE, who formerly wrote on the economy and public policy for the *Wall Street Journal*, is a distinguished fellow in economics at The Heritage Foundation

## Also by Horace Cooper

*How Trump is Making Black America Great Again:*
*The Untold Story of Black Advancement in the Era of Trump*

# PUT Y'ALL BACK IN CHAINS

## HOW JOE BIDEN'S POLICIES HURT BLACKS

## HORACE COOPER

BOMBARDIER
BOOKS

Published by Bombardier Books
An Imprint of Post Hill Press
ISBN: 978-1-63758-706-5
ISBN (eBook): 978-1-63758-707-2

Put Y'all Back in Chains:
How Joe Biden's Policies Hurt Black Americans
© 2023 by Horace Cooper
All Rights Reserved

Cover Design by Matt Margolis

Post Hill Press
New York • Nashville
posthillpress.com

Published in the United States of America
1  2  3  4  5  6  7  8  9  10

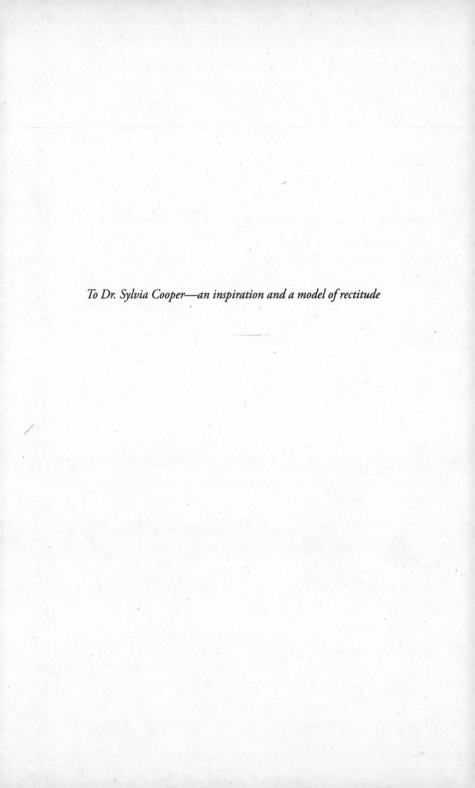

*To Dr. Sylvia Cooper—an inspiration and a model of rectitude*

# TABLE OF CONTENTS

# INTRODUCTION

In the fall of 2019, Biden's campaign was tattered and failing. Despite his best efforts, Biden's third try at the White House was struggling. To many analysts, it was looking a lot like the first two in 1988 and 2008.

Let's review:

In 1987, Biden was the Chairman of the Senate Judiciary Committee, where he was working with Senator Ted Kennedy to thwart Reagan's appointment of Robert Bork to the Supreme Court and simultaneously setting up a run for his first presidential campaign.

Robert Bork was a sitting judge on the most prestigious federal appeals court: the D.C. Circuit. A former Yale Law School professor, Bork was a highly regarded constitutional scholar. Court watchers predicted that he might provide the critical fifth vote to overturn *Roe v. Wade*.

Joe Biden's academic credentials weren't as impressive: he had earned a BA at the University of Delaware and later received his law degree from Syracuse University. Unlike the Supreme Court, politics doesn't require exceptional academic credentials.

Biden likely considered that his high profile as Chair of the Committee overseeing the nomination could only aid his nascent presidential run. For this reason, Biden publicly promised that Judge Bork would have a "full and fair" hearing. However, at the same time, he had not so privately promised civil rights groups (in order to aid his presidential campaign) that he would lead the opposition to the nomination.[1] At the time, even the *Washington Post*—no friend of Robert Bork—editorialized about Biden's cyn-

---

1    Kelly Sadler, "Want to Destroy Democracy? Look to the Left," *Washington Times*, June 29, 2022, https://www.washingtontimes.com/news/2022/jun/29/want-to-destroy-democracy-look-to-the-left/.

icism, writing, "As the Queen of Hearts said to Alice, 'Sentence first—Verdict Afterward.'"[2]

But Biden's presidential campaign ended as quickly as it began. For a candidate known for being a long-winded gaffe-machine,[3] it shouldn't be a surprise that it was this very trait that took him down. Biden's presidential campaign was tripped up by a speech he gave at the Iowa State Fair in September 1987,[4] which was copied almost word for word from one that had been given by British Labor Party Leader Neil Kinnock.[5] Maybe Biden thought that it wouldn't be noticed, since Kinnock was based in the UK and he was in the USA.

But the press noticed, and once they started digging around, they discovered that there were many instances of misappropriation and falsehoods by Biden, going all the way back to his law school days. For instance, he was forced to admit that he had given speeches by Hubert Humphrey and Robert Kennedy, presented as his own. Further digging revealed that he'd misrepresented his class ranking in law school. In fact, he'd barely graduated.[6] It was also uncovered that Biden had publicly said in a debate that he'd

---

2    Michele L. Norris, "Judge Bork and the Democrats," *Washington Post*, July 10, 1987, https://www.washingtonpost.com/archive/opinions/1987/07/10/judge-bork-and-the-democrats/a5da635a-6912-45a7-bd10-0ce462892e27/.

3    Michelle Cottle, "Straight Man," *New Republic*, May 6, 2009, https://newrepublic.com/article/61661/straight-man.

4    James Risen and Richard E. Meyer, "No Time to Cite Source, He Says: Biden Stirs Row by Using Lines From Briton's Talk," *Los Angeles Times*, September 13, 1987, https://www.latimes.com/archives/la-xpm-1987-09-13-mn-7557-story.html.

5    Tamara Keith, "For Joe Biden, 1987 Brought Triumph In The Wake Of Political Setback," NPR, December 21, 2019, https://www.npr.org/2019/12/21/789323826/for-joe-biden-1987-brought-triumph-in-the-wake-of-political-setback.

6    Daniel Funke, "Ad Watch: Fact-checking a Video About Biden's Academic Record," *Politifact*, May 7, 2020, https://www.politifact.com/article/2020/may/07/ad-watch-fact-checking-video-about-bidens-academic/. Biden graduated 76th of 85.

never supported tuition tax credits—the bete noire of the teacher's unions—but his voting record showed otherwise.[7] It seemed that Biden's willingness to dissemble was widespread.

Shortly after his 1988 campaign began, it was over.

The 2008 campaign wasn't much better. Running in a primary that was a Who's Who of prominent Democrats—including Barack Obama, Bill Richardson, Hillary Clinton, John Edwards, and Chris Dodd—Biden positioned himself as the "national security" candidate.

Once again, he talked himself out of the race. One of his biggest gaffes occurred in trying to damn Obama with faint praise, calling him "the first mainstream African-American who is articulate and bright and clean and a nice-looking guy.[8]" The pushback by Democrats was intense. His campaign management abilities weren't much better—he fell well short of the $20 million fundraising goal that he had said he'd need to compete in the early primary states, raising just over $11 million instead. He would get blown out of the water in the Iowa Caucuses, scoring less than 1 percent of the vote, and dropped out shortly thereafter.

Proving his commitment to the "triumph of hope, over experience," Biden ran for a third time in 2019. But the sophomore who had boasted to classmates, at the famed Archmere Academy in Claymont, Delaware, that he wanted to be President of the United States found himself, yet again, spending time in his latest campaign explaining his exaggerations and gaffes instead of pushing his platform.

First, in the summer of 2019, there was "segregationist-gate," based on Biden's wistful memory of working with segregationist

7    Risen and Meyer, "No Time to Cite Source."

8    Xuan Thai and Ted Barrett, "Biden's description of Obama draws scrutiny," CNN, February 9, 2007, https://www.cnn.com/2007/POLITICS/ 01/31/biden.obama/.

Senators Eastland and Talmadge. "I was in a caucus with James O. Eastland," Biden boasted. "He never called me 'boy,' he always called me 'son.'" Then he praised his own ability to work with Talmadge, saying that he was "one of the meanest guys I ever knew," but "Well guess what? At least there was some civility. We got things done. We didn't agree on much of anything. We got things done. We got it finished.[9]" Blacks and progressives—key constituencies of the party—were horrified.

Then, near the end of July, during the second presidential primary debate, Biden said that illegal immigrants wouldn't be a priority and that they should "get in line" and wait to enter the country legally. Later, in August, he explained that "poor kids are just as bright and just as talented as white kids.[10]" These gaffes fed into his reputation as a blowhard and raised concerns about what his core beliefs really were.

But the rank and file had additional criticisms. They worried that the 77-year-old Biden was too old to be President. A whisper campaign started about his mental agility, and some commentators openly wondered if this campaign would end the way the two others had. In response, before the year was out, he'd be forced to release medical records showing that he was healthy, with no significant medical issues.

Unsurprisingly, the early primaries were especially brutal to Biden. In Iowa, Biden ended up in fourth place, behind Pete Buttigieg, Bernie Sanders and Elizabeth Warren. In New

9    Eric Bradner, "Joe Biden Recalls Working With Segregationist Senators: 'At Least There Was Some Civility'," CNN, June 19, 2019, https://www.cnn.com/2019/06/19/politics/joe-biden-senate-segregationists-civility/index.html.

10   Adam Edelman and Mike Memoli, "Biden says 'poor kids are just as bright and just as talented as white kids'," *NBC News*, August 9, 2019, https://www.nbcnews.com/politics/2020-election/biden-says-poor-kids-are-just-bright-just-talented-white-n1040686.

Hampshire, he did worse, placing fifth behind all of those he'd lost to in Iowa, and now even behind Amy Klobuchar.

What was a murmur then became a roar: media observers were saying openly that third time might not be the charm for Joe Biden. Other insiders were suggesting that he adopt a "second ballot strategy"—since he wouldn't be able to win the nomination outright, he should stay in the race long enough to win at a brokered convention.

And then Biden's campaign had an epiphany, realizing that the first primaries were dominated by non-black voters, even though blacks are the Democratic base. If the campaign could get blacks to vote for Biden, he would have enough support to win the primary outright.

It worked. Biden worked behind the scenes to get South Carolina Rep. Jim Clyburn's endorsement. In a passionate speech, Clyburn told Democrat primary voters, "I'm fearful for my daughters and their future and their children and their children's future.[11]" On primary day, Biden would win 61 percent of the vote. Fifty-six percent of the voters that day were black.

The rest is history. Thanks to the backing of blacks, Biden—the "law and order" author of the 1988 crime bill and lifelong opponent of busing—would go on to win the 2020 primary. He would then win the election, fulfilling his childhood dream.

But what of black voters? In many ways, what should have been seen as a great accomplishment for blacks has turned into a nightmare:

---

11    Donna M. Owens, "Jim Clyburn changed everything for Joe Biden's campaign. He's been a political force for a long time," *Washington Post*, April 1, 2020, https://www.washingtonpost.com/lifestyle/style/jim-clyburn-changed-everything-for-joe-bidens-campaign-hes-been-a-political-force-for-a-long-time/2020/03/30/7d054e98-6d33-11ea-aa80-c2470c6b2034_story.html.

Biden's shifts in policies created turmoil for most Americans, but especially for blacks.

Biden bragged that he would reverse Trump's policies, and he did. Blacks would find out the hard way what this meant.

Since 2017, Blacks have seen record low unemployment. Record numbers were able to buy their first home or new automobile or start their own business.

But by the summer of 2022, much of their successes had been wiped away. According to the Employment Policy Institute, the black-white unemployment gap had risen to 2.2 to 1 (blacks are unemployed 2.2 times the rates of whites)—higher than it had been in the last year of the Trump Administration. The policies of Joe Biden have led to record levels of inflation, which have hit blacks the hardest. Biden's mismanagement of the supply chain has created scarcity at the grocery store, and gasoline prices have jumped to levels never seen in the U.S. before. Through it all, blacks have been among the worst to suffer.

This outcome isn't simply bad luck or coincidence. Galatians 6:7 must be remembered: "Be not deceived; God is not mocked: for whatsoever a man soweth, that shall he also reap.[12]"

Blacks, as well as other Americans, have been severely economically damaged—not by the pandemic, but by falling for the idea that policies that confiscate wealth and punish those who are successful, treating us all based solely on group identities (thereby rejecting the idea that Americans are individuals), is the best way for everyone to succeed.

Perhaps the most dangerous idea of all is that these policies could occur at the hands of a central government located in Washington that would create and ensure prosperity is provided to the people at large. This scheme has never worked anywhere or

---

12    Galatians 6:7, https://www.kingjamesbibleonline.org/Galatians-6-7/.

anytime it has been tried. In fact, it can never work. Add to that the toxic notion that our physical characteristics are the primary factors about us as citizens, which has been poisonous for blacks and further limited achievement. History shows that punishing achievers by confiscating their wealth so that bureaucrats can redistribute it only makes everyone poorer.

The failure of this idea is obvious when looking at how America—and in particular, blacks—prospered from 2017 to early 2020 due to policies that reward thrift, risk, and achievement. Unlike most recent U.S. economic growth spurts, during the Trump years, the least among us—underserved groups, including blacks and the working class in general—gained ground faster than everyone else. Yet today, the policies Biden promotes have yielded the opposite effect, and blacks have been hardest hit.

The following chapters will explain his policies and their effects. Americans, especially black Americans, have been put back in chains.[13]

---

13   Maggie Haberman, "They're going to put y'all back in chains," Burns & Haberman Blog, *Politico*, August 14, 2012, https://www. politico.com/blogs/burns-haberman/2012/08/theyre-going-to-put-yall-back-in-chains-updated-132073. "Romney…said in the first 100 days, he's going to let the big banks once again write their own rules. Unchain Wall Street. They're going to put y'all back in chains."

# CHAPTER ONE

# BIDENOMICS IS LYNCHING BLACK AMERICANS' ECONOMY

Perhaps the greatest measure of President Joe Biden's destructive anti-black policies is his unacceptably poor stewardship of the economy. Having inherited the hottest economy in a generation, America might now be headed for a double-dip recession, which disproportionately hurts black Americans.

Going into the COVID-19 pandemic, black employment was setting records on a near-monthly basis, hitting marks that in some cases had not been seen in half a century, and in other cases had never been seen at all.[1] The massive disruptions caused by the virus and the government-mandated lockdowns—promoted by an elite professional class that enjoyed the benefits of remote work in white-collar jobs—was devastating to working- and middle-class workers, who are disproportionately minorities.[2] However, by the second quarter of 2020, employment was sharply rebounding, and the economic recovery was well under way when President Biden was sworn into office in January 2021.[3]

1   "The Employment Situation—February 2020," U.S. Department of Labor, Bureau of Labor Statistics, March 6, 2020, https://www.bls.gov/news.release/archives/empsit_03062020.pdf.

2   "Profile Of The Labor Force By Educational Attainment," U.S. Department of Labor, Bureau of Labor Statistics, August 2017, https://www.bls.gov/spotlight/2017/educational-attainment-of-the-labor-force/pdf/educational-attainment-of-the-labor-force.pdf.

3   "The Employment Situation—January 2021," U.S. Department of Labor, Bureau of Labor Statistics, February 25, 2021, https://www.bls.gov/news.release/archives/empsit_02052021.pdf.

That was the critical moment when the federal government decided to make a sharp turn backwards to heavy regulation and expanded government welfare programs—policies not put in place in decades. This approach has undeniably stalled the jobs recovery.

According to the U.S. Bureau of Labor Statistics, many of the gains that blacks made during the Trump years have been lost. By the end of December 2021, black unemployment was twice as high as that of whites.[4] After dropping to a record low of 5.4 percent, it reached 7.1 percent in December 2021.[5]

Two years before, pre-pandemic, the labor market had been as tight as it is today. One might think this is good news. A worker shortage *should* give workers leverage for higher wages, strengthening the social fabric. Prior to the pandemic, unemployment rates overall had reached their lowest level in over thirty years, and the number of total population working also set records. Additionally, both the employment growth and wage increases were greatest among the groups who traditionally fare the worst in the workplace: women, young workers, minorities, and the less educated. This reduces welfare utilization and crime levels in urban communities, which makes them more attractive places for business and residential development, which in turn creates even more jobs and can lead to higher levels of marriage and family stability.

However, today's worker shortage has resulted in a labor market so tight that—as Federal Reserve Chairman Jay Powell said—

---

4    Kristen Broady and Anthony Barr, "December's Jobs Report Reveals a Growing Racial Employment Gap, Especially For Black Women," Brookings Institution, January 11, 2022, https://www.brookings.edu/blog/the-avenue/2022/01/11/decembers-jobs-report-reveals-a-growing-racial-employment-gap-especially-for-black-women/.

5    "US Unemployment Rate: Black or African American, 5.80% for Sep 2022," YCharts, October 7, 2022, https://ycharts.com/indicators/us_unemployment_rate_black_or_african_american.

it is simply "unhealthy."[6] Fewer Americans are working; the labor force participation rate—the measure of the percentage of working-age Americans in the workforce—is lower now that it was pre-pandemic.[7] Consequently, the tight labor market isn't helping those who could benefit the most but instead has enriched those already well-entrenched in the workforce. The present tight labor force isn't reducing welfare use, and it is generally more concentrated in the suburbs or rural parts of the country. In other words, thee poor, young, and minorities do not benefit.

Another major consequence of the present overly-tight labor market is that the price of almost any service that requires labor is substantially more costly. This situation disproportionately hurts working- and welfare-class households. When significantly fewer people are working, the compensation for those who *are* working is dramatically higher. This is very beneficial if you're employed in a high-paying job, but everyone else will face significantly higher prices for everything, from eating out to going to the movies to grocery shopping. Likewise, middle- and upper-income families are not only more likely to be employed now, but they can also absorb these hikes, while those with lower or no income—especially blacks—cannot.

Why is this tight labor market different? The Biden Administration's anti-growth policies are the chief cause. They place more emphasis on government making payments directly to Americans, instead of creating an environment where more jobs can be created (letting people find their own prosperity in

6    https://fortune.com/2022/03/16/labor-market-unhealthy-tight-jerome-powell-rate-hikes-recession/

7    Mitra Toossi, "Labor Force Projections To 2022: The Labor Force Participation Rate Continues To Fall," Monthly Labor Review, U.S. Bureau of Labor Statistics, December 2013, https://www.bls.gov/opub/mlr/2013/article/labor-force-projections-to-2022-the-labor-force-participation-rate-continues-to-fall.htm.

the private sector as a result). The results are slow or zero wage growth, a lower job participation rate, and inflation that has completely overtaken wage growth—families that take home more income find that their household expense increases have erased their gains. Thus, the Biden policies have created stagflation: high inflation with limited economic growth. America has only seen this phenomenon once before: in the 1970s, when a moderately high inflation period was impacted by the embargo of oil by the Organization of Petroleum Exporting Countries (OPEC).

## OIL PRICE SPIKES

In 1973, President Nixon supported the state of Israel in the Yom Kippur War. The oil-producing countries of the Middle East responded by ending oil sales to America. This embargo hit an already weak economy. The price of oil shot up nearly 400 percent. Though the embargo only lasted through 1974, oil prices never returned to their pre-embargo level; they stayed more than 33 percent higher for nearly a decade.[8] At the same time, the Federal Reserve adopted a policy of keeping interest rates low to stimulate the economy. The embargo caused moderate inflation and slow growth to turn into explosive inflation, and economic growth all but stalled. Economists say that America's low economic growth, the expanding welfare state, funding for the Vietnam War, a declining manufacturing sector, and rising inflation joined with the oil embargo to knock America's economy flat.[9] This stagflation lead to Americans' economic suffering for nearly a decade.

---

8    Edward Heath, quoted in James T. Patterson, *Grand Expectations: The United States, 1945-1974* (New York: Oxford University Press, 1996).

9    "Definition of Stagflation," Economics Help, https://www.economicshelp.org/blog/glossary/stagflation/.

Signs point to a similar phenomenon today. Biden has expanded the welfare state with more than a trillion dollars in payments and subsidies, mostly in the name of COVID-19 mitigation. He's pushing for increasing military payments to Ukraine. He's ignored the domestic manufacturing industry and enacted anti-growth taxes on corporate America.

These policies are a reversal of the economic measures adopted during Trump's presidency. From 2017 through early 2020, the labor market was tight in a *positive* way, leading to meaningful wage growth across the board for the first time in decades.[10] However, in 2021 and 2022, there was a significant net reduction in the number of people in the job market compared to pre-pandemic levels,[11] which is now leading to what should fairly be called over-competition for too few workers, leading to huge price spikes and employers who can't find workers at a price they can pay. Even the workers themselves are frustrated, with many dropping out of the workforce. Some are taking early retirement, others are relying on a single source of household income, and still others are moving to areas with a lower cost of living. In sum, a collection of wrongheaded policies have chased people out of the workforce, leading to supply-chain disruptions and contributing to the highest inflation in forty years.

In a deeply destructive move for black America, left-wing policymakers have used the pandemic to experiment with much higher unemployment benefits. Coupled with far-left regulatory schemes such as the push for "environmental justice" and war on the fos-

---

10    "The Employment Situation—February 2020," U.S. Department of Labor, Bureau of Labor Statistics, February 6, 2020, https://www.bls.gov/news. release/archives/empsit_03062020.pdf.

11    "The Employment Situation – December 2021," U.S. Department of Labor, Bureau of Labor Statistics, January 7, 2022, https://www.bls.gov/news.release/ archives/empsit_01072022.pdf.

sil-fuel industry, this policy has made it harder for working-class people (particularly black men) to stay gainfully employed.

The high unemployment benefits mean that millions of Americans are now paid *more* to *not work* than they would earn if they took a job. Some Washington politicians, and their supporters at far-left think tanks, continue to argue that high unemployment benefits are not affecting employment. However, more centrist and conservative-leaning research institutions and think tanks overwhelmingly recognize the obvious: expanded unemployment benefits discourage labor participation.

The question is to what degree these policies have pushed workers out of the workforce permanently.[12] Some might ask: Why work when you can get the same, or more, money to catch up on Netflix from the comfort of your own couch? There are a few problems with this approach. First of all, the money for payments eventually runs out; indeed, it already has in most states. This puts average workers—and disproportionately, black workers—further behind than if they had gotten back to work as soon as possible. Everyone but progressives knows that staying in the workforce is the fastest way to improve one's skills and experience, and thereby increase one's earning potential.

Secondly, not having a job, or work of any kind, creates a toxic situation. The habit of having a job improves the habit of working professionally with other people and developing skills. Shutting that engine off for a lengthy period of time leaves people less valuable as employees—hence, less competitive—once they do get around to job hunting.

---

12    Sophia Campbell, Nasiha Salwati, and Louise Sheiner, "Hutchins Roundup: Pandemic Unemployment Benefits, Corporate Tax Cuts, And More," Brookings Institution, December 23, 2021, https://www.brookings.edu/blog/up-front/2021/12/23/hutchins-roundup-pandemic-unemployment-benefits-corporate-tax-cuts-and-more/.

America is a free-market country. Notwithstanding the dreams of progressives, the American ethos is not socialist. Misleading working-class Americans, especially blacks—who need high-growth policies the most in order catch up—likely leads to a heightened willingness to conclude that America is systemically unfair and unjust. Is this the outcome that progressives seek?

Third, businesses, especially small businesses, will adapt to having fewer workers, either by increasing automation or by shuttering their doors. This means more chaos for a community and the job market at large.

Last but not least, giveaway programs are rife with fraud. In March 2022, the Department of Justice reported that more than $8 billion in fraud was either being investigated or charged.[13] And this is likely the tip of the iceberg. Total fraud exceeds $100 billion, according to testimony by Michael Horowitz, Department of Justice Inspector General and chair of the Pandemic Response Accountability Committee before the Senate Homeland Security Committee.[14] As infamous bank robber Willie Sutton[15] might say, defrauding the feds' pandemic assistance programs happened because that's where the money is.

---

13    Tony Romm, "Justice Department Reports More Than $8 Billion In Alleged Fraud Tied To Federal Coronavirus Aid Programs," *Washington Post*, March 10, 2022, https://www.washingtonpost.com/us-policy/2022/03/10/justice-department-coronavirus-aid-fraud/.

14    Natalie Alms, "There's No Final Number Yet For Pandemic Fraud, Oversight Leaders Tell Congress," FCW, March 21, 2022, https://fcw.com/congress/2022/03/theres-no-final-number-yet-pandemic-fraud-oversight-leaders-tell-congress/363400/.

15    "Willie Sutton: The Colorful Character Who Said He Robbed Banks 'Because That's Where The Money Is' Was One Of The First Fugitives Named To The FBI's Top Ten List," Federal Bureau of Investigation, accessed October 28, 2022, https://www.fbi.gov/history/famous-cases/willie-sutton.

## UNIVERSAL BASIC INCOME: A UNIVERSALLY STUPID IDEA

Left-wing policymakers have a long-term strategy to implement Universal Basic Income (UBI): direct payments to every person of working age, able-bodied or not, with the goal of creating a future utopia where most people don't need to work. The lion is going to lie down with the lamb in peace and harmony before that ever happens. Meanwhile, this scheme would lead to the biggest skill-atrophying that Americans have ever seen.

UBI is a bad idea all around. It creates the wrong incentives and stings taxpayers in the process, and for blacks, it's a lose-lose situation. The justification most often given for UBI is that automation will eventually render most human jobs obsolete, and therefore, a vast system of government handouts is needed to take care of millions of people whose jobs will have been replaced by robots.[16]

Democrat Andrew Yang based almost his entire 2020 presidential run on this premise.[17] But this fearmongering is contradictory to the reality of what is actually likely to happen. Automation has been expanding for over a century, and the effects have been fairly consistent. Some workers do indeed get displaced by new technologies, but new job categories of work always emerge, usually not far geographically from the old ones.

In the late nineteenth century, opponents of the automobile industry predicted that it would destroy the agricultural, horse-breeding, and buggy (or carriage) industries, as well as the

---

16    Katharine Miller, "Radical Proposal: Universal Basic Income to Offset Job Losses Due to Automation," Stanford University, Institute for Human-Centered AI, October 20, 2021, https://hai.stanford.edu/news/radical-proposal-universal-basic-income-offset-job-losses-due-automation.

17    Kevin Roose, "His 2020 Campaign Message: The Robots Are Coming," *New York Times*, February 2, 2018, https://www.nytimes.com/2018/02/10/technology/his-2020-campaign-message-the-robots-are-coming.html.

related jobs associated with horse-drawn travel, thus leading to an economic downturn. But the birth and expansion of the automobile had untold positive ripple effects: industries that supported automobile manufacturing appeared all over the country. The rubber industry exploded. Even the federal and state governments got into the act of creating thousands of new jobs as they funded new roads and highways.

In the middle of the twentieth century, critics of the burgeoning computer industry feared that computers would overwhelm society, predicting that humans might be replaced by machines, or—more ominously—become slaves to them. In fact, the fear of computers was so severe that "computerphobia" became an actual term referencing this apprehension.[18]

These concerns were unwarranted. Data storage has dramatically lowered the cost of business operations and led to significantly improved working conditions, while expanding the number of office jobs and improving efficiency in data organization and data access. The ability of computers to handle untold tasks for not only industries but also households has expanded economic growth and made the computer an essential tool for modern life.

## ROBOTS ARE ALREADY HERE

Contrary to the plots of movies like *I, Robot* or *The Terminator*, the robotics industry is not a serious threat to Americans or to our economy. Robots and related technology will likely give companies needed tools for monitoring and managing, potentially even enabling them to have viable substitutes for tedious jobs. Instead of overthrowing civilization, robots could make it far easier for

---

18   Adrienne LaFrance, "When People Feared Computers," *Atlantic*, March 30, 2015, https://www.theatlantic.com/technology/archive/2015/03/when-people-feared-computers/388919/.

Americans to keep manufacturing in America rather than out-sourcing to other countries. No matter what jobs humans continue to carry out, having more jobs in America not only helps the U.S. economy as a whole but also black Americans in particular—since their employment participation rate is lower than the overall rate, any new jobs will increase the pool of options for them.

Liberals would like Americans to panic about an imaginary jobs apocalypse, and in anticipation, they've proposed new, complicated, and incredibly expensive federal benefits programs. This approach is likely to be fiscally ruinous.

For years, responsible people have warned of the limits of the federal government's ability to incur tens of trillions of dollars in debt. President Biden's policies have already inflicted on Americans a forty-year high in inflation. If that isn't bad enough for working families, all Americans should understand that inflation is not just a crisis today but a warning of much worse if the federal government continues to cut trillion-dollar checks.

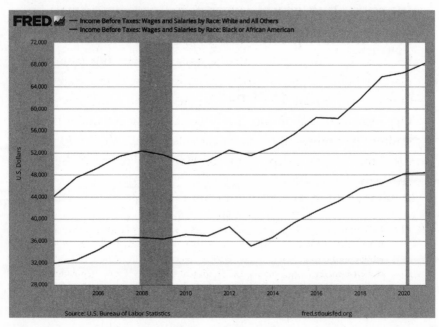

This would be devastating for blacks, who have already trailed whites in income and wages for decades. Stagflation caused by these handouts would pull the rug out from under black families.

The really sneaky part here is that the Left has a strategic rationale for promoting anti-robot hysteria: its policies will create a permanent underclass that progressives can count on for support for decades to come because people without productive work become people without ambition. For liberal politicians grasping for ever more power, it is a dream scenario. Black citizens, who today have jobs and are making progress in society—and most black people were making *remarkable* progress during the Trump presidency—would be disproportionately victimized by this approach. Creating a client population of tens of millions of welfare recipients, whose only "job" is to vote for politicians that maintain and expand the handouts, is wonderful for political office holders. For black Americans, it's a nightmare.

## INDEPENDENT CONTRACTORS: AN OPPORTUNITY FOR BLACKS THREATENED BY BUREAUCRACY

Fortunately, UBI remains off the table for now. But labor regulations being cranked out at all levels of government are very much a live threat. The Biden Administration—with the U.S. Department of Labor and the National Labor Relations Board leading the charge—is trying to throttle workers' ability to work for companies as independent contractors,[19] known as the "gig economy."[20]

---

19    Levi Sumagaysay, "Gig work could change under Biden's Labor secretary. Here's how," *MarketWatch,* May 4, 2021, https://www.marketwatch.com/story/gig-work-could-change-under-bidens-labor-secretary-and-heres-how-11620141865.

20    Robert Longley, "Gig Economy: Definition and Pros and Cons," Thoughtco, March 15, 2019, https://www.thoughtco.com/gig-economy-4588490.

For years, independent contractors have enjoyed the freedom to come and go in ways that those in traditional jobs cannot. Leftists want to throw up roadblocks for them, and they are succeeding at the state as well as the federal level. California, home of many crazy leftist schemes, is just one of the states trying to make life harder for middle-class people. The workers taking advantage of gig-economy opportunities are disproportionately minorities and disproportionately black.[21]

This is not the first time that the Left has promoted policies that cripple blacks. In fact, much of the modern legislation to "help" American workers was enacted primarily to aid whites by obstructing competition from black workers.

While most Americans take for granted that the minimum wage and the forty-hour work week came about as a result of an effort to improve the lives of working Americans, this is simply not true. In fact, these measures were rooted in the anti-black racism of the day and were actually part of an effort to benefit white workers at the expense of black tradesmen.[22] These policies helped to create persistent high unemployment for blacks then, and when new versions of these laws and regulations are advocated today, they should shed a light on the real motivations of so-called progressives.

Many Americans, including blacks, don't realize that today's high black unemployment is a relatively new phenomenon. From the end of the Civil War to just prior to the Depression, blacks (especially men) saw ballooning job opportunities. Some blacks

---

21    "The Gig Economy," Marketplace-Edison Research Poll, Edison Research, December 2018, http://www.edisonresearch.com/wp-content/uploads/2019/01/Gig-Economy-2018-Marketplace-Edison-Research-Poll-FINAL.pdf.

22    Horace Cooper, "The Untold, Racist Origins of 'Progressive' Labor Laws," Capital Research Center, June 2014, https://capitalresearch.org/app/uploads/2014/06/LW1406-final-for-posting-140528.pdf.

chose to negotiate wage payments with their former slaveholders. Others fled the plantation to engage in completely different types of work,[23] such as the merchant marines and tradesman jobs like plumbing and boot-making. Later in the nineteenth century, as the Industrial Revolution exploded in America, blacks jumped in to take advantage by holding crucial jobs in industry.[24]

The movement by blacks from the South to the manufacturing jobs of the North was most pronounced near the turn of the twentieth century. What began in the 1880s as a trickle grew larger and larger,[25] and by 1910, nearly 500,000 southern blacks had moved north in what would be known as the Great Migration.[26] According to the New York Journal of Commerce, by 1923, the number of whites outnumbered blacks in South Carolina for the first time in the existence of the United States.[27] Cities in the North experienced a population boom. Detroit's population ballooned from 465,755 in 1910 to nearly a million by 1920,[28] the black population during that period increasing seven-fold.[29] The Associated Press reported at the time that the Black migration

---

23    "The African American Odyssey: A Quest for Full Citizenship. Reconstruction and Its Aftermath," Library of Congress, https://www.loc.gov/exhibits/african-american-odyssey/reconstruction.html.

24    Asha Banerjee and Cameron Johnson, "African American Workers Built America," The Center for Law and Social Policy, February 26, 2020, https://www.clasp.org/blog/african-american-workers-built-america/.

25    Theodore Kornweibel, "An Economic Profile of Black Life in the Twenties," *Journal of Black Studies* 6, no. 4 (June 1976): 307.

26    Peter Kalinski, "African American Workers at Ford Motor Company," (updated in 2020 with additional text by Curator of Transportation Matt Anderson), The Henry Ford Museum of American Innovation, February 26, 2013, https://www.thehenryford.org/explore/blog/african-american-workers-at-ford-motor-company/.

27    W.E.B. Du Bois, "The Hosts of Black Labor," *The Nation* 116, (May 9, 1923): 539-41.

28    Kalinski, "Ford Motor Company."

29    Kalinski, "Ford Motor Company." The black population in Detroit increased from 5,741 to 40,838.

north was so significant that the state of North Carolina canceled more than fifty highway construction projects.[30] The Ford Motor Company was the single largest employer of blacks in the US from 1920 to 1930.[31]

At the beginning of the twentieth century, blacks held a position that other racial groups envied: black men were more likely to be employed than any other men,[32] black children were as likely as whites to be born in two-parent married households,[33] and white men were much more likely to be in federal prison than blacks.[34] The number of black millionaires exploded. In fact, there were more black millionaires in the first half of the twentieth century than there would be in the next twenty-five years, even though the black population grew a great deal over that time frame.[35]

## THE ROARING 20S

During the very period that blacks were making a major relocation from the South, U.S. Senator Warren G. Harding won a landslide election as President, a repudiation of the economic and social policies of progressive Woodrow Wilson.

---

30    Victoria B. Turner, "Industrial Relations and Labor Conditions," *Monthly Labor Review* 16, no. 6 (June 1923): 1278, https://www.jstor.org/stable/41828652# metadata_info_tab_contents.

31    Kalinski, "Ford Motor Company."

32    Amity Shlaes, *The Forgotten Man: A New History Of The Great Depression* (New York: Harper Collins, 2007).

33    Thomas Sowell, *Black Rednecks and White Liberals* (San Francisco: Encounter Books, 2005), 161.

34    Margaret Werner Cahalan and Lee Anne Parsons, "Historical Corrections Statistics in the United States,1850–1984," U.S. Department of Justice, Bureau of Justice Statistics, https://bjs.ojp.gov/content/pub/pdf/hcsus5084.pdf.

35    Center for Social Policy, *A Dream Deferred: The Economic Status of Black Americans.* A Working Paper, Washington: Center for the Study of Social Policy, 1983, http://pi.lib.uchicago.edu/1001/cat/bib/554030.

Harding believed that the U.S. economy needed room to grow and that federal expenditures should be curtailed.[36] He appointed as Treasury Secretary the industrialist and philanthropist Andrew Mellon, who believed in economic growth and publicly advocated policies similar to those derived from today's Laffer Curve. Mellon believed that if taxes on business were lowered, the feds would receive higher revenues because business expansion would yield more funds for the nation at large to use.[37] Successfully pushing debt and tax reduction, and a balanced budget, Mellon oversaw rapid economic growth and prosperity in the American economy that came to be known as the "Roaring Twenties."

America's total wealth more than doubled between 1920 and 1929, and from 1922 to 1929, Gross National Product (GNP) expanded by 40 percent.[38]

Blacks overwhelmingly benefited from these policies.

It was during this period that the population shifted to an urban rather than rural life.[39] This was also the period of the Jazz Age and the Harlem Renaissance.[40] The African American population in Harlem grew over 40 percent between 1910 and 1930: from 50,000 to over 200,000 [41] During this period, there was a

36    Eugene P. Trani, "Warren G. Harding: Domestic Affairs," Miller Center, University of Virginia, accessed October 30, 2022, https://millercenter.org/president/harding/domestic-affairs.

37    "Andrew W. Mellon (1921–1932)," U.S. Department Of The Treasury, https://home.treasury.gov/about/history/prior-secretaries/andrew-w-mellon 1921-1932.

38    "The Roaring Twenties," The History Channel, https://www.history.com/topics/roaring-twenties/roaring-twenties-history.

39    History, "The Roaring Twenties."

40    Femi Lewis, "Black History Timeline: 1920–1929," updated July 02, 2019, ThoughtCo, https://www.thoughtco.com/african-american-history-timeline-1920-1929-45440.

41    "Black Capital: Harlem in the 1920s," The New York State Museum, accessed November 21, 2022, http://www.nysm.nysed.gov/exhibitions/ongoing/black-capital-harlem-1920s-0.

dramatic increase in the number of Blacks buying homes, and at a faster rate than whites.[42]

Most federal labor law in the United States originated from efforts to saddle black men with extra burdens and limitations, in order to—as racists of the day often put it—"protect white jobs."[43] These laws, in one form or another, remain on the books today and continue to hamper the ability of blacks, especially men, to enjoy gainful employment. Yet the Left hails these laws for their supposed ability to aid America's working class, and their baleful effects continue.

The effect of these laws was to undo what was perhaps one of the most remarkable phenomena in American history: Black men at the start of the twentieth century were the most likely to be employed among all racial groups.

That bears repeating: The unemployment rate for blacks—even as late as 1930—was lower than the rate for whites.[44]

The intrusion by the federal government that occurred early in the twentieth century proved to be so sufficiently enduring that, even a hundred years later, blacks (especially men) are disproportionately limited in the U.S. workforce. Yet the advocates for government intervention in the economy now proclaim themselves the strongest advocates of blacks and the working class and claim that the economy needs more intrusion because America is so bigoted and irredeemably racist.

That's a slur against Americans as well as denial of the facts. No reasonable person would argue that Americans, as a people,

---

42    William J. Collins and Robert A. Margo, "Race and Home Ownership from the End of the Civil War to the Present—Preliminary Draft," November 2010, https://www.bu.edu/econ/files/2013/03/101122_sem777_Robert-Margo-Paper-1.pdf. Figure 1: Rates of Owner-Occupancy, 1870-2007: Households Headed by Males, Ages 25-64, in Labor Force, Not in School ("Core Sample").

43    Cooper, "Untold, Racist Origins."

44    Shlaes, *The Forgotten Man*.

undermine the interests of blacks today more than they did a hundred years ago. If that were the case, why was black employment so robust in the 1920s—fewer than sixty years after the Civil War? It isn't the views of Americans that explain today's economic disadvantage of blacks; it's the existence of failed economic theories. Today's Left would have Americans believe that the policies that racists used nearly a century ago to *thwart* the economic interests of blacks should now be used to *help* blacks.

Just as a hammer nails and a shovel digs, heavy-handed economic regulation kills—yesterday and today.

Let's review the history: Progressive icon Woodrow Wilson screened the pro-Ku-Klux-Klan movie *Birth of a Nation* at the White House, and simultaneously, the KKK became one of the nation's most influential groups in Washington.

The idea of restricting blacks' access to "white jobs" through federal regulation was planted then; it took root in the 1920s, and it blossomed during President Roosevelt's New Deal—a "deal" created in significant part by an Alabama Klansman named Hugo Black. The ability of government to manipulate the economy and, by doing so, to harm blacks was shown to be a workable model.

This pattern was repeated in the 1960s and early 1970s. With the advent of the "Great Society," and federal programs like Aid to Families with Dependent Children (welfare), Food Stamps, Head Start, and affirmative action, blacks lost ground compared to the general population.[45]

---

45    Horace Cooper, *How Trump is Making Black America Great Again* (New York: Post Hill Press, 2020), https://posthillpress.com/book/how-trump-is-making-black-america-great-again-the-untold-story-of-black-advancement-in-the-era-of-trump.

## THE GIG ECONOMY: A BOON FOR BLACK AMERICANS THAT'S UNDER ATTACK

Today, this approach continues. The Left's latest target is the independent contractor industry—also called the "gig economy"—that allows Americans to be their own bosses, set their own schedules, and control their own work activities.

When a major theme of the Leftwing media is that blacks—especially black men—can't get a break in corporate America, the gig economy provides a viable alternative. Typically, there's no box to check or even a background review—people either want your assistance or they don't. Given the obstacles to "standard" employment placed in their path by progressives, it is no wonder that blacks have disproportionately chosen this field.[46]

And now, the Biden Administration is waging war on this industry.[47] One might think it's a *good* thing that modern technology has created the opportunity for people almost anywhere to be able to jump into work with companies that coordinate deliveries or to undertake many other forms of work that can be done from home. A normal person might say, "Oh good! People can make money in dozens of different industries, even without a college degree, by taking on work that suits their schedule and their interests. That's freedom. That's opportunity."

But leftists say, "That's horrible! Where is the HR Department? Where are the 500 pages of paperwork for 'on-boarding' that raise

---

46    "Contingent and Alternative Employment Arrangements—May 2017," U.S. Bureau of Labor Statistics, June 7, 2018, https://www.bls.gov/news. release/pdf/conemp.pdf. Agency temps, on-call, and contract company employees are more likely to be African American or Hispanic.

47    Nandita Bose, "U.S. Labor Secretary supports classifying gig workers as employees," Reuters, April 29, 2021, https://www.reuters.com/world/us/exclusive-us-labor-secretary-says-most-gig-workers-should-be-classified-2021-04-29/.

the costs of trying to do business? It's way too easy for gig workers to come and go! Let's make it more difficult!"

Take California, for example. Under the state's new "AB5" law, independent contractors must not only show that they set their own work hours and operate a separate business; they must also prove that they provide services to the business or customer that is outside the core functions of the business or customer paying them. The core functions test is essential. For example, if a waste management company has a need for part-time contractors during a holiday, under the new rule, anyone they bring on to assist them with garbage removal would have to be an employee. Before that, they could literally let any person show up and join the crew and then pay them at the end of the day. The waste management company can hire accountants or lawyers as independent contractors, but it can't hire "contractors" to help with trash pick up since that's a core function. Additionally, a contractor couldn't be used to drive buses for a bus company as that is a core function of the bus business, even if the contractor only worked weekends or was a standby substitute. Similarly, a bakery can't let a non-employee cook handle extra demand during the Christmas season. To be clear, AB5 doesn't bar companies from hiring anyone. It only governs whether they are considered employees or contractors.

Under AB5, few would qualify as independent contractors—which is the goal of the California law. While it doesn't ban gig workers, it simply makes it very difficult to legally be one.

Passed in January of 2020, AB5 is the most anti-independent-contractor law in the nation[48]

Independent contractors provide significant flexibility in the US economy. These gig workers can be hired or dismissed rel-

---

48    Stephen Fishman, J.D., "California's Historic AB5 Gig-Worker Law," NOLO Network, accessed October 28, 2022, https://www.nolo.com/legal-encyclopedia/california-gig-worker-law-AB-5.html.

atively easily, allowing small and large companies to expand or contract easily.

AB5 changes that equation.

Hiring employees (not gig workers) requires interviews and background checks. Employees also present legal liabilities: under the legal doctrine of *respondeat superior*, employers are responsible for the actions of their employees. In contrast, employers are not responsible for the actions of gig workers.

The Left claims that American companies are systemically racist. If so, why make it harder to get paid for the work you're able to do? Gig work eliminates the need for background checks and often even the interviews, since the relationship with the company isn't permanent.

There are other downsides to laws like AB5. Being designated as an "employee" adds between 20 percent and 30 percent to labor costs, since employers are required to pay Social Security and Medicare taxes, unemployment and disability insurance, workers' compensation, and other employment-related expenses. Blacks (as well as other marginalized workers such as those with felony convictions or high-school dropouts of all races) are typically the losers under this scheme since their market value might not exceed these costs. The Left forgets that the only reason one gets hired is if one brings sufficient value to the employer to cover all of his administrative and tax costs, as well as the actual cost of the labor one provides. Employers don't set salaries arbitrarily. Whatever the job, the salary offered assumes that the employer will do better than break even when hiring an employee. For instance, if you are an employer and you pay someone 25k a year, you are only doing so if you, the employer, expect to benefit more than 25k from the arrangement. Employers will not stay in business if they benefit less than $25k.

The employer's assessment doesn't stop with the salary. He must pay health and taxes for his employee. These can add between 15 percent and 30 percent to the bottom line. Thus, the employer must receive in value from the worker $25k + taxes + medical, or nearly $29k. If the employee doesn't provide more in value to the employer than 29k, a prudent employer won't hire.

Gig work or independent contractors bridge the gap.

Gig workers easily undercut full-time employees by as much as 40 percent, since they often don't require training or supervision or payment of any employment taxes and they can be paid hourly or monthly. In other words, the business only has to pay for what he needs as long as he needs it. When you as an independent contractor can offer to work for up to 40 percent less, you have a big advantage in the market. In fact, blacks have found this area of work very attractive; today they are 11.8 percent of gig workers.[49] Expanding an anti-freedom and anti-worker agenda nationwide not only harms blacks but also demonstrates how the Biden Administration is perpetuating the same anti-black-worker policies that the Left has done for more than a hundred years.

It may be the case that the federal court system will eventually shut down this attempt to kill the gig economy. Until then, policymakers in many cities and states, as well as the Biden Administration, are creating a chilling effect for many companies and job-seekers looking to earn a living. Blacks—especially those with arrest records—are disproportionately paying the price.

---

49    "Courier/Independent Contractor Demographics And Statistics In The Us," Zippia, https://www.zippia.com/courier-independent-contractor-jobs/demographics/.

## COVID-19 LOCKDOWNS: STILL AWFUL

Not since the Spanish flu of 1918 has a pandemic affected American society the way COVID-19 has. According to the Centers for Disease Control and Prevention (CDC), the H1N1 virus was first identified in U.S. military personnel in the spring of 1918[50] and eventually infected more than 500 million people—one third of the planet's total population. More than 675,000 Americans would die from the Spanish flu.[51]

The strategies then for combatting the disease looked remarkably similar to those undertaken over the past two years. There was a mask mandate, and schools, theaters, and businesses were ordered closed.[52] In New York City, the health commissioner even ordered businesses to open and close on staggered shifts to avoid overcrowding the subway.[53] Even President Woodrow Wilson would get infected.[54]

Make no mistake—the Spanish Flu was serious. In 1918, the average life expectancy in America dropped by a dozen years thanks to the H1N1 outbreak.[55] In 1918, there were no vaccines, or even antivirals like Tamiflu, that could treat or reduce the effects of the flu. America would have three waves of the Spanish flu[56]

---

50    "History of 1918 Flu Pandemic," Centers for Disease Control and Prevention (CDC), last updated March 21, 2018, https://www.cdc.gov/flu/pandemic-resources/1918-commemoration/1918-pandemic-history.htm.

51    CDC, "1918 Flu Pandemic."

52    "Spanish Flu," History Channel, October 12, 2010, updated December 22, 2021, https://www.history.com/topics/world-war-i/1918-flu-pandemic.

53    History, "Spanish Flu."

54    Meilan Solly, "What Happened When Woodrow Wilson Came Down With the 1918 Flu?," *Smithsonian*, October 2, 2020, https://www.smithsonianmag.com/smart-news/what-happened-when-woodrow-wilson-came-down-1918-flu-180975972/.

55    History, "Spanish Flu."

56    History, "Spanish Flu."

before it suddenly stopped. (Notably, whites were the hardest hit by the pandemic[57].)

However, even without viable medical treatments, the economic impact was modest. America's GDP shrank by only 1.5 percent[58], and there was little to no job loss.[59] The contrast with COVID-19's effects on the U.S. economy bears some examination. This time a pandemic caused the U.S. economy to shrink by 19.2 percent[60], and a staggering 22.4 million Americans lost their jobs. Those losers were disproportionately black.[61] More than 1 million Americans have succumbed to COVID-19 since 2020. At nearly 150k deaths, blacks were more likely than whites to die from COVID-19.[62] One obvious conclusion is that the government's mitigation response explains the difference between the impact of the Spanish flu and COVID-19 today.

57    Thomas A. Garrett, "Economic Effects of the 1918 Influenza Pandemic," Federal Reserve Bank of St. Louis, November 2007, https://www.stlouisfed.org/-/media/project/frbstl/stlouisfed/files/pdfs/community-development/research-reports/pandemic_flu_report.pdf.

58    Steve Maas, "Social and Economic Impacts of the 1918 Influenza Epidemic," National Bureau of Economic Research, May 2020, https://www.nber.org/digest/may20/social-and-economic-impacts-1918-influenza-epidemic.

59    Harlan Ullman, "Economic Recovery From Coronavirus: Lessons From 1918-1923," *New Atlanticist*, May 1, 2020, https://www.atlanticcouncil.org/blogs/new-atlanticist/economic-recovery-from-coronavirus-lessons-from-1918-1923/.

60    Lucia Mutikani, "U.S. economy contracted 19.2% during COVID-19 pandemic recession," Reuters, July 29, 2021, https://www.reuters.com/business/us-economy-contracted-192-during-covid-19-pandemic-recession-2021-07-29/.

61    Jhacova Williams, "Laid Off More, Hired Less: Black Workers in the COVID-19 Recession," *The Randblog*, Rand Corporation, September 29, 2020, https://www.rand.org/blog/2020/09/laid-off-more-hired-less-black-workers-in-the-covid.html.

62    Latoya Hill and Samantha Artiga, "COVID-19 Cases and Deaths by Race/Ethnicity: Current Data and Changes Over Time," Kaiser Family Foundation (KFF), August 22, 2022, https://www.kff.org/coronavirus-covid-19/issue-brief/covid-19-cases-and-deaths-by-race-ethnicity-current-data-and-changes-over-time/.

The response of the Biden Administration has been particularly harmful to blacks. On November 4, 2021, it announced that all businesses with one hundred or more employees would have to require their employees to either be vaccinated against COVID-19 or submit to regular testing. Not only did the policy contradict the Administration's public commitments made earlier in the year, but it also disproportionately harmed black workers.[63] As Jonathan Tobin explains in *Newsweek*, blacks are less likely to be vaccinated than the general population but are more likely to hold the blue-collar or working-class positions disproportionately affected by this requirement.[64]

If the requirements of the U.S. Constitution had been followed, the impact of shutdowns would have been limited, but sadly at the peak of pandemic lockdowns, thirty-nine states imposed quasi-martial law—ordering people to stay indoors for all but essential activities—which was remarkably destructive to their lives and to the economy. The federal government paid out trillions of dollars in emergency payments so that people could stay home. Governors exercised emergency powers that their own state constitutions never authorized. Federal and state courts, which should have insisted that these actions ultimately be barred, waited on the sidelines. Cases against these edicts were either never brought or courts issued very narrow rulings to only restrict government action if it directly restricted the First Amendment.

Their excuse was that the pandemic was such a significant threat, and the "dictatorial" executive orders were so straightforward and commonsensical, that interference by the courts was unnecessary. But if these rules and policies were so straightforward

63    Williams, "Laid Off More."
64    Jonathan Tobin, "Vaccine Mandates Will Have a Disparate Impact on Minorities," *Newsweek*, August 17, 2021, https://www.newsweek.com/vaccine-mandates-will-have-disparate-impact-minorities-opinion-1619755.

and commonsensical, the governors of all fifty states could have called special sessions of their state legislatures, and in seventy-two hours, the rules could all have been adopted properly. Similarly, Washington could have done the same thing.

Of course, the rules were not all straightforward and commonsensical, and often there was no way to appeal their implementation. Many businesses and individuals suffered as a result of courts refusing to do their job of blocking unconstitutional edicts.

Students—especially black students—suffered the most. Inner-city schools failed to meet their obligations to the neediest (disproportionately black) Americans, and the social consequences will likely be long-lasting. Children who rely on schools for meals went hungry, those with special needs went without support, reading and mathematics assessments showed marked declines,[65] and the primary mission of schools to equip children to become independent citizens of the future went unfulfilled. Since black kids are more likely to be in public schools (private schools often stayed open), they bore the brunt of the shutdowns.

Congressional Democrats rammed through a trillion-dollar COVID-19 bill, which has little to do with addressing the COVID-19 pandemic or its economic fallout. Instead, Washington bureaucrats were given free rein to try out untested schemes to subsidize government workers at the federal, state, and local levels. Perhaps the worst of these was a program to pay workers more to stay home than they would earn by working. More than $350 billion was spent by the American Rescue Plan—Biden's signature COVID-19 relief bill—which provided economic impact assistance for individuals and families as well as augmented unemployment assistance to them.

---

65  Sarah Schwartz, "Students' Math and Reading Plummet, Erasing Years of Gains, National Assessment Finds," *Education Week*, September 01, 2022, https://www.edweek.org/leadership/students-math-and-reading-plummet-erasing-years-of-gains-national-assessment-finds/2022/09.

In July 2021, President Biden declared the pandemic over.[66] Less than a month later, he announced that it was back.[67] The reversal of policy was swift and brutal.

Subsequently, some cities and states continued to prevent workers from returning to work well after infection and death rates dropped, even into 2022. While many jobs can now be done remotely, some industries, such as restaurants and hotels, need human workers on site, and they are usually blue-collar workers.

Liberal policymakers did everything they could to make a full return to work in person more difficult. Bad enough were the inconsistent mandates for how businesses could operate, what hoops workers needed to jump through in order to be able to report for work, and what they needed to do once they got there. The businesses themselves were also at the mercy of health inspectors who may or may not have been up-to-date on the latest instructions from Dr. Anthony Fauci and the CDC. Social-distancing measures were inconsistently applied and enforced. Workers themselves were not able to keep up with the frequent changes to the rules. Customers were repeatedly frustrated.

Following Dr. Fauci and the CDC, deep blue states and cities set up draconian rules that in New York State and California hit those least able to make demands on employers—hourly and blue-collar workers. High-income white-collar workers had the ability and the backing of the left to work at home, vaccinated or not. But first responders, nurses, and police were suspended or fired if they refused the vaccine. These covid19 policies mostly

66    Jennifer Jacobs and Sophia Cai, "Biden Declares Success in Beating Pandemic in July 4 Speech," Bloomberg, July 4, 2021, https://www.bloomberg.com/news/articles/2021-07-04/biden-to-appeal-for-vaccinations-after-u-s-missed-july-4-target.

67    Benjamin Wallace-Wells, "What Happened to Joe Biden's 'Summer of Freedom' from the Pandemic?" *New Yorker*, August 12, 2021, https://www.newyorker.com/news/annals-of-inquiry/what-happened-to-joe-bidens-summer-of-freedom-from-the-pandemic.

persist in large urban centers, where black people make up larger shares of the overall population.

Americans—particularly blacks—were caught flatfooted.

First, HIPAA (The Health Insurance Portability and Accountability Act of 1996), the law which protects information about a patient's medical condition and status, was ignored. Enacted by Congress to ensure that patients and consumers could control the use and access of their own health information,[68] HIPAA was intended to restore trust in the health care system and encourage Americans to access medical care without fear by mandating that an "individual's past, present or future physical or mental health or condition, and the provision of health care to the individual was not to be disclosed."[69]

The impetus for legislating HIPAA was America's experience with HIV/AIDS (Human Immunodeficiency Virus Infection and Acquired Immunodeficiency Syndrome). In June of 1981, five previously healthy young men in Los Angeles were diagnosed with what would soon become known as HIV/AIDS.[70] Within months, the AIDS epidemic was announced. In response many state and local governments created registries as part of their efforts to track the spread of the virus, sometimes abusing the information. One state attempted to use its registry to determine whether any of its public school teachers were infected.[71] Another state sought to use its registry to identify whether prisoners or individuals recently

---

68    "Summary of the HIPAA Privacy Rule," U.S. Department of Health & Human Services, https://www.hhs.gov/hipaa/for-professionals/privacy/laws-regulations/index.html.

69    HHS, "HIPAA Privacy Rule."

70    "HIV Historical Timeline," U.S. President's Emergency Plan for AIDS Relief (PEPFAR), https://hivhistory.org/.

71    Amy L. Fairchild, PhD, MPH,a, et al, "Public Goods, Private Data: HIV and the History, Ethics, and Uses of Identifiable Public Health Information," U.S. National Institutes of Health's National Library of Medicine (NIH/NLM), accessed October 28, 2022, https://www.ncbi.nlm.nih.gov/pmc/articles/PMC1804110/.

arrested had the virus.[72] Yet another state enacted a statute to allow law enforcement to subpoena any and all HIV/AIDS test results.[73]

Privacy advocates sought what the executive director of AIDS Action called a "firewall between the health departments and people living with AIDS," to protect the privacy of these individuals.[74] The Equal Employment Opportunity Commission issued guidance prohibiting employers from asking employees about their HIV status "or any other medical condition."[75]

For more than 20 years, the consensus held that the health-care privacy of individuals was paramount. But then along came COVID-19.

In January 2021, the Occupational Safety and Health Administration (OSHA) issued guidance that contravened both HIPAA and the EEOC,[76] and before 2021 was over, the Equal Employment Opportunity Commission (EEOC) had updated its rules to allow for employers to inquire specifically about vaccine status and fire those who don't comply.[77]

---

72   Fairchild, "Public Goods, Private Data."

73   Fairchild, "Public Goods, Private Data."

74   Daniel Zingale (Executive Director, AIDS Action) to Lawrence O. Gostin (Professor of Public Health Law, Georgetown University), March 16, 1999, https://www.ncbi.nlm.nih.gov/pmc/articles/PMC1804110/#B53.

75   "Living with HIV Infection Your Legal Rights in the Workplace Under the ADA," U.S. Equal Employment Opportunity Commission (EEOC), issue Date: December 1, 2015, https://www.eeoc.gov/laws/guidance/living-hiv-infection-your-legal-rights-workplace-under-ada.

76   "Protecting Workers: Guidance on Mitigating and Preventing the Spread of COVID-19 in the Workplace," Occupational Safety and Health Administration (OSHA), guidance posted January 29, 2021; Update to reflect the July 27, 2021 Centers for Disease Control and Prevention (CDC) mask and testing recommendations for fully vaccinated people, https://www.osha.gov/coronavirus/safework.

77   Allen Smith, J.D., and Lisa Nagele-Piazza, J.D. SHRM-SCP, "Employers React to Workers Who Refuse a COVID-19 Vaccination," *The Society for Human Resource Management,* February 3, 2022, https://www.shrm.org/resourcesandtools/legal-and-compliance/employment-law/pages/if-workers-refuse-a-covid-19-vaccination.aspx.

These changes pulled the rug out from under American work-ers and hit blacks fairly hard. Many blacks were unwilling to take the vaccine. In fact, only 10 percent of all vaccine and boosters shots ultimately went to black Americans.[78] By contrast, 55 per-cent of the shots were administered to whites.[79]

The unemployment rate of blacks exploded during this period. Having reached the official lowest level since the Department of Labor starting keeping records, these gains were reversed.[80] Not unlike the effects of the Great Recession during Obama's presi-dency, black worker unemployment during the COVID-19 pan-demic reached double digits.[81] A late 2020 Rand study warned policymakers about the potential impact on black unemployment of hiring and firing decisions during the pandemic, reminding its readers that after the Great Recession, it took more than ten years for black employment to drop to "pre-recession" levels.[82] The Left, which constantly focuses on racial disparities, conveniently ignored this warning and left blacks at the mercy of their employ-ers by encouraging job-killing covid-19 mitigation policies.

The federal government, which is the single largest employer of blacks—although they make up 12.4 percent of the U.S. population, they make up more than 18 percent of the federal workforce[83]—adopted rules that were quite harsh. Biden issued

78    Nambi Ndugga et al, "Latest Data on COVID-19 Vaccinations by Race/Ethni-city," Kaiser Family Foundation (KFF), July 14, 2022, https://www.kff.org/coronavirus-covid-19/issue-brief/latest-data-on-covid-19-vaccinations-by-race-ethnicity/.

79    Ndugga, "COVID-19 Vaccinations by Race/Ethnicity."

80    Williams, "Laid Off More."

81    Williams, "Laid Off More."

82    Williams, "Laid Off More."

83    "Strengthening The Federal Workforce," Office of Management and Budget, May 5, 2021, https://www.whitehouse.gov/wp-content/uploads/2021/05/ap_5_strengthening_fy22.pdf.

an executive order which mandating COVID-19 vaccines for all federal employees.[84] This order was in effect for nearly six months before federal employees filed the *Feds for Medical Freedom v. Biden* suit in Texas.[85] Federal Judge Jeffrey Vincent Brown issued a nationwide injunction against the order in January of 2022.[86]

These federal employees argued that no president in U.S. history had every required civil servants to undergo any medical procedure as a condition for employment.[87] Although an initial ruling by the Fifth Circuit Court of Appeals overturned Judge Brown's injunction in April of 2022, the employees appealed to the full circuit and the ban remained in place through the fall of 2022.[88] The case reached the full Fifth Circuit Court of Appeals in September and will likely be appealed to the U.S. Supreme Court in early 2023, regardless of the outcome in the Fifth Circuit.

Sadly, the NAACP and the Leadership Conference on Civil and Human Rights was silent about the mandate impact on

---

84  "Feds for Medical Freedom v. Biden," Case Summary, Constitutional Accountability Center (CAC), accessed October 28, 2022, https://www.theusconstitution. org/litigation/feds-for-medical-freedom-v-biden/.

85  Bill Mears and Tyler Olson, "Biden Still Pushing Federal Worker Vaccine Mandate Despite Eased CDC Guidelines," *Fox News,* August 19, 2022, https://www.foxnews.com/politics/biden-admin-still-pushing-federal-worker-vaccine-mandate-cdc-eased-quarantine-prevention-guidelines.

86  "Feds for Medical Freedom et al v. Biden, Jr. et al, No. 3:2021cv00356—Document 36 (S.D. Tex. 2022)," Justia Law, https://law.justia.com/cases/federal/district-courts/texas/txsdce/3:2021cv00356/1855108/36/.

87  Cameron Langford, "Fifth Circuit Lifts Injunction Against Biden Administration's Federal Employee Vaccine Mandate," *Courthouse News Service*, April 7, 2022, https://www.courthousenews.com/fifth-circuit-lifts-injunction-against-biden-administrations-federal-employee-vaccine-mandate/.

88  Brendan Pierson, "DOJ Urges Appeals Court to Uphold Federal Employee Vaccine Mandate," Reuters, September 13, 2022, https://www.reuters.com/legal/government/appeals-court-will-weigh-reviving-federal-employee-vaccine-mandate-2022-09-13/.

blacks. Even the ACLU refused to support these workers.[89] Once again, blacks were on the short end of the stick.

## BIDEN'S POLICIES LEAD TO RUNAWAY INFLATION

A consequence of the White House's COVID-19 policies was rampant inflation. In the fall of 2021, economists warned Biden that there was a heightened risk of high inflation unless he reversed course. Instead, the White House pushed ahead full steam. Treasury Secretary Janet Yellen was trotted out to shut down the concerns of economists that the "American Rescue Plan," and Biden's executive orders involving oil and gas exploration, would harm the economy, including raising fuel prices.[90]

In a press briefing in November 2021, White House press secretary Jen Psaki flatly denied that Biden's policies were an inflation concern: "No economist out there is projecting that [the Build Back Better bill] will have a negative impact on inflation."

Politifact—no friend of conservatives—called this statement a lie.[91] "I'm an economist, and I disagree," Douglas Holtz-Eakin, president of the American Action Forum, explained to Politifact.[92]

---

89     David Cole and Daniel Mach, "Civil Liberties and Vaccine Mandates: Here's Our Take," American Civil Liberties Union (ACLU), September 2, 2021, https://www.aclu.org/news/civil-liberties/civil-liberties-and-vaccine-mandates-heres-our-take.

90     Michael Collins and Joey Garrison, "'Paying The Price': Biden And Top Aides Misread Threat of Inflation as Warning Signs Gathered," *USA Today*, June 3, 2022, https://www.usatoday.com/story/news/politics/2022/06/03/white-house-misread-warning-signs-inflation/7468471001/.

91     Louis Jacobson, "Jen Psaki Incorrect in Saying No Economist Thinks Biden Bill Will Boost Inflation," *Politifact*, November 18, 2021, https://www.politifact.com/factchecks/2021/nov/18/jen-psaki/jen-psaki-wrong-say-no-economist-thinks-b/.

92     Jacobson, "Psaki Incorrect."

Well-known economist Larry Summers,[93] as well as those from Bank of America[94] and JPMorgan Chase,[95] all maintained that the Biden's program would cause inflation.

The Biden Administration had been warned that its policies were likely to cause inflation. And when it came, it came with a vengeance, hitting a forty-year high. Once it was clear that inflation was headed to levels not seen since the presidency of Jimmy Carter, the White House was forced to reverse course. In January of 2022, President Biden declared that it was the Federal Reserve's job to reduce inflation.[96]

## THE INFLATION TORNADO DESTROYING BLACK HOUSEHOLDS

*"I know families all across America are hurting because of inflation. I want every American to know that I am taking inflation very seriously."*

— PRESIDENT JOE BIDEN[97]

93    Matt Egan, "Larry Summers Sends Stark Inflation Warning to Joe Biden," CNN, May 27, 2021, https://www.cnn.com/2021/05/26/economy/inflation-larry-summers-biden-fed/index.html.

94    David J. Lynch and Tyler Pager, "Biden Team Struggles to Promote Economic Message as Inflation Persists," *Washington Post*, October 30, 2021, https://www.washingtonpost.com/us-policy/2021/10/30/biden-team-struggles-promote-economic-message-inflation-persists/.

95    Jacob Manoukia, "The Fed, Taxes And Inflation: How Can They Disrupt The Stock Market?" J.P. Morgan Wealth Management, June 18, 2021, https://Www.Jpmorgan.Com/Wealth-Management/Wealth-Partners/Insights/The-Fed-Taxes-And-Inflation-How-Can-They-Disrupt-The-Stock-Market.

96    Katia Dmitrieva, "Biden Says Stemming Inflation is Fed's Job, Backs Policy Shift," Bloomberg, January 19, 2022, https://www.bloomberg.com/news/articles/2022-01-19/biden-says-price-control-is-fed-s-job-backs-shift-in-policy?leadSource=uverify%20wall.

97    "Biden Blasts GOP as Having No Plan on Inflation," Reuters, May 10, 2022, https://www.yahoo.com/news/biden-blasts-gop-having-no-190144006.html.

The dramatic arrival of high inflation—a situation reminiscent of the days of the Betamax and rotary phones—caught America, including President Biden, unprepared.

A survey released on May 12, 2022 by Pew Research found that, by a wide margin, Americans viewed inflation as the top problem facing the country today. Seven in ten Americans believe inflation is a huge problem, followed by the affordability of health care and the risk of violent crime.[98]

Though viewed with alarm across the nation's income spectrum, rising inflation places a disproportionate burden on lower-income households—especially the soaring costs of food, housing, and energy—Federal Reserve Board Governor Lael Brainard noted in a speech in early April of 2022.[99] Lower-income households spend 77 percent of their income on necessities, more than double the 31 percent of income spent by higher-income households in these categories, she added.[100]

The wealthy, irrespective of race or ethnicity, may be annoyed by inflation, but higher prices pose no real threat to their livelihoods. That picture changes dramatically, however, at the lower rungs of the income ladder, and because black Americans are disproportionately represented in lower-income brackets, it stands to reason that they bear the heaviest burden of inflation.

98     Carroll Doherty and Vianney Gómez, "By a Wide Margin, Americans View Inflation as the Top Problem Facing the Country Today," Pew Research Center, May 12, 2022, https://www.pewresearch.org/fact-tank/2022/05/12/by-a-wide-margin-americans-view-inflation-as-the-top-problem-facing-the-country-today/.

99     Federal Reserve System Governor Lael Brainard, "Variation in the Inflation Experiences of Households" (Institute Research Conference, Minneapolis, Minnesota, April 05, 2022), https://www.federalreserve.gov/newsevents/speech/brainard20220405a.htm.

100    Rachel Siegel, "Fed official: Inflation Falls Hardest on Poorer Families," *Washington Post,* April 5, 2022, https://www.washingtonpost.com/us-policy/2022/04/05/fed-inflation-poor/.

# A HIDDEN TAX

*"The main point that I can't stress enough is that inflation is a hidden tax.... It robs people of their purchasing power, transferring it to the federal government. This is how the Biden Administration is paying for trillions of dollars of unfunded government expenses."*

— E.J. ANTONI, a research fellow at the Heritage Foundation's Center for Data Analysis[101]

Well before the annual numbers were released, Project 21 member Chris Aarps, a young black commentator, explained on Newsmax that inflation was a cruel tax that hit Americans hard, especially the working class.[102] According to the U.S. Bureau of Labor Statistics, by the summer of 2022, grocery prices had not only risen 13.5 percent over the previous twelve months—bread by 16.2 percent, chicken by 16.6 percent, and eggs by 2.9 percent—but also 39.8 percent from the year before.[103]

Paul Kupiec, resident scholar at the American Enterprise Institute, explains that inflation is a hidden tax that redistributes wealth to the federal government. "Inflation is a real tax, just as real and at times nearly as important as the income tax," he wrote in *The Hill* in November 2021. "While inflation clearly does reduce the purchasing power of your earnings and fixed-income

---

101   EJ Antoni interviewed by Michelle Cordero, "Biden's Recession," in *Heritage Explains* (podcast), produced by Heritage Foundation, August 1, 2022, https://www.heritage.org/markets-and-finance/heritage-explains/bidens-recession.

102   "'Inflation is a Cruel Tax,' Says Project 21's Christopher Arps," *Wake Up America*, Newsmax, December 15, 2021, https://www.youtube.com/watch?v=0VVcUM5NwoM.

103   Katie Wedell, "More People Are Paying for Groceries With Buy Now, Pay Later Apps as Inflation Pinches," *USA Today*, September 14, 2022, https://www.msn.com/en-us/money/other/more-people-are-paying-for-groceries-with-buy-now-pay-later-apps-as-inflation-pinches/ar-AA11P5Bu.

asset values, it also redistributes purchasing power from businesses and households to the federal government."[104] This hidden tax especially impacts black households. The highest median household income in the U.S. in 2020 was among Asians, at $94,903. For non-Hispanic whites, the comparable figure was $74,912, for Hispanics (of any race) $55,321, and blacks $45,870.[105]

Americans derive their wealth from many means besides salaries and wages. Homeownership is a major component of individual wealth in the U.S., and disparities in homeownership therefore play a decisive role in determining how wealth is distributed across demographic groups. In 2019, the homeownership rate among white, non-Hispanic Americans was 73.3 percent, compared with 57.7 percent among Asian and Pacific Islander Americans, 57.5 percent among Hispanics, and 42.1 percent among blacks.[106] The already low rate of black homeownership is made worse by inflation's corrosive effects on purchasing power. Inflation pushes aspirations for first time homeownership out of reach for most blacks.

In response to inflation, the Federal Reserve began aggressively raising interest rates in 2022. Mortgage rates rose at their fastest pace in thirty-five years, making home purchases in late 2022 much more expensive than even at the beginning of 2022. The rate for a standard 30-year fixed-rate mortgage passed the 5 percent mark in April for the first time since 2011.[107] Consider,

104 Paul Kupiec, "The Inflation Tax is Not Only Real, It's Massive," *The Hill,* November 4, 2021, https://thehill.com/opinion/finance/580043-the-inflation-tax-is-not-only-real-its-massive/.

105 "Current Population Survey, 2020 and 2021 Annual Social and Economic Supplements," U.S. Census Bureau, https://www.census.gov/newsroom/press-releases/2022/current-population-survey-tables.html.

106 "Homeownership Rates Show That Black Americans Are Currently the Least Likely Group to Own Homes," USA Facts, July 28, 2020, https://usafacts.org/articles/homeownership-rates-by-race/.

107 Tobias Burns, "Mortgage Rates Top 5 Percent for the First Time in Decade," *The Hill,* April 14, 2022, https://thehill.com/policy/finance/3267686-mortgage-rates-top-5-percent-for-the-first-time-in-decade/.

the average rate was less than 3.5 percent for a mortgage in January of 2022.[108]

Renters were in a worse situation. Rent prices skyrocketed. Prices already had risen nearly 11 percent in 2021, and by the middle of 2022, they'd risen another 13 percent.[109]

According to the National Multifamily Housing Coalition (NMHC), the US has a serious housing shortage.[110] Notably, this problem preceded Biden's disastrous inflationary policies. The NHMC argues, "That shortage is the result of decades of failed housing policy at all levels of government. And it was exacerbated by the housing bust that followed the Great Recession of 2008 when new apartment construction plummeted."[111] The NMHC estimates that by 2030, the U.S. will need to have built an average of 328,000 new apartments every year to meet expected future demand,[112] but today's high inflation poses a significant barrier to reaching that goal. "The supply shortage is further exacerbated by rapidly rising for-sale housing prices that are preventing would-be

108 Melissa Brock, "Mortgage Interest Rates Forecast For 2022," Rocket Mortgage, September 23, 2022, https://www.rocketmortgage.com/learn/mortgage-interest-rates-forecast.

109 Kate Dore, "Rent Prices Are Soaring In These 5 U.S. Metros. Here's What To Know Before Moving to a Cheaper Area," CNBC, August 2, 2022, https://www.cnbc.com/2022/08/02/rent-prices-are-soaring-in-these-5-metros-what-to-know-before-moving-.html.

110 Matthew Berger, "Low-Income Housing Tax Credit," The National Multifamily Housing Council (NMHC), February 10, 2022, https://www.nmhc.org/advocacy/issue-fact-sheet/low-income-housing-tax-credit-fact-sheet/.

111 "NAA and NMHC Statement on the Biden Administration's Housing Supply Action Plan," The National Apartment Association (NAA), May 16, 2022, https://www.naahq.org/naa-and-nmhc-statement-biden-administrations-housing-supply-action-plan.

112 "Apartment Supply Shortage," The National Multifamily Housing Council (NMHC), August 2018, https://www.nmhc.org/contentassets/0662d3fe113046bb89019d0dfabfb271/apartment_supply_shortage_2018_08_fact_sheet.pdf.

first-time house buyers from moving out of apartments."[113] In the spring of 2022, CNET confirmed what many households—especially those of color—have felt. "Overall rent prices are growing faster than incomes, leading to affordability issue for renters across the country."[114] Realtor.com predicted that rents would increase by 17 percent by the end of 2022.[115] Today, since blacks own homes at lower rates compared to other racial and ethnic groups, blacks are renters at higher rates than other groups.

Food is right at the top of the list of life's necessities. Since inflation began its dramatic rise in the U.S. in 2021, visits to the grocery store have become much more expensive. Food inflation saw its largest annual increase since March 1981—rising at 8.8 percent year over year—with a recent Bank of America analysis forecasting that U.S. food inflation will hit 9 percent by the end of 2022.[116] Staples like bread, milk, meat, fruit and vegetables have been caught up in the inflationary spiral, with Bank of America analysts predicting "sustained price increases later this year."

Farmers are having to cope with the cost of fertilizers and pesticides rising almost 50 percent since the spring of 2021.[117] Fertilizer prices have also been affected by the higher cost of natural gas, which is critical to the production of nitrogen-based fertil-

---

113   "Talking Points: Rising Rents," The National Multifamily Housing Council (NMHC), March 2022, https://www.nmhc.org/globalassets/communications/resources/rising-rent-talking-points-2022-03.pdf.

114   Alix Langone, "Rent Increases by Nearly 20% Across the US: What Renters Need to Know," CNET, March 31, 2022, https://www.cnet.com/personal-finance/mortgages/rent-increases-by-nearly-20-across-the-us-what-renters-need-to-know/.

115   Alex Galbraith, "Trends," Realtor.com, May 19, 2022, https://www.realtor.com/news/trends/no-relief-in-sight-average-rents-continued-to-soar-in-april/.

116   Will Daniel, "Don't Expect The Huge Rise in Food Prices to Slow Anytime Soon, Bank of America Says," *Fortune*, April 21, 2022, https://fortune.com/2022/04/21/inflation-food-rise-2022-bank-of-america-says/.

117   *Risk Review 2022*, Federal Deposit insurance Corporation, https://www.fdic.gov/analysis/risk-review/2022-risk-review/2022-risk-review-full.pdf.

izers. Fertilizers and chemicals represent 10 to 20 percent of total costs for U.S. farmers, according to Bank of America.[118]

Various factors, including an acute shortage of truck drivers, have pushed up the Consumer Price Index (CPI) for gasoline and fuel oil by 48.7 and 106.7 percent respectively, year-over-year.[119] The resulting rising costs to consumers can be seen in supermarkets all across the country.

Even necessities like clothing have been hit by inflation. The CPI showed prices for apparel rising 5.4 percent year over year.[120] While this increase is lower than the current overall 8.3 inflation rate, clothes are essential for everyone. For families with limited means, budgeting for new clothes—even in the local thrift shop—increasingly involves making hard choices.

However, when inflation reared its ugly head, America wasn't prepared. Blacks, rural residents, and workers without a college degree were hardest hit by the inflation shock that arose in the midst of the pandemic. According to Project 21, inflation added $433 per month to costs for the average American and, because blacks earn less than other racial groups, it is easy to see that black families shoulder an especially high burden with high inflation.[121]

Having on average less money to spend on life's necessities, black Americans find themselves, through inflation, increasingly transferring what wealth they have to a federal government whose policies are at the root of the devalued currency that undermines

118   Daniel, "Huge Rise in Food Prices."
119   Bureau of Labor Statistics, "Consumer Price Index News Release," August 10, 2022, https://www.bls.gov/news.release/archives/cpi_08102022.htm.
120   Arthur Friedman, "Retail Apparel Prices Follow April's Easing Inflation," *Sourcing Journal*, May 11, 2022, https://sourcingjournal.com/market-data/apparel-data/retail-apparel-prices-inflation-fed-adobe-biden-april-2022-344152/.
121   David Ridenour, "Inflation is Causing Black Americans to Leave the Left," National Center for Public Policy Research, September 21, 2022, https://mailchi.mp/nationalcenter/inflation-is-causing-black-americans-to-leave-the-left?e=991c4d6e67.

their very livelihoods. Thus, despite his claims to the contrary, Biden's inflationary policies have had a real impact on America—especially blacks.

## GOOD NEWS ABOUT CONGRESS: IT'S TOO BUSY ARGUING TO DO MORE DAMAGE

Will Rogers was a popular humorist and actor in the early twentieth century. One of his best lines was commenting that "papers say: 'Congress is deadlocked and can't act.' I think that is the greatest blessing that could befall this country."[122]

Congress did succeed in passing two major pieces of legislation in 2021: the ironically named American Rescue Plan—an infrastructure bill that does little for roads, but a lot for boondoggle passenger-rail systems and bike lanes—and the climate bill passed in the summer of 2022 that was far smaller than the $2 trillion dollar plan that Biden originally proposed.[123]

When Joe Biden was running for President, his campaign slogan was "Build Back Better"—a transparent attempt to mimic Donald Trump's "Make America Great Again." When Democrats won control of the White House while also clinging to power in Congress, Biden immediately threw his hat in with Vermont Senator Bernie Sanders and the other furthest-left members of Congress to slap the Build Back Better label onto a $6 trillion monstrosity of a bill. This bill would have injected every nutty leftist idea on healthcare, education, welfare, and global warming into hundreds of new federal programs. Even worse, the bill

---

122  "Is a deadlocked Congress good for the country?" Will Rogers Today, December 29, 2013, https://www.willrogerstoday.com/is-a-deadlocked-congress-good-for-the-country/.

123  Katy Glueck and Lisa Friedman, "Biden Announces $2 Trillion Climate Plan," *New York Times*, February 1, 2021, https://www.nytimes.com/2020/07/14/us/politics/biden-climate-plan.html.

would have essentially abolished the successful Trump tax cuts and raised taxes higher than they had been at any time under previous president Barack Obama.[124] Biden's economic policies are so extreme they make the progressive Obama look like a moderate in comparison.

The Build Back Better Act immediately flopped like a fish out of water and within a few months was pared back to $3.5 trillion. However, it wasn't really being pared back—Democrats used accounting tricks to game the budget scoring to make the bill seem cheaper,[125] and it still contained damaging new regulatory mandates on workers and businesses.

When September 2021 rolled around, the White House, in desperation, hit on a new talking point: The Build Back Better Act didn't cost anything at all. It was free, you see, because the tax increases—that would hammer small businesses and force thousands of layoffs—would pay for the gigantic new spending programs.

No one in Washington seems to actually believe this claim. Even progressives admit that they don't really care how high the price tag is. For example, Rep. Alexandria Ocasio-Cortez (D-NY) explained, "I think that one of the ideas that's out there is fully fund what we can fully fund, but maybe instead of doing it for 10 years, you fully fund it for five years."[126] Happily, their numbers

124 "Heritage Experts: President Biden's 'Build Back Better Plan' Represents the Largest Tax Increase, Federal Power Grab in Decades," *Heritage Foundation* March 31, 2021, https://www.heritage.org/press/heritage-experts-president-bidens-build-back-better-plan-represents-the-largest-tax-increase.

125 Glenn Kessler, "Biden's claim that his spending plan 'costs zero dollars'," *Washington Post*, September 28, 2021, https://www.washingtonpost.com/politics/2021/09/28/bidens-claim-that-his-spending-plan-costs-zero-dollars/.

126 Caroline Vakil, "Ocasio-Cortez says it's possible to shorten years on funding programs to compromise on reconciliation bill," *The Hill*, October 3, 2021, https://thehill.com/policy/energy-environment/575066-ocasio-cortez-says-its-possible-to-shorten-years-on-funding-programs-to-compromise-on-reconciliation-bill/.

weren't high enough for the bill to pass the U.S. Senate, where it remained dead in the water until proposals by Senator Manchin dramatically revived it. Almost all the tax increases were stripped out, and even wasteful programs were pitched over the side to the point that the bill that passed in the summer was a mere shadow of the original plan.[127]

Although some Democratic senators, who were either worried about losing their own elections in November 2022 or simply didn't like the idea of losing their pretend 50–50 "majority," quietly urged their party leaders to drop the whole package or pass a much smaller bill. The latter option was chosen.

## BIDEN'S ECONOMIC POLICIES THAT HURT BLACK AMERICANS GO BACK TO WOODROW WILSON

America's preeminent progressive President was Woodrow Wilson. Elected in 1912, he promoted dramatic changes that transformed America. Starting with what he called the "New Freedom," he took aim at corporations, banks, and tax policy.[128] The Sixteenth Amendment, which legalized a federal graduated income tax, was also ratified during his presidency, Wilson used this new authority to impose an income tax. Claiming that the old tax system of tariffs—paid indirectly by traders internationally, based on consumption—was unfair, Wilson presented the graduated (or "progressive," as we call it today) income tax as a revenue system that would instead focus on the ability to pay.[129]

---

127 "'A recipe for absolute destruction': Democrats scramble to avoid electoral blowback after Manchin halts Biden agenda," CNN, December 21, 2021, https://www.cnn.com/2021/12/20/politics/moderate-democrats-manchin-2022/index.html.

128 "Woodrow Wilson's New Freedom," The Independence Hall Association, accessed November 1, 2022, https://www.ushistory.org/us/43g.asp.

129 Steven A. Bank, "Federal Income tax of 1913," *Encyclopedia.com*, https://www.encyclopedia.com/history/encyclopedias-almanacs-transcripts-and-maps/federal-income-tax-1913.

While the GOP pushed for a flat tax rate, progressives insisted on a graduated income tax that would be a tool for redistributing wealth.[130] Today the Internal Revenue Service (IRS) and the progressive tax is a heavy burden on not only America's economy in general, but more importantly a weight disproportionately borne by black households. Even though the IRS doesn't keep audit records on the basis of race, a far higher percentage of taxpayers in predominantly black counties are audited versus those in white ones.[131]

Additionally, it was at Wilson's direction that the Federal Reserve was created.[132] It has the power to impose banking policy and set interest rates. Today it has near complete control over America's money and banking. The Federal Reserve makes the inflationary financing of budget deficits easy, as well as the ability of Washington to repay its debts more easily with inflated dollars.[133] Its members serve fourteen-year appointed terms, all but insulating the Federal Reserve from political influence once they join the Board of Governors.[134] Being able to set interest rates without regard to the impact on poor populations hurts blacks especially.

As President, Wilson held a screening of the racist movie *Birth of a Nation* at the White House. [135] Afterwards, he proclaimed of

---

130    Bank, "Federal Income tax of 1913."

131    Dorothy A. Brown, "The IRS Is Targeting the Poorest Americans," *The Atlantic*, July 27, 2021, https://www.theatlantic.com/ideas/archive/2021/07/how-race-plays-tax-policing/619570/.

132    Matthew Caggia, "Wilson's New Freedom," **Caggia Social Studies**, accessed October 20, 2022, http://www.caggiasocialstudies.com/AHText/17-5.pdf.

133    Hans F. Sennholz, "The Federal Reserve System," Foundation for Economic Education (FEE), April 1, 1972, https://fee.org/articles/the-federal-reserve-system/.

134    "Structure of the Federal Reserve System," Federal Reserve System, last updated October 3, 2022, https://www.federalreserve.gov/aboutthefed/structure-federal-reserve-board.htm.

135    Cooper, *Making Black America Great Again.*

the movie: "It is like writing history with lightning, and my only regret is that it is all so terribly true."[136]

Even more galling was that after having openly sought the support of black voters during his campaign in 1912, Wilson reversed the policies of GOP presidents and re-segregated all departments of the federal government.[137] The effect on blacks was significant. In 1912, Washington, DC was a place where a flourishing black middle class lived and nearly a third of the overall population of the city was black.[138]

Wilson dramatically changed that. All federal jobs would require photos.[139] Many blacks in the federal government during Wilson's presidency were either downgraded or discharged during his presidency.[140] Take the case of James C. Napier. In 1912, every single dollar printed by the Bureau of Engraving and Printing bore his signature as Register of the Treasury.[141] A year later, he was forced out and replaced by a white supporter of Wilson.[142]

Progressive President Woodrow Wilson not only oversaw the initial implementation of the income tax, he increased it for individuals and corporations several times, along with passing new excise taxes in the lead-up to World War I and after U.S. entry into the conflict. When the war ended, war production fell off

---

136 Rachel Janik. "'Writing History With Lightning': *The Birth of a Nation* at 100," *Time*, February 8, 2015, https://time.com/3699084/100-years-birth-of-a-nation/.

137 Saladin Ambar, "Woodrow Wilson: Domestic Affairs," Miller Center, University of Virginia, https://millercenter.org/president/wilson/domestic-affairs.

138 "Wilson and Race," President Woodrow Wilson House, https://www.woodrowwilsonhouse.org/wilson-topics/wilson-and-race/.

139 "Woodrow Wilson and Race in America," *American Experience*, PBS, https://www.pbs.org/wgbh/americanexperience/features/wilson-and-race-relations/.

140 Ambar, "Woodrow Wilson."

141 Eric S. Yellin, "How The Black Middle Class Was Attacked by Woodrow Wilson's Administration," The Conversation, February 8, 2016, https://theconversation.com/how-the-black-middle-class-was-attacked-by-woodrow-wilsons-administration-52200.

142 PBS, "Woodrow Wilson and Race in America."

sharply, but the higher taxes remained. The U.S. entered a deep recession in 1920 and 1921, and millions saw their wages fall or lost their jobs.[143] Millions of blacks had migrated north from the rural South to work in factories devoted to armament production, so the economic crisis from the recession of 1920 hit black Americans particularly hard, compounding the effects of Wilson's policies segregating the civil service and eliminating positions for blacks.[144]

## BIDEN CHANNELS THE GHOST OF WOODROW WILSON

What the Biden Administration hasn't learned is that new regulations and taxes on critical service industries will disproportionately hurt black Americans. Biden campaigned on a pledge that he wouldn't raise taxes on those with incomes below $400k.[145] But like so many other promises, it too was set aside. More interested in controlling the energy sector than the concerns of poor and working class Americans, Biden promoted and signed into law the falsely named "Inflation Reduction Act" which imposed new energy taxes on natural gas production, crude oil and coal. All of these taxes will be paid by American households regardless of whether they make less than 400k.[146]

---

143  Andrew Beattie, "A Concise History of Changes In U.S. Tax Law," Investopedia.com, December 16, 2020 (updated July 23, 2022), https://www.investopedia.com/articles/tax/10/concise-history-tax-changes.asp.

144  Judson MacLaury, "The Federal Government and Negro Workers Under President Woodrow Wilson," U.S. Department of Labor, March16, 2000, https://www.dol.gov/general/aboutdol/history/shfgpr00.

145  Greg Iacurci, "Biden reiterates $400,000 tax pledge to fund agenda," CNBC, March 2, 2022, https://www.cnbc.com/2022/03/02/biden-reiterates-400000-tax-pledge-to-fund-agenda.html.

146  Mike Palicz, "Biden Breaks $400K Tax Pledge," Americans for Tax Reform, August 16, 2022, https://www.atr.org/biden-breaks-400k-tax-pledge/.

## LIBERALS GET A FAILING GRADE ON HELPING WORKERS

Biden promised in 2020 to have a platform to help the working class, especially those on the front line of the COVID-19 pandemic. He promised to make their workplaces safer, get them more personal protective equipment (PPE), and provide them with "premium pay" for their sacrifice.[147] No one guessed that his solution would be to force these front-line workers out of the workforce in order to do it. His pandemic mitigation policies targeted the very workers that he had pledged to assist. He and his party promoted mandatory COVID-19 testing, stay-at-home orders, and vaccine passports—all of which crippled this sector of the workforce. The Electronic Frontier Foundation (a digital rights group) explains that the policies hurt lower-income groups, who were less likely to own smartphones or access to testing and vaccines.[148] As a result it was these people who wouldn't be able to work, shop, or even attend school. Even the ACLU, which had remained silent as governments used so-called "emergency powers" to implement pandemic mitigation measures, decried these policies because of their effect on the working class.[149]

Some 53 million Americans[150], or 44 percent of all workers, hold working class jobs. A higher percentage of blacks make up

---

147   "Joe Biden's 4-point Plan for Our Essential Workers," Biden/Harris campaign website, https://joebiden.com/joe-bidens-4-point-plan-for-our-essential-workers/.

148   Darius Tahir, "Vaccine passports pose ethical thicket for Biden administration," *Politico*, March 17, 2021, https://www.politico.com/news/2021/03/17/vaccine-passports-ethics-biden-administration-476384.

149   Jay Stanley, "There's a Lot That Can Go Wrong With 'Vaccine Passports'," *American Civil Liberties Union*, March 31, 2021, https://www.aclu.org/news/privacy-technology/theres-a-lot-that-can-go-wrong-with-vaccine-passports.

150   Martha Ross, Nicole Bateman, and Alec Friedhoff, "A Closer Look At Low-Wage Workers Across The Country," Brookings Institution, March 2020, https://www.brookings.edu/interactives/low-wage-workforce/.

the working class than the population at large.[151] Consequently, policies that harm the working class hurt blacks more. According to the BLS, some 7.3 million Americans are out of work due to COVID-19 fear or forced furloughs due to COVID-19.[152]

## PROGRESSIVE POLICIES KILL JOBS

The data is now in: Progressivism liberalism has failed at every step to help the economy move past the COVID-19 pandemic. (Indeed, it's unclear if progressives even *want* the economy to move past the pandemic.) Out-of-control spending and crushing new regulations on workers and businesses are making life harder on large sections of blue-collar Americans.

It is intensely ironic that a President supposedly elected with such a high percentage of black Americans would hammer them disproportionately. Regardless of the intent—no one is a mind-reader—it is a fact that the policies of the Biden Administration are hitting working-class Americans hardest, and because blacks make up a high percentage of the working class, they are hitting black Americans hardest.

Sadly, this is nothing new. Progressives have been obsessed with centrally planning the economy even before the first major progressive planner, Woodrow Wilson, occupied the White House. Just like Wilson, the progressives of today experiment with the lives and livelihoods of Americans at the middle and the bottom

---

151 Alex Rowell, "What Everyone Should Know About America's Diverse Working Class," The Center for American Progress Action Fund, December 11, 2017, https://www.americanprogressaction.org/article/everyone-know-americas-diverse-working-class/.

152 "Measuring Household Experiences during the Coronavirus Pandemic," U.S. Census Bureau, September 14, 2022, https://www.census.gov/data/experimental-data-products/household-pulse-survey.html.

eration Legend

ding to former Attorney General Bill Barr, Operation
moved violent criminals, domestic abusers, carjackers, and
ckers from nine cities that were experiencing stubbornly
e and took illegal firearms, narcotics, and illicit mon-
streets. By most standards, many would consider these
resounding success, especially amid a global pandemic.[7]
tion Legend was originally announced in Kansas City,
nd Cleveland, Ohio. More than 6,000 arrests—includ-
volving 460 homicides—occurred through December
ly 3,000 firearms and "more than 32 kilos of heroin,
fentanyl, 300 kilos of methamphetamine, 135 kilos of
$11 million in drug and other illicit proceeds have
since the program began in July 2020"[8]

General William P. Barr Announces Results of Operation Legend,"
artment of Justice, December 23, 2020, https://www.justice.gov/
orney-general-william-p-barr-announces-results-operation-legend.
rney Justin Herdman Announces Final Update on Operation Legend,"
nt of Justice, Northern District of Ohio, December 28, 2020,
w.justice.gov/usao-ndoh/pr/us-attorney-justin-herdman-announces-
te-operation-legend.

of the income ladder. In Wilson's time, they openly explained that they did so to harm the financial interests of blacks.

These plans never work, for the simple reason that a dynamic economy with millions of people is constantly shifting. One cannot create a plan from Washington to set rules for the countless adjustments that businesses and workers make every day across the country. Indeed, these attempts only create misery. Even the best of the progressive plans are not actually good—they're simply the least bad. That is to say, the ones that are the least ambitious and draconian do the least damage.

Black Americans have seen their prospects fall with the imposition of leftist schemes and rise when those schemes fade. With lower average wages, blacks are more reliant on a strong economy that allows businesses to hire quickly.

# CHAPTER TWO

# BIDEN EMBRACES THE WOKE

*"Go Woke, Go Broke"*[1]

When Joe Biden was inaugurated on January 20, 2021, he pledged in his inaugural address that he would work to unite America. Standing on the West Front of the Capitol, Biden told America that "to restore the soul and secure the future of America requires so much more than words. It requires the most elusive of all things in a democracy: unity…." He added, "Without unity, there is no peace. Only bitterness and fury. No progress, only exhausting outrage. No nation, only a state of chaos. This is our historic moment of crisis and challenge, and unity is the path forward."[2] Yet within hours of his inauguration, President Biden began to put in place a divisive agenda that is the antithesis of unity, and created the raison d'être of the November 8, 2022, shellacking his party received.

Biden was woke, and his party went broke!

One of his first agenda items attacked patriotism. Calling it "counter-factual," President Biden abolished the 1776 Commission created by his predecessor and in the process, distanced the White House from the nation's founding and the unity those principles embody.[3] Established in September 2020, the 1776 Commission

was created to promote patriotic education the dean of Hillsdale College's Van And Government, was named executive direct other notable members include former Development Secretary Ben Carson, Hill Larry Arnn, and Project 21 Member, Caro just how much the project is impacting the end of President Biden's first year, s had introduced their version of the 17 mote patriotism in their public schools of "critical race theory."[4]

## NO JUSTICE FOR ALL

President Biden also set up a new dom the country's "domestic extremism" th admits that the foreign terror threa Furthermore, while there are eight hu Matter (BLM) "protest" trials under 2020 death of George Floyd, those ca tic terrorism, but four cases involvir extremism are.[6] Furthermore, while lated during his presidency, Presiden continue the remarkably successful program that former President Tru

Op

**More tha
2,000**
Arrests

**More tha
450**
Federal
Defendant
Charged

Accor
Legend re
drug traff
high crim
ies off the
results as a

Opera
Missouri, a
ing cases i
2020. Nea
17 kilos of
cocaine an
been seized

1 "When Brands Go Woke, Do They Go Broke?," The Chartered Institute of Marketing, February 3, 2020, https://www.cim.co.uk/content-hub/editorial/when-brands-go-woke-do-they-go-broke/.

2 "Inaugural Address by President Joseph R. Biden, Jr.," The White House, accessed November 23, 2022, https://www.whitehouse.gov/briefing-room/speeches-remarks/2021/01/20/inaugural-address-by-president-joseph-r-biden-jr/#:~:text=And%20now%2C%20a%20rise%20in,Unity.

3 Peter Wood, "America Isn't Make-Believe," *The American Mind,* January 26, 2021, https://americanmind.org/memo/america-isnt-make-believe/.

4 Jake Silverstein, "The 1619 Project and *New York Times*, November 12, 2021, magazine/1619-project-us-history.htm

5 "Terrorism," FBI: What We Investigat November 23, 2022, https://www.fbi Nicholas Harrington, and Seth G. Jo the United States," CSIS, June 17, 20 terrorism-problem-united-states.

6 Ben Weingarten, "Woke and Weak: Adversaries," *Newsweek*, January 25, woke-weak-biden-punishes-america

7 "Attorney
U.S. Dep
opa/pr/at

8 "U.S. Atto
Departmc
https://w
final-upda

However, President Biden and his woke followers can't see the good of a program like Operation Legend because they are focused on the skin color of the criminals. Progressives have a fixation on race, and in the process, they've re-created racial divisions from previous centuries. In the summer of his first year in office, President Biden made an astonishing announcement: "According to the intelligence community, terrorism from white supremacy is the most lethal threat to the homeland today...."[9] While marking the United Nation's International Day for the Elimination of Racial Discrimination (created to memorialize a 1960 massacre in South Africa), Biden issued a statement claiming that "racism and white supremacy are ugly poisons that have long plagued the United States."[10]

After South Carolina's Senator Tim Scott, a black man, gave the GOP's official response to the State of the Union, progressives were outraged. In the course of his response, Senator Scott declared that America is not a racist place, and he also took issue with the left-wing practice of using discrimination to fight discrimination.[11] The next day, Vice President Kamala Harris declared, "What we know from the intelligence community, one of the greatest threats to our national security is domestic terror-

9    Maanvi Singh and Joan E Greve, "Biden Declares White Supremacists 'Most Lethal Threat' to US as He Marks Tulsa Race Massacre - As It Happened," *Guardian,* June 1, 2021, https://www.theguardian.com/us-news/live/2021/jun/01/joe-biden-tulsa-oklahoma-race-massacre-us-politics-live.

10   President Joseph Biden, "Statement on the International Day for the Elimination of Racial Discrimination," The White House, March 21, 2021, https://www.whitehouse.gov/briefing-room/statements-releases/2021/03/21/statement-by-president-biden-on-the-international-day-for-the-elimination-of-racial-discrimination/.

11   Ben Gittleson, "Vice President Kamala Harris: We Must 'Speak Truth' About History of Racism in America," *ABC News,* April 29, 2021, https://abcnews.go.com/Politics/vice-president-kamala-harris-speak-truth-history-racism/story?id=77391730.

ism manifested by white supremacists."[12] When pressed whether that meant that America was a racist country, Harris backtracked, saying on *Good Morning America*, "No, I don't think America is a racist country."[13]

Is this so-called threat a greater risk to the homeland than covert actions within America by Russia, China, or threats from al-Qaida and ISIS? What about the violence by groups like Antifa, whose role in the BLM riots of 2020 caused billions in damage?

According to the White House's 2021 National Strategy for Countering Domestic Terrorism, the data show that the homeland security threat includes "self–proclaimed 'militias' and militia violent extremists…anarchist violent extremists, who violently oppose all forms of capitalism, corporate globalization, and governing institutions," as well as those who hold "single-issue ideologies related to abortion–, animal rights–, environmental–… as well as other grievances—or a combination of ideological influences."[14]

Even the report doesn't demonstrate that white supremacists are the greatest threats. In fact, militias don't all involve whites.

## THE NOT F**KING AROUND COALITION

The Not F**ing Around Coalition (NFAC), an all-black, Atlanta-based militia group, made headlines in 2020. Its stated purpose was "to protect, self-police and educate Black communities on

---

12   Katie Davis, "Kamala Harris Says 'White Supremacy Terrorism' Is One of 'Greatest National Security Threats'—But US 'Isn't Racist'," *The Sun*, April 29 2021, https://www.the-sun.com/news/2796882/kamala-harris-white-supremacy-terrorism-national-security-threats/.

13   Gittleson, "Harris: We Must 'Speak Truth'."

14   "National Strategy for Countering Domestic Terrorism," National Security Council, Executive Office of the President, June 2021, https://www.whitehouse.gov/wp-content/uploads/2021/06/National-Strategy-for-Countering-Domestic-Terrorism.pdf.

firearms and their constitutional rights."[15] According to Professor Thomas Mockaitis of De Paul University and author of *Violent Extremists: Understanding the Domestic and International Terrorist Threat*, the NFAC "echoes the Black Panthers but they [sic] are more heavily armed and more disciplined...."

NFAC founder John Fitzgerald Johnson issued a call to arms on social media for a rally planned for July 25, 2022, which included "Black boots, black pants, black button-down shirt, black mask, shotgun, semi-automatic or rifle...."[16] In a federal criminal complaint filed against Johnson in 2020, tapes reveal him saying, "The only way to stop police violence is to identify and locate the homes of police, burn the houses to the ground, kill the officer, their [sic] family members, and associates...."[17]

The Brotherhood Movement.

---

15    Thomas Mates, "What is the NFAC? A Look at Black Militia Group Police Say Is Connected to Suspected Shooter of Daytona Officer," Clickorlando.com, June 27, 2021, https://www.clickorlando.com/news/local/2021/06/26/what-is-the-nfac-a-look-at-black-militia-group-connected-to-suspected-shooter-of-daytona-officer/.

16    Nicole Chavez, Ryan Young, and Angela Barajas, "An All-Black Group Is Arming Itself and Demanding Change. They Are the NFAC," CNN, October 25, 2020, https://www.cnn.com/2020/10/25/us/nfac-black-armed-group/index.html.

17    Mates, "What is the NFAC?"

The Brotherhood Movement is a militia group that believes in "education, black economics, community engagement, conflict resolution." Its Facebook page shows the clenched fist—a common image associated with communism and black "resistance."[18] In 2021, a "pro-CRT" (CRT stands for Critical Race Theory) member of the Brotherhood Movement showed up at a Fort Worth, Texas, school board meeting, threatening critical race theory critics by explaining that he had "1,000 soldiers ready to go, locked and loaded."[19]

## RISE OF THE MOORS

In the summer of 2021, a story broke early one Saturday morning about the arrest of 11 members of Rise of the Moors, after a major armed confrontation on I–95 with SWAT teams and Massachusetts state police. Members of the heavily-armed Rise of the Moors told police that they were not carrying gun licenses and that they do not recognize U.S. laws.[20] In fact, they refuse to pay taxes, get driver's licenses, or register firearms.[21] According to the group's website, the organization is based in Pawtucket, Rhode

---

18    "The Brotherhood Movement," Facebook, accessed November 23, 2022, https://www.facebook.com/TheBrotherhoodMovement.

19    Ariel Zilber, "Ex-Member of Black Militia Group The Brotherhood Is Kicked out of Texas School Board Meeting After Threatening Anti-CRT Parents by Saying He's Got '1,000 Soldiers Ready to Go, Locked and Loaded'," *Daily Mail*, November 15, 2021, https://www.dailymail.co.uk/news/article-10203843/Pro-CRT-parent-ex-member-black-militia-group-threatens-anti-CRT-parents.html.

20    Tate Delloye, "A Refusal to Acknowledge US Laws, Belief In Ufos and Selling Fake Passports to Pay for Their Abandoned House HQ: The Inside Story of the 'Rise of The Moors' Militia Who Hit the Headlines After Stand-Off With Massachusetts Cops," *Daily Mail*, July 1, 2021, https://www.dailymail.co.uk/news/article-9718235/The-inside-story-Rise-Moors-militia-nine-hour-stand-Massachusetts-cops.html.

21    "Rise of the Moors FAQ," Rise of the Moors, accessed November 23, 2022, http://www.riseofthemoors.org/faq.html.

Island, and its views have exploded on Facebook and YouTube.[22] The Southern Poverty Law Center—no friend of conservatives— lists the group as an active anti-governmental sovereign-citizen group "known to retaliate against government authorities through financial means—a process called 'paper terrorism.'"[23]

Notably, none of these groups gets much attention from the mainstream media nor from President Biden's Justice Department. Nor has the White House highlighted eco-terrorism as a threat. In fact, the White House has refused to acknowledge or publicly condemn what the FBI once called in 2005 "the most active criminal extremist elements in the United States."[24] Even today the FBI explains: "domestic terrorists may be motivated to violence by single-issue ideologies"—including "environmental extremism."[25] In 2009, an American animal-rights activist, Daniel Andreas of San Diego, became the first "domestic terrorist" to be placed on the FBI's Most Wanted Terrorists list.[26] Additionally, a 2020 edition of the Journal of Strategic Security reports that "recent extremist organizations are showing a more violent anti-progress and pro-environment agenda."[27]

---

22   Rise of the Moors, http://www.riseofthemoors.org/.

23   "Moorish Sovereign Citizens," The Southern Poverty Law Center (SPLC), accessed November 23, 2022, https://www.splcenter.org/fighting-hate/extremist-files/group/moorish-sovereign-citizens.

24   John E. Lewis, "Testimony," Federal Bureau of Investigation (FBI), May 18, 2004, https://archives.fbi.gov/archives/news/testimony/animal-rights-extremism-and-ecoterrorism.

25   Dr. Cynthia Miller-Idriss, "The Dynamic Terrorism Landscape And What It Means For America," The House Committee on Homeland Security, February 2, 2022, https://homeland.house.gov/imo/media/doc/miller-idriss_testimony_full_020222.pdf.

26   Lorraine Elliott, "Ecoterrorism," Encyclopaedia Britannica Online, accessed October 27, 2022, https://www.britannica.com/topic/ecoterrorism.

27   Paola Andrea Spadaro, "Climate Change, Environmental Terrorism, Eco-Terrorism and Emerging Threats," *The Journal of Strategic Security (JSS)* 13, no. 4 (2020), https://digitalcommons.usf.edu/cgi/viewcontent.cgi?article=1863&context=jss.

# TREE SPIKING

*George Alexander was 23 years old. His job was to split logs. He was a victim of a tree spike. Though he was nearly three feet away when the log he was sawing hit the spike, the saw exploded. One half of the blade was lodged in the log. The other half hit Alexander in the head, tearing through his safety helmet and face shield. His face was slashed from eye to chin. His teeth were smashed and his jaw was cut in half.*

— JACK ANDERSON and DALE VAN ATTA,
"Tree Spiking an 'Eco-Terrorist' Tactic,"
*The Washington Post*, March 5, 1990[28]

Searching for tree spikes is now a way of life in the logging industry. Tree spiking is when a nail or a metal rod is driven into a tree, sometimes hidden in the bark. When a logger saws into the tree and hits the spike, it can shatter the chain saw and send shards of metal flying.

Meet Tracy Stone-Manning. When she was a graduate student, she used her thesis to argue that America should follow the Chinese Communist government's lead in placing limits on the number of children Americans can have.[29] Apparently humans were displacing grizzly bears. It was also during this period that Stone-Manning sent a letter to the U.S. Forest Service informing the service that there were spiked trees in the Clearwater National

---

28    Jack Anderson and Dale Van Atta, "Tree Spiking an 'Eco-Terrorist' Tactic," *The Washington Post*, March 5, 1990, https://www.washingtonpost.com/archive/local/1990/03/05/tree-spiking-an-eco-terrorist-tactic/a400944c-a3a0-4c03-ab99-afada6f44e7a/.

29    Debbie Lesko and Steve Pierce, "Tree Spiking? Population Control? Tracy Stone-Manning is Too Extreme to Lead BLM," *AZCentral*, August 13, 2021, https://www.azcentral.com/story/opinion/op-ed/2021/08/13/tracy-stone-manning-too-extreme-lead-bureau-land-management/8102411002/.

Forest in Idaho.[30] After a criminal investigation, it was determined that Stone-Manning was not only a senior member of the eco-terrorist group Earth First but had mislead law enforcement about her role in the tree spiking. Though she admitted that she "composed the letter," she claimed that she had no idea that the letters could be treated as a threat, had no actual knowledge of the spikes' locations, and further explained that she was acting more as a whistleblower than a co-conspirator when she sent the letters.[31]

The investigator hired by the U.S. Department of Agriculture (USDA) concluded otherwise. After a multi-year investigation, the investigator discovered evidence that Stone-Manning had planned the spike letter project from its inception and had likely played a key role in the tree spikes that were actually planted in Post Office Timber Sales trees.[32]

In 2021, the White House nominated Tracy Stone-Manning to head the Bureau of Land Management, and she was confirmed in the fall of that year.[33]

---

30  Caitlyn Kim, "A Tree Spiking Incident From the 1980s Is Looming Over Biden's BLM Nominee," Coloradio Public Radio (CPR), July 21, 2021, https://www.cpr.org/2021/07/21/tree-spiking-eco-terrorism-tracy-stone-manning-buearu-of-land-management/.

31  Lesko and Pierce, "Tree Spiking?"

32  Michael W. Merkley, "Letter to Senators Joe Manchin and John Barasso," (letter, 2021), 1-4, https://www.energy.senate.gov/services/files/03E32662-AF39-43BE-9109-48809E1E56EB.

33  "Tracy Stone-Manning," Bureau of Land Management (BLM), accessed November 23, 2022, https://www.blm.gov/bio/tracy-stone-manning.

# EARTH LIBERATION FRONT

*From destroying evidence to fleeing the country, none of Mr. Dibee's tactics stopped us from making sure he was held accountable for his malicious and destructive actions.*[34]

— KIERAN L. RAMSEY, Special Agent in Charge of the FBI in Oregon, April, 2022

At a 2005 hearing before the Public Works Committee examining eco-terrorism, Republican Senator James Inhofe from Oklahoma explained that both the Department of Justice and the Department of Homeland Security agreed that eco-terrorism was a severe problem, naming the Earth Liberation Front (ELF) and the Animal Liberation Front (ALF) as among the severe threats to the homeland.[35]

One of those radicals was Joseph Mahmoud Dibee. He was active in a group that called itself "the Family," which, according to the FBI, committed crimes in the name of ELF, causing an estimated $40 million in damages from 1995 to 2005.[36] In the spring of 2022, Dibee, a fugitive for more than twelve years, was finally forced to answer for his eco-terrorism. In one instance, his arson resulted in a loss of more than $1.2 million at Cavel West, a meat-processing plant in Redmond, Oregon.[37]

Eco-terrorism doesn't just create problems for the specific companies that are targeted. It can have broader effects on the

---

34     "Pacific Northwest Environmental Extremist and Arsonist Pleads Guilty," Department of Justice, District of Oregon, April 21, 2022, https://www.justice.gov/usao-or/pr/pacific-northwest-environmental-extremist-and-arsonist-pleads-guilty.

35     Merkley to Manchin and Barasso.

36     DOJ, "Environmental Extremist."

37     Conrad Wilson, "Eco-Activist and Former International Fugitive Joseph Dibee Pleads Guilty in 1997 Oregon Arson," OPB, April 21, 2022, https://www.opb.org/article/2022/04/21/joseph-dibee-environmental-terrorism-oregon-washington-earth-liberation-front-animal/.

nation's economy and American society. Opposition to oil pipelines is just such an issue. In 2016 and 2017, environmentalists tried to halt construction of the Dakota Access Pipeline under the Missouri River. Nearly a thousand people were arrested.[38] One extremist tactic has been to target emergency pipeline shut-off valves. Such an unplanned closure can lead to damage to the pipeline, or worse, a ground leak. When America faces unprecedented prices at the pump, such eco-terrorism can ripple throughout the economy.

Jessica Reznicek, a self-proclaimed "climate activist" decided to move beyond protests and vandalism. In 2016, she committed herself to stopping the construction of the Dakota Access Pipeline, no matter the cost. Now serving an eight-year sentence, Reznicek managed to get through security fences so that she could set fire to equipment, and then she used chemicals to burn holes into the pipeline itself. Climate activists used shunts, made of wire and magnets, to trigger a train's automatic brakes in order to cause it to derail. In the fall of 2021, eco-terrorist Ellen Brennan Reiche was convicted of using a shunt on a rail line that carried crude oil.[39]

Though the White House tries to downplay it, home-grown eco-terrorism—a leftist ideology—is perhaps the greatest threat facing the homeland besides Islamic acts of terror. Authors of a 2020 research paper, "Climate Change, Environmental Terrorism, Eco-Terrorism and Emerging Threats," used open-source data to show that "environmental terrorism represents an increasing secu-

---

38   "Probe into Dakota Access Protest Continues 4 Years Later," *ABC News*, February 13, 2021, https://abcnews.go.com/US/wireStory/probe-dakota-access-protest-continues-years-75876369.

39   "Bellingham, Washington Woman Convicted of 'Shunt' Attack on BNSF Railroad," Department of Justice, Western District of Washington, September 9, 2021, https://www.justice.gov/usao-wdwa/pr/bellingham-washington-woman-convicted-shunt-attack-bnsf-railroad.

rity threat...."[40] Published in the *Journal of Strategic Security*, the paper identified climate change as a key driver of eco-terrorism and warned that "either through war or acts of terror" this motivation could be "used to exert fear in the population to achieve organizational aims."[41]

Finally, it is noteworthy that the White House highlights "white supremacy" in stark contrast to the post-9/11 consensus that foreign terrorist organizations are the greatest threat to the homeland. Last spring, American Enterprise Institute Fellow Katherine Zimmerman issued a stern warning that jihadist terror groups remain a serious threat.[42] She identified the botched withdrawal from Afghanistan and the COVID-19 pandemic as key drivers of the growing reach of ISIS and the Islamic state.[43] She claims that COVID-19 mitigation efforts are a key driver of anti-government hostility used by ISIS recruiters.[44] According to the George Washington University Program on Extremism, since 9/11, more than two hundred persons have been charged in the U.S. with ISIS-related activities.[45]

This is the real threat that President Biden's racially divisive "white supremacy" claim ignores.

---

40  Spadaro, "Climate Change, Environmental Terrorism."

41  Spadaro, "Climate Change, Environmental Terrorism."

42  "Global Terrorism Threat Has Not Gone Away, Says AEI Fellow," *Security Matters*, May 15, 2022, https://govmatters.tv/terrorism-threat-us-national-strategy-isis-islamic-state-jihad-covid-19-afghanistan-iraq-syria-aei-american-enterprise-institute-katherine-zimmerman/.

43  Katherine Zimmerman, "Afghanistan Is Set to Become a Sanctuary For Extremists," *The Hill,* September 2, 2021, https://thehill.com/opinion/national-security/570416-afghanistan-is-set-to-become-a-sanctuary-for-extremists/.

44  *Security Matters*, "Global terrorism threat."

45  The Cases, The Program on Extremism, George Washington University, accessed October 26, 2022, https://extremism.gwu.edu/cases.

## THE REAL DOMESTIC EXTREMISM RECORD

- *The average age of charged individuals was 28.*

- *Arrests occurred in 33 states and the District of Columbia.*

- *The average prison sentence was 13.1 years.*

- *40% were accused of traveling or attempting to travel abroad.*

- *29% were accused of plotting domestic terror attacks.*

- *57% were arrested in an operation involving an informant and/or an undercover agent.*

- *189 individuals have pleaded or were found guilty.*

GWU on Program Extremism[46]

## BUILDING BACK BAD

Though many Americans thought the worst of the pandemic was over, a newly elected President Biden tried to push through Congress a budget-busting agenda that would put trillions more into the U.S. economy, pay Americans to delay re-entry into the work place, prevent landlords from charging tenants, and make billions in payments to left-wing special interests. All of these hurt economic growth, create greater long-term debt for the US, and undermine capitalism—the very tools needed for Americans (especially blacks) to thrive.

Candidate Biden promised that he could get enacted a comprehensive package, called Build Back Better, that would allow

---

46    Lorenzo Vidino and Seamus Hughes, "ISIS in America: From Retweets to Raqqa," The Program on Extremism, George Washington University, December 2015, https://extremism.gwu.edu/isis-america.

him to be regarded as a historic progressive figure. It was a nearly $4 trillion budget-reconciliation package made up of far-left priorities—priorities that weren't close to being bipartisan. In fact, they couldn't even garner the support of all Democrats. But President Biden decided that, as the pandemic wound down, now was the time "to imagine and build a new American economy for our families and the next generation."[47]

President Biden's plan includes support for state, local, and tribal governments to provide education and first responder grants, universal and free pre-school for all three- and four-year-olds, day-care for senior citizens, and $300 monthly payments to nearly 40 million households, while also extending unemployment insurance.

BBB also proposes what the White House calls the largest climate change initiative in American history. This "Green New Deal" includes billions in payments and subsidies for wind turbines, solar panels, and electric cars. Making sure to make a left turn into impoverished communities, the plan creates a Clean Energy and Sustainability Accelerator agency to invest in projects around the country, while delivering 40 percent of the benefits of investment to disadvantaged communities. BBB also included generous affordable housing grants, expanded the Earned Income Tax Credit (EITC) to include an additional 17 million Americans, and provided new and expanded availability of the school lunch program.

BBB dramatically expands the role of Washington in healthcare administration. This would mean billions paid in prescription drug grants as well as billions more in grants for insurance premiums—and let's not forget the billions in hearing benefits to

---

47    "Build Back Better: Joe Biden's Jobs and Economic Recovery Plan for Working Families," Biden/Harris, accessed November 24, 2022, https://joebiden.com/build-back-better/.

Medicare. Although loved by the hospital and insurance industry, the costs for the taxpayer were staggering. The health provisions (not including Medicare) would cost more than $550 billion.[48] President Biden also pledged with BBB to create a Public Health Jobs Corps that would create 100,000 new jobs.[49]

The Congressional Budget Offices assessed the House-passed version and concluded that, if made permanent, this proposal would add $3 trillion to the deficit.[50]

You might imagine that this plan was everything and more that progressives could ever have dreamed they could achieve. But you'd be wrong. Senator Bernie Sanders argued that Democrats should take this opportunity to spend much more. He advocated a $6 trillion version of the "Build Back Better Act" that contained everything including immigration reform. In his words, it dealt with "the existential threat of climate change…the cost of pre-scription drugs, mak[ing] sure elderly people can chew their food because we expand Medicare to dental care, hearing aids and eyeglasses…."[51]

48  Phillip L. Swagel to Hon. Jason Smith, "Provisions in Reconciliation Legislation That Would Affect Health Insurance Coverage of People Under Age 65," Congressional Budget Office, October 19, 2021, https://energycommerce.house.gov/sites/democrats.energycommerce. house.gov/files/documents/Letter_Honorable_Jason_Smith.pdf.

49  "FACT SHEET: Biden-Harris Administration to Invest $7 Billion from American Rescue Plan to Hire and Train Public Health Workers in Response to COVID-19," White House Briefing Room, May 13, 2021, https://www. whitehouse.gov/briefing-room/statements-releases/2021/05/13/fact-sheet-biden-harris-administration-to-invest-7-billion-from-american-rescue-plan-to-hire-and-train-public-health-workers-in-response-to-covid-19/.

50  Phillip L. Swagel to Hon. Lindsey Graham and Hon. Jason Smith, "Budgetary Effects of Making Specified Policies in the Build Back Better Plan," Congressional Budget Office, December 10, 2021, https://www. cbo.gov/system/files/2021-12/57673-BBBA-GrahamSmith-Letter.pdf.

51  Alexander Bolton, "Sanders: Democrats Considering $6 Trillion Spending Package," The Hill, June 17, 2021, https://www.sanders.senate.gov/ in-the-news/sanders-democrats-considering-6-trillion-spending-package/.

Like much of the President's agenda, BBB fell flat. As in so many other instances, the White House refused to choose between getting some of its agenda passed by Congress or getting everything that it wanted, so it lost due to expensive and unpopular parts of the agenda, such as the Green New Deal, and in the end, BBB died.

Expansions of school lunch programs and greater medical benefits would likely have been quite well received by blacks who make up the base of President Biden's party. But President Biden wouldn't say no to the progressives on the other issues to just get those measures. For black America, dropping BBB, instead of taking much smaller pieces, was just another example of being pushed to the back of the political bus.

## NO GASOLINE LEFT IN THE TANK

Next, President Biden embraced sharp new restrictions on America's domestic oil and gas industry, along with a legion of growth-killing energy regulations that were very popular with progressives. Shortly after his inauguration, he rejoined the Paris Climate Accords, canceled the Keystone Pipeline, and committed to wholesale restrictions on the use of public lands for oil exploration.[52]

Not surprisingly, this led to a dramatic rise in gas prices at the pump. The price would reach $5 a gallon before receding.[53] This woke policy backfired. A Rasmussen poll in the spring of

---

52    Executive Office of the President, "Protecting Public Health and the Environment and Restoring Science to Tackle the Climate Crisis," Federal Register, January 25, 2021, https://www.federalregister.gov/documents/2021/01/25/2021-01765/protecting-public-health-and-the-environment-and-restoring-science-to-tackle-the-climate-crisis?aff_id=1314.

53    "US Retail Gas Price," Ycharts, October 10, 2022, https://ycharts.com/indicators/us_gas_price.

2021 revealed that a majority of Americans rejected climate regulation and wanted Washington to work to bring fuel prices down instead,[54] and by the close of summer, fuel prices had become one of the leading concerns of the American people.

The high gas prices harmed blacks the most.[55] As a 2021 Bank of America report indicated, the inflation spikes on food and energy hurt blacks more than other Americans, as blacks spend more of their money on energy, food, and household items—all of which are affected by out-of-control gas prices.[56]

It has often been said that energy is the lifeblood of the economy. Though access to electricity is taken for granted by most Americans, people are now having to pay considerably more for it—a trend that is likely to continue unless the Biden Administration reverses course.

## ENVIRONMENTAL RACISM—A SOLUTION IN SEARCH OF A CAUSE

Biden's Environmental Protection Agency (EPA) says environmental justice "is the fair treatment and meaningful involvement of all people regardless of race, color, national origin or income

---

54   "Voters More Worried About Gas Prices Than Climate Change," Rasmussen Reports, May 9, 2022, https://www.rasmussenreports. com/public_content/politics/partner_surveys/may_2022/ voters_more_worried_about_gas_prices_than_climate_change.

55   Kandace Redd, "'We Need Help Right Now' | People of Color Hit Hardest by Inflation, Gas Prices," ABC 10 News, March 15, 2022, https://www.abc10.com/ article/news/community/race-and-culture/study-inflation-hits-communities-of-color-more-than-others/103-6e1e851d-cf0c-4bd9-9b77-21de3a14262f.

56   Logan Pellegrom, "What To Know About Inflation, as US Hits 40-Year High," Central Michigan University, February 11, 2022, https://www. cmich.edu/news/details/what-to-know-about-inflation-as-us-hits-40-year-high; Abbianca Makoni, "People of Color Amongst Those Getting Hit the Hardest by 2021 Inflation—Study," People of Color in Tech (POCIT), accessed November 26, 2022, https://peopleofcolorintech.com/front/ people-of-color-amongst-those-getting-hit-the-hardest-by-2021-inflation-study/.

with respect to the development, implementation and enforcement of environmental laws, regulations, and policies."[57] This official explanation bears little correlation with the actual practice. Environmental justice is in reality a political tool exercised predominantly by progressive whites in the federal bureaucracy and in the academy.

From the outset, the Biden Administration recognized the potential of environmental justice to help propel its regulatory agenda, especially its climate policies. Environmental justice provisions were included in Biden's Executive Order 14008, issued on January 27, 2021, just a few days after he took office. E.O. 14008 is entitled "Tackling the Climate Crisis at Home and Abroad" and, among its many provisions, includes Sec. 219, which addresses environmental justice. It also created two new White House councils—the White House Environmental Justice Interagency Council and the White House Environmental Justice Advisory Council—to address EJ implementation and solicit "expert advice and recommendations."[58] Under this directive, the federal government has sought to create environmental justice training academies and new mapping tools to highlight environmental racial disparities.[59]

As a result of the President's order, environmental justice has been elevated to a position of unprecedented prominence in determining the decisions of the EPA.

---

57    "Learn About Environmental Justice," U.S. Environmental Protection Agency, last updated on September 6, 2022, https://www.epa.gov/environmentaljustice/learn-about-environmental-justice.

58    "About the White House Environmental Justice Advisory Council," The White House, https://www.whitehouse.gov/environmentaljustice/white-house-environmental-justice-advisory-council/.

59    "What is the EJ Academy?," U.S. Environmental Protection Agency (EPA), July 11, 2022, https://www.epa.gov/oh/ej-academy.

## LET THEM EAT CAKE

Under the guise of protecting racial minorities from being exposed to environmental hazards, these unelected and unaccountable activists promote policies that ultimately make those minorities they claim to work for wards of the state, thereby denying them full participation in society. For example, the Biden EPA hands out millions in grants to so called community activists to use in predominantly minority communities for "feel good" discussions.[60] The very communities that are most beset by violent crime, high out-of-wedlock birth rates, and poor public schools can now at least hear lectures about environmental justice in their own neighborhoods. But lectures don't alleviate poverty.

Washington should be working to direct new investments and private sector job creation in these communities, instead of highlighting them as places to avoid. Consider: if the EPA denies a permit for a manufacturing facility on the grounds that its carbon emissions would have a disparate impact on people of color, it will be blocking an important avenue these people have to improve their lives. In fact, the criteria used by the EPA to make environmental justice determinations are inherently subjective and can be enlisted to serve political objectives. For example, the more conservative parts of the country can easily be prevented from having new plants built, while allowing them in the more liberal areas.

Take the case of Flint, Michigan. For months, this Rust Belt city's residents were unable to drink city water because it had been contaminated by lead, a potent neurotoxin that can cause brain damage in children. Flint's aging, corroded underground iron

---

60    "EPA Seeks Input on New Environmental Justice-Focused Pollution Prevention Grant Opportunity Funded by $100 Million Investment from President Biden's Bipartisan Infrastructure Law," U.S. Environmental Protection Agency (EPA), September 1, 2022, https://www.epa.gov/newsreleases/epa-seeks-input-new-environmental-justice-focused-pollution-prevention-grant.

water pipes had become a breeding ground for human pathogens, with the pipes corroded to the point that they all but prevented chlorine's ability to disinfect the water. This disaster was ignored by city, state, and federal officials until it was too late. The contaminated water was eventually linked to seventy-two cases of Legionnaires' disease that resulted in twelve deaths.[61]

In truth, these tragic results were the result of systemic incompetence by three levels of government that failed to address a problem that had been unfolding for years. The fact that the EPA, even then the lead agency on environmental justice, played such a prominent role in the Flint disaster is a reflection of the misplaced priorities of a wasteful and flawed program.

If you thought that we'd learned anything from Flint, take a look at Jackson, Mississippi. In early September of 2022, torrential rains caused Jackson's waste-water treatment plant to be shuttered, leaving more than 150,000 residents (out of 160,000) without drinking water.[62] For more than a decade, the waste water treatment plant had been the center of a political dispute over who should bear responsibility for its needed repairs. Jackson—which is 82 percent black—was able to fall through the cracks, even as Biden was bragging about "pushing investments to areas with high pollution levels and economic distress."[63]

For nearly two years, the Biden White House ignored Jackson. Now that the treatment center has failed, instead of taking responsibility to fix the problem, the White House complains that the

61    David Shultz, "Was Flint's Deadly Legionnaires' Epidemic Caused by Low Chlorine Levels in the Water Supply?" *Science*, February 5, 2018, https://www.science.org/content/article/was-flint-s-deadly-legionnaires-epidemic-caused-low-chlorine-levels-water-supply.

62    Zack Colman, "Jackson's Water Emergency Exposes A Dilemma For Biden," *Politico*, September 3, 2022, https://www.politico.com/news/2022/09/03/biden-jackson-federal-cash-00054562.

63    Colman, "Jackson's Water Emergency."

GOP legislature shouldn't impose mandatory repair requirements on Jackson (designed to ensure that the repairs actually occur).[64]

A grave environmental injustice was inflicted on the residents of this majority black city at a time when federal environmental justice grants were being lavished on activist groups and an assortment of governmental entities around the country.

"Cancer Alley" in Louisiana is another case in point. In the 1990s, reports of high cancer rates in parishes stretching for eighty-five miles along the Mississippi River led to the area being dubbed "Cancer Alley." Local petrochemical plants were seen as the likely cause, and the region's substantial African American population was thought to be especially threatened by the plants' emissions. The "Cancer Alley" narrative seemed to confirm the points Carol Browner was making at the time as she set about creating EPA's environmental justice program. But when scientists at Louisiana State University Medical Center and the Louisiana Tumor Registry took a closer look, they found that people in "Cancer Alley" did not develop cancer any more often than the residents of the rest of South Louisiana, or even the rest of the nation.

These policies have already hurt working-class households, harming blacks the most.

## DIE (AKA DIVERSITY EQUITY AND INCLUSION) BEFORE NATIONAL SECURITY

In yet another woke action, President Biden pushed the progressive Diversity, Equity, And Inclusion (DEI) agenda on the nation's military. He nominated defense contractor Lloyd Austin as Secretary of Defense and had him initiate an extremism "stand-down" and DIE

---

64    Hannah Northey, "Mississippi Water Crisis Triggers Blame Game," *Politico*, August 31, 2022, https://www.politico.com/news/2022/08/31/blame-game-rages-as-water-system-crashes-in-miss-capital-00054372.

training for the entire Defense Department.[65] Military service members wasted 5,889,082 man-hours going through this training.[66]

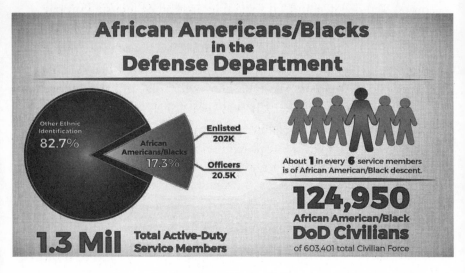

US Dept of Defense.[67]

As a payoff acknowledging the Left's antipathy toward the military, this move did nothing for blacks. Yet, not only are blacks, and especially black men, over-represented in the military,[68] but as an American Enterprise Institute study titled "Black Men

65 Paul D. Shinkman, "Pentagon Orders 'Stand-Down' to Address Extremism in the Ranks," *U.S. News and World Report,* February 3, 2021, https://www.usnews.com/news/national-news/articles/2021-02-03/pentagon-orders-stand-down-to-address-extremism-in-the-ranks.

66 "Under Biden, Military Spent Nearly 6 Million Man-Hours On 'Woke' Training," Senator Marsha Blackburn, February 15, 2022, https://www.blackburn.senate.gov/2022/2/under-biden-military-spent-nearly-6-million-man-hours-on-woke-training.

67 "African American History in the Defense Department: African Americans in Times of War," *U.S. Department of Defense,* accessed October 20, 2022, https://dod.defense.gov/News/Special-Reports/African-American-History-archive/.

68 Richard V. Reeves and Sarah Nzau, "Black Americans are Much More Likely to Serve the Nation, in Military and Civilian Roles," Brookings Institution, August 27, 2020, https://www.brookings.edu/blog/up-front/2020/08/27/black-americans-are-much-more-likely-to-serve-the-nation-in-military-and-civilian-roles/.

Making it in America" revealed, military service is a significant tool of economic mobility for many black men.[69] Wasting time on the stand-down and DEI training, instead of focusing on pay raises and new benefits, demoralizes servicemembers and threatens national security. The stand-down is in stark contrast to the Defense Department's past record of opportunity for blacks. This training does promote the false impression that military service and extremism are linked. It will more likely make recruiting more difficult and cause some blacks to miss out on the amazing leadership skills they can acquire in service to the nation.

## VIRUS GONNA VIRUS

Perhaps none of President Biden's failed policies represented wokeness more than his COVID-19 policies. Throughout his first year in office, he pushed hard to continue COVID-19 mitigation policies that were ultimately shown to be destructive to the economy, set back the education of school children, and decimated the restaurant industry, all while crippling America's supply chain.

With fanfare, President Biden signed a nearly $2 trillion COVID-19 bill in March 2021.[70] He bragged that it was accomplished with no support from the GOP, and his bill sent a payment of $1,400 to almost every American, extended $300-per-week unemployment payments, and provided another $20 billion in vaccine payments, as well as $25 billion for rental and utility

---

69   W. Bradford Wilcox, Wendy R. Wang, and Ronald B. Mincy, "Black Men Making It In America: The Engines of Economic Success for Black Men in America," American Enterprise Institute, June 2018, https://www.aei.org/wp-content/uploads/2018/06/BlackMenMakingItInAmerica-Final_062218.pdf.

70   Jacob Pramuk, "Biden Signs $1.9 Trillion Covid Relief Bill, Clearing Way for Stimulus Checks, Vaccine Aid," CNBC, March 11 2021, https://www.cnbc.com/2021/03/11/biden-1point9-trillion-covid-relief-package-thursday-afternoon.html.

payment assistance.[71] Perhaps the icing on the cake was the nearly $400 billion in grants to state, local, and tribal governments.[72]

Almost immediately, there were warning signs. Critics pointed out that almost half of the school funds to encourage classroom re-openings wouldn't be spent until 2024.[73] The Committee for a Responsible Federal Budget identified more than $650 billion in non-pandemic-related funding. In fact, it included nearly $90 billion for union-supported pension plans alone.[74]

Perhaps the most significant outcome from this decision is the explosive inflation that hurts Americans and was a key driver of the Democrats' rout in November 2021. The measure ended up being poorly targeted, used borrowed money, and ultimately did nothing to improve the nation's long-term economic outlook.

After promising that our time with COVID-19 mitigation efforts would end around Independence Day[75] and admitting that he didn't have the power to issue a federal vaccine mandate, President Biden abruptly changed course.[76]

71   Pramuk, "Covid Relief Bill."

72   Richard Rubin, "Biden Administration to Start Doling Out $350 Billion in Aid to State, Local Governments," *Wall Street Journal*, May 10, 2021, https://www.wsj.com/articles/biden-administration-to-start-doling-out-350-billion-in-aid-to-state-local-governments-11620666000.

73   Jonathan Nicholson, "'Wasteful,' 'Poorly Targeted'—Critics Rip Stimulus Bill's Price Tag, Contents," *MarketWatch*, February 22, 2021, https://www.marketwatch.com/story/wasteful-poorly-targeted-critics-rip-stimulus-bills-price-tag-contents-11614007215.

74   Rich Lowry, "Biden's Covid Relief Bill Might Be Good Politics, But It's Bad Policy," *Politico*, March 10, 2021, https://www.politico.com/news/magazine/2021/03/10/bidens-relief-bill-bad-policy-475216.

75   Anthony Zurcher, "Covid Pandemic: Biden Eyes 4 July as 'Independence Day' From Virus," BBC, March 12, 2021, https://www.bbc.com/news/world-us-canada-56368328.

76   Rachel Siegel et al. "Millions of Workers, Businesses to Face Biden's New Coronavirus Vaccine and Testing Rules," *Washington Post*, September 10, 2021, https://www.washingtonpost.com/business/2021/09/10/biden-vaccine-mandate-workers-businesses/.

The reversal would prove to be devastating. While claiming to follow the science, his Administration pushed new COVID-19 policies that encouraged "COVID-19 passports"[77] and lockdowns. Within a few months, polling showed that Americans, disheartened by the shift, now distrusted federal health agencies at record levels.[78]

Lawsuits were filed against the airline mask mandate, as well as against the vaccine mandate Biden ordered for large employers. Even military servicemembers filed suits against the DOD vaccine mandate.[79] By early 2022, a CNBC poll showed that Americans disapproved of Biden's handling of the pandemic, which had been one of his strongest areas of support up to that point.[80]

By 2022, the results were in: blacks were, once again, hardest hit. Even the Centers for Disease Control and Prevention admitted that blacks lost their jobs at higher levels and consequently experienced elevated financial instability.[81] Extended school clo-

77    In many places across America, citizens were expected to carry proof of their compliance with Covid19 protocols referred to as Covid-19 passports.

78    "The Public's Perspective on the United States Public Health System," Harvard T.H. Chan School of Public Health, Robert Wood Johnson Foundation, May 2021, https://cdn1.sph.harvard.edu/wp-content/uploads/sites/94/2021/05/RWJF-Harvard-Report_FINAL-051321.pdf.

79    Efthimios Parasidis, "COVID-19 Vaccine Mandates at The Supreme Court: Scope and Limits of Federal Authority," Health Affairs, March 8, 2022, https://www.healthaffairs.org/do/10.1377/forefront.20220303.102051/; Charlie Savage and Heather Murphy, "Federal Judge Strikes Down Mask Mandate for Planes and Public Transit," New York Times, April 18, 2022, https://www.nytimes.com/2022/04/18/us/politics/federal-mask-mandate-airplanes.html.

80    Thomas Franck, "Biden Disapproval Hits New High as Voters Give Him Bad Grades on Economy, New CNBC/Change Poll Says," CNBC, January 4, 2022, https://www.cnbc.com/2022/01/04/biden-disapproval-rating-high-voters-blame-him-on-economy-cnbc-poll.html.

81    "Unintended Consequences of COVID-19 Mitigation Strategies," Centers for Disease Control and Prevention (CDC), December 10, 2020, https://www.cdc.gov/coronavirus/2019-ncov/community/health-equity/racial-ethnic-disparities/disparities-impact.html.

sures created nutrition challenges for the students, disproportion-ately black, who relied on school lunches for meals.[82] And per-haps worse, black students fell behind in math and reading.[83] Of some 4.4 million students tested in third grade to eighth grade, black children lost the most ground academically, according to the NWEA (formerly the Northwest Evaluation Association).[84]

The federal vaccine mandate for government employees also affected blacks, who work for federal and state government agen-cies at higher levels than the population as a whole.[85] President Biden's order made it far easier for black government employees to lose their jobs due to behavior that wasn't even related to the workplace, such as a requirement to send in COVID-19 testing results from home, despite the fact that Biden didn't even direct federal employees to return to the workplace until April 2022.[86]

82    Lisa Held, "The Pandemic Reveals Racial Gaps in School Meal Access," Civil Eats, January 26, 2021, https://civileats.com/2021/01/26/did-pandemic-disruptions-to-school-meal-programs-leave-out-students-of-color/.

83    Erin Einhorn, "When Covid-19 Closed Schools, Black, Hispanic and Poor Kids Took Biggest Hit in Math, Reading," NBC, December 1, 2020, https://www.nbcnews.com/news/education/when-covid-19-closed-schools-black-hispanic-poor-kids-took-n1249352.

84    Erin Einhorn, "When Covid-19 closed schools, Black, Hispanic and poor kids took biggest hit in math, reading," NBC News, November 30, 2020, https://www.nbcnews.com/news/education/when-covid-19-closed-schools-black-hispanic-poor-kids-took-n1249352.

85    "Executive Branch Employment by Gender and Race/National Origin, September 2006–September 2017," U.S. Office of Personnel Management, accessed November 26, 2022, https://www.opm.gov/policy-data-oversight/data-analysis-documentation/federal-employment-reports/reports-publications/executive-branch-employment-by-gender-and-racenational-origin/.

86    Jory Heckman, "Biden COVID Plan Directs More Federal Employees to Resume In-Person Work in April," Federal News Network, March 3, 2022, https://federalnewsnetwork.com/workforce/2022/03/biden-covid-plan-directs-more-federal-employees-to-resume-in-person-work-in-april/.

## CHARLIE FOXTROT

Though blacks serve disproportionately in the military, Biden engaged in reckless decision-making with our military operations, damaging our nation's reputation and that of our servicemembers.

Military service is a key means that blacks have used to reach the middle class for decades. Poor oversight of the military and America's foreign policy undermines the attractiveness of military service. Biden's managed to do both.

In the summer of 2021, President Biden abandoned Afghanistan without a plan, and in the disarray, thirteen American military servicemembers lost their lives. On August 31, 2021, readers of *Bloomberg News* awoke to this headline: "U.S. Withdrawal Leaves Afghanistan in Crisis and Uncertainty."[87] In one particularly desperate episode, Afghans desperate to flee their country ran along a departing U.S. Airforce transport plane and even clung to it as it taxied down a runway.[88]

President Biden was more interested in credit than in responsibility. In the summer of 2021, he explained, "I'm now the fourth United States President to preside over American troop presence in Afghanistan: two Republicans, two Democrats. I will not pass this responsibility on to a fifth."[89] The chaotic Afghanistan departure ended up being a disaster all around. President Biden robbed the White House of the political victory of achieving an

---

87   Justin Sink and Nick Wadhams, "U.S. Withdrawal Leaves Afghanistan in Crisis and Uncertainty," Bloomberg, August 30, 2021, https://www.bloomberg.com/news/articles/2021-08-31/biden-s-withdrawal-leaves-afghanistan-in-crisis-and-uncertainty.

88   Hal Bernton, "Dramatic Video of C-17 at Kabul Airport Shows People Clinging to JBLM-Based Plane," *Seattle Times*, August 16, 2021, https://www.seattletimes.com/seattle-news/dramatic-video-of-c-17-at-kabul-airport-shows-people-clinging-to-outside-of-jblm-based-plane/.

89   Cameron Peters, "The US Military is Finally Withdrawing from Afghanistan," *Vox*, April 25, 2021, https://www.vox.com/2021/4/25/22402539/afghanistan-military-withdrawal-final-biden-september-11th.

exit that most Americans wanted, while sending the signal to U.S. adversaries that America can't be trusted to keep its promises.

But wokeness overrode all. The State Department at one point even announced that the Administration would consider recognizing the odious Taliban, if it allowed a woman to be in the new government.[90] In a stunning example of pride coming before a fall, mere months before the total collapse of Afghanistan, the State Department flew the gay pride flag over the Kabul embassy.[91]

This disaster isn't just a humanitarian one for the people of Afghanistan. At the same time, the White House abandoned American citizens, many of whom have yet to be returned home. A 2022 U.S. Senate Foreign Relations Committee report indicated that more than 9,000 Americans were left behind.[92] Meanwhile, President Biden has prioritized homing up to 30,000 Afghan refugees at military bases in the U.S.[93]

President Biden claimed that he'd largely followed the Pentagon's advice, yet almost to a man the nation's generals have denied this claim, stating that they warned him that withdrawal was not advisable.[94] In testimony before the U.S. Senate Armed

90    Tammy Bruce, "Biden's 'Woke' Afghanistan Strategy," *The Washington Times*, August 17, 2021, https://www.washingtontimes.com/news/2021/aug/17/bidens-woke-afghanistan-strategy/.

91    Pranshu Verna, "State Department Authorizes U.S. Embassies to Fly the Pride Flag," *New York Times*, June 21, 2021, https://www.nytimes.com/2021/04/23/us/us-embassy-pride-flag.html.

92    "Left Behind: A Brief Assessment of the Biden Administration's Strategic Failures during the Afghanistan Evacuation," The United States Senate Committee on Foreign Relations Minority Report, February 2022, https://www.foreign.senate.gov/imo/media/doc/Risch%20Afghanistan%20Report%202022.pdf.

93    Ben Weingarten, "Biden's Afghanistan Bungle: Wrong Man, Right Thing, Worst Way," *Newsweek*, August 18, 2021, https://www.newsweek.com/bidens-afghanistan-bungle-wrong-man-right-thing-worst-way-opinion-1620352.

94    Andrew Clevenger, "Pentagon Told Biden Not to Withdraw from Afghanistan," *Roll Call*, September 28, 2021, https://rollcall.com/2021/09/28/pentagon-told-biden-not-to-withdraw-from-afghanistan/.

Services Committee, Joint Chiefs of Staff Chairman General Mark Milley and U.S. Central Commander General Kenneth McKenzie explained why they thought the withdrawal was a mistake.[95]

President Biden defended himself by telling the nation that "Afghanistan political leaders gave up and fled the country. The Afghan military collapsed, sometimes without trying to fight. If anything, the developments of the past week reinforced that ending U.S. military involvement in Afghanistan now was the right decision."[96] But these facts were known before the withdrawal order was given. President Biden has long been a skeptic of what America's military could achieve in Afghanistan, going back to his time in the Obama White House.[97]

Rather than assess America's military and national security needs, President Biden wanted to demonstrate his anti-war bona fides and achieve recognition in history. His withdrawal date was to be officially commemorated on September 11th.[98]

## TRUST AND DON'T VERIFY

Throughout the first two years of his term, President Biden pushed for a disastrous new Iran nuclear deal, at one point even using Russia as his primary negotiator.

The Joint Comprehensive Plan of Action (JCPOA)—known as the Iran nuclear deal—was first entered into by President Barack Obama and all permanent members of the UN Security Council

---

95    Clevenger, "Pentagon Told Biden."
96    Ken Dilanian et al, "CIA Warned of Rapid Afghanistan Collapse. So Why Did U.S. Get It So Wrong?" *NBC*, August 17, 2021, https://www.nbcnews.com/politics/national-security/cia-warned-rapid-afghanistan-collapse-so-why-did-u-s-n1277026.
97    Andrew Prokop, "Why Biden Was So Set on Withdrawing from Afghanistan," *Vox*, August 18, 2021, https://www.vox.com/2021/8/18/22629135/biden-afghanistan-withdrawal-reasons.
98    Peters, "Withdrawing from Afghanistan."

(and Germany) with the goal of dismantling Iran's nuclear program, as well as gaining permission for inspections in exchange for billions of dollars' worth of sanctions relief.[99]

President Biden was so desperate for a deal that his negotiators agreed in principle to be only observers at European organized talks.[100] And, crucially, in the original Iran nuclear deal, Russia was responsible for helping Iran to implement the agreement, including being responsible for shipping out Iran's excess enriched uranium. Now Russia sits in the catbird seat, because if it refuses to continue play this role, the deal between Iran and the US is once again undermined. Russia has made it clear that it wants some exemptions from the sanctions the U.S. placed on Russia after its February 24, 2022, invasion of Ukraine, as its price for assisting the U.S.[101]

Iran has made demands as well. The Central Bank of Iran (CBI) ensures that the Islamic Revolutionary Guard Corps (IRGC) receives financing to fund Islamic terror organizations. A key aim of Iran is to ensure that both the CBI and IRGC are no longer designated as foreign terrorist organizations.

Naftali Bennett, Israel's Prime Minister at the time, repeatedly argued that the deal will "likely create a more violent, more volatile Middle East."[102] As Republican Senator Ted Cruz from Texas has explained:

---

99   Kali Robinson, "What Is the Iran Nuclear Deal?" Council on Foreign Relations, July 20, 2022, https://www.cfr.org/backgrounder/what-iran-nuclear-deal.

100  Michael Hirsh, "Did Biden Wait Too Long to Engage Iran?" *Foreign Policy*, February 24, 2021, https://foreignpolicy.com/2021/02/24/biden-iran-nuclear-deal-trump/.

101  "France, Britain, Germany Warn Iran Deal Could Collapse Due To Russian Demands," *Radio Free Europe/Radio Liberty*, March 12, 2022, https://www.rferl.org/a/russia-iran-nuclear-deal-collapse/31749667.html.

102  "US Rejects Bennett's Criticism of Iran Nuke Talks: 'We Cannot Make the Same Mistake'," *Times of Israel*, February 21, 2022, https://www.timesofisrael.com/us-rejects-bennetts-criticism-of-iran-nuke-talks-cannot-make-the-same-mistake/.

This Iran deal if and when it is announced will be a massive win for Vladimir Putin. Because the Biden administration has been eager to tell Putin and tell the Ayatollah, of course, we will have a carveout for the Iran deal on Russia sanctions which means Putin will make billions in oil and gas transactions, in nuclear transactions and weapons transactions.[103]

In the spring of 2022, a bipartisan group of senators voted to require that any nuclear agreement with Tehran address Iran's support for terrorism in the region, specifically that that the U.S. continue to sanction the IRGC as a terror sponsor.[104] Democrats in the House agreed. Eighteen of them, led by Representative Josh Gottheimer of New Jersey, held a press conference to maintain that President Biden should not enter into a deal that allows Iran to continue its terrorist activities across the region, and that will not stop Iran's quest for a nuclear weapon.[105]

The original deal didn't end Iran's nuclear ambitions; it only slowed them down. It is silent on Iran's acquisition of ballistic missiles, and it doesn't include inspection at any time for any reason.

Is it any wonder that recruiting numbers have dropped across the board in the military?[106]

---

103  "President Biden Under Attack for Working with Russia on Iran Deal During Ukraine Invasion: 'Insane'," *News Center Nigeria,* March 10, 2022, https://newscenterng.com/2022/03/10/president-biden-under-attack-for-working-with-russia-on-iran-deal-during-ukraine-invasion-insane/.

104  Andrew Desiderio, "Congress Fires Its First Warning Shot on Biden's Iran deal," *Politico,* May 5, 2022, https://www.politico.com/news/2022/05/05/congress-warning-biden-iran-deal-00030448.

105  "House Democrats Join Criticism Of Biden's New Iran Deal," *Iran International,* April 6, 2022, https://www.iranintl.com/en/202204068353.

106  Drew Friedman, "Several military branches poised to miss recruitment targets for fiscal 2022," Federal News Network, September 28, 2022, https://federalnewsnetwork.com/defense-main/2022/09/several-military-branches-poised-to-miss-recruitment-targets-for-fiscal-2022/.

# IDENTITY POLITICS UBER ALLES

Joe Biden promised and then carried out his pledge to appoint a black woman—not the best and smartest lawyer he could find, but a person of a specific gender and skin color—to the Supreme Court. Before that, he created a "court-packing committee" to consider increasing the Supreme Court's size, to allow him to put more progressives on the Court.

President Biden nominated Ketanji Brown Jackson, a former public defender and D.C. Circuit judge, a staunch progressive who checked the identity boxes and would vote reliably to the left of the judge she was replacing, Justice Stephen Breyer. In fact, Brown is so "woke" that she couldn't tell the Senate Judiciary Committee what a woman is[107]—her answer: "I'm not a biologist."[108]

Her record is troubling. The role of a judge is to decide cases impartially and to avoid allowing personal views to cloud one's judgment. Jackson's sentencing history—especially in cases involving child pornography—demonstrate that she struggled with this responsibility. Using the U.S. Sentencing Commission's data,[109] an analysis of Jackson's sentencing decisions in child porn cases showed that her sentences were significantly more lenient than those of other federal judges: she issued sentences one-third lighter than other judges for production of child porn, 57 percent

---

107   Joseph Curl, "Liberals Finally Learn The Meaning of The Word 'Woman'," *Washington Times*, May 11, 2022, https://m.washingtontimes.com/news/2022/may/11/liberals-finally-learn-the-meaning-of-the-word-wom/.

108   "What Happened on Day 2 of Judge Ketanji Brown Jackson's Confirmation Hearings," NBC, March 22, 2022, https://www.nbcnews.com/politics/supreme-court/blog/ketanji-brown-jackson-confirmation-hearings-live-updates-rcna20973.

109   *Federal Sentencing of Child Pornography: Non-Production Offenses* (Washington, DC: United States Sentencing Commission, June 2021), https://www.ussc.gov/sites/default/files/pdf/research-and-publications/research-publications/2021/20210629_Non-Production-CP.pdf.

lighter than other judges for possession of child porn, and 47 percent lighter than other judges for distribution of child porn.[110]

This is striking, as black children have almost twice the risk of sexual abuse as white ones.[111] According to U.S. Bureau of Justice statistics, sex trafficking is overwhelmingly a phenomenon affecting minority girls as well.[112] That a black woman could be blind to these concerns is remarkable. That President Biden could be more interested in "shattering ceilings" than protecting black children is, sadly, not surprising.

## BIDEN'S GENDER BENDER

Biden changed the USDA's farm producer survey to find out which farmers identify as transgender, whether they changed their gender identity, or to disclose their sexual orientation.[113] Yet blacks have complained for decades that the USDA denied loans and credit to blacks, leading to a large loss of landownership particularly among Black farmers.[114]

---

110　Thomas Jipping, "Here's What We Know About Judge Jackson's Record on Child-Pornography Sentences," *Heritage Foundation*, April 1, 2022, https://www.heritage.org/courts/commentary/heres-what-we-know-about-judge-jacksons-record-child-pornography-sentences.

111　A.J. Sedlak et al, *Fourth National Incidence Study of Child Abuse and Neglect (NIS–4): Report to Congress, Executive Summary.* (Washington: U.S. Department of Health and Human Services, Administration for Children and Families, 2010).

112　Tracey Kyckelhahn et al, "Characteristics of Suspected Human Trafficking Incidents, 2007–08," Bureau of Justice Statistics, January 2009, https://bjs.ojp.gov/library/publications/characteristics-suspected-human-trafficking-incidents-2007-08.

113　"Hawley Exposes Biden's Woke Farming Agenda," Senator Josh Hawley, February 17, 2022, https://www.hawley.senate.gov/hawley-exposes-bidens-woke-farming-agenda.

114　#TeamEbony, "$1.2 Billion Settlement Given to Black Farmers," Ebony, October 7, 2013, https://www.ebony.com/12-billion-settlement-given-to-black-farmers-981/.

## RACIST BRIDGES TO NOWHERE

His Department of Transportation sought to use the bipartisan transportation and infrastructure bill to "combat the climate crisis…and advance equitable access to transportation."[115] Specifically Transportation Secretary Pete Buttigieg was allowed to crusade against "racist highways."[116] Instead of sending actual construction and transportation projects to urban centers, Biden's DOT has implemented new "equity" planning and permitting mandates that will delay expanded transportation options where they are needed most.[117]

## KILLING THE WAGES OF BLACK WORKERS

The President all but abandoned the nation's Southern border, including announcing that he would repeal Title 42 of the U.S. Code—a key anti-illegal-border-crossing tool—as well as refusing to even make a visit to the Southern border. This despite a growing consensus that unfettered immigration correlates with lower wages, higher unemployment, and increased levels of incarceration for blacks.[118]

115    Jessica Wehrman, "Republicans: Biden Forcing 'Woke' Agenda in Infrastructure Law," *Roll Call,* February 9, 2022, https://rollcall.com/2022/02/09/republicans-biden-forcing-woke-agenda-in-infrastructure-law/.

116    Tara McKelvey, "Biden's Unlikely Plan to Use Roads to Fight Racism," *BBC*, August 10, 2021, https://www.bbc.com/news/world-us-canada-58106414.

117    "Planning Topics," Transportation Planning Capacity Building, accessed November 28, 2022, https://www.planning.dot.gov/planning/topic_transportationequity.aspx.

118    George J. Borjas, Jeffrey Grogger, and Gordon H. Hanson, "IMMIGRATION AND THE ECONOMIC STATUS OF AFRICAN-AMERICAN MEN," (UC Sand Diego, 2009), https://gps.ucsd.edu/_files/faculty/hanson/hanson_publication_immigration_men.pdf.

## JIM CROW RETURNS

In May 2022, President Biden announced plans that would cripple charter schools.[119] Even though most of the nearly 4 million students enrolled in charter schools are black and Hispanic, the new proposed rules seek to ascertain whether the charter schools exacerbate school segregation and whether they undermine use of nearby local schools.[120] This puts the cart before the horse. Would black and brown parents fleeing poorly performing schools be expected to stay behind so that the race number crunchers won't give their local public school a "bad" race percentage? And why not ask the nearby local schools whether their poor performance is pushing parents and students out?

## WHEN THE INFLATION REDUCTION ACT DOESN'T

Finally, even after President Biden's version of the Green New Deal failed to get the support of all Senate Democrats, he continued to push for a "lite" version that included corporate and income tax hikes to soak the rich. Passed in the midst of record high levels of inflation, Biden named the job killing monstrosity, the Inflation Reduction Act. The Penn-Wharton University of Pennsylvania Budget Model concluded that in the near term it would increase

---

119    Erica L. Green, "New Biden Administration Rules for Charter Schools Spur Bipartisan Backlash," *New York Times*, May 13, 2022, https://www.nytimes.com/2022/05/13/us/politics/charter-school-rules-biden.html.

120    Proposed rule: "Proposed Priorities, Requirements, Definitions, and Selection Criteria: Expanding Opportunity through Quality Charter Schools Program: Grants to State Entities; Grants to Charter Management Organizations for the Replication and Expansion of High-Quality Charter Schools; etc.," Department of Education, March 14, 2022, https://www.regulations.gov/document/ED-2022-OESE-0006-0001.

inflation, reduce GDP for the next decade, and unleash a torrent of IRS agents on America.[121] All three outcomes will hurt blacks.

## CONCLUSION

Rejected by most Americans, President Biden's divisive agenda is warmly embraced by a narrow group of Americans—the so-called "problem-solving class," which purportedly exists to improve the lot of the have-nots. Rather than helping the poor, being a member of the problem-solving class means having the financial wherewithal to afford a luxury home, luxury car, and luxury vacation, and spends more of its time discovering more problems, whether real or imagined, than solving the problems it has already found.

The problem-solving class has existed for decades, but in the Biden Administration, it has found new life and financial support. What some analysts refer to as the diploma divide is the growing difference in political outlook between Americans whose income is based on their ability to produce goods or services that others willingly buy and those whose income stems from identifying and "serving" communities in need. They are trained to self-censor, behave as if they are important, and rigorously act as followers, not leaders.

Increasingly, some of those with diplomas have sought out obscure areas of study (think of gender studies, peace studies, African-American studies, and even dance as majors) that in an earlier era would leave them desperately unlikely to find stable employment, but now those who comfortably use terms like "Latinx" and "pregnant people" can find a home in the prob-

---

121 "SENATE-PASSED INFLATION REDUCTION ACT: ESTIMATES OF BUDGETARY AND MACROECONOMIC EFFECTS," Penn Wharton, August 12, 2022, https://budgetmodel.wharton.upenn.edu/issues/2022/8/12/senate-passed-inflation-reduction-act.

lem-solving class. Not surprisingly, this cohort loves President Biden and his woke agenda. Untested Washington schemes to regulate America are their bread and butter.

There's only one problem. The woke agenda doesn't fix what ails America. In fact, it makes everything far worse than it needs to be.

# CHAPTER THREE

# RUNNING FOR THE BORDER
# HOW BIDEN'S OPEN BORDER
# POLICIES HARM BLACKS

During the 2020 presidential campaign, candidate Biden claimed that "[President] Trump has waged an unrelenting assault on our values and our history as a nation of immigrants. It's wrong, and it stops when Joe Biden is elected president."[1] He pledged that if elected, he would undo President Trump's policies and instead:

- ✔ Modernize America's immigration system
- ✔ Welcome immigrants in communities across America
- ✔ Reassert America's commitment to asylum seekers and refugees
- ✔ Tackle the root causes of irregular migration
- ✔ Implement effective border screening

American media and elites praised Biden, and he never faced pushback on his immigration pledges. While his policies were indeed popular with the *New York Times* and the progressive gentry, they were awful for the average American and would hit black workers—especially men—the hardest.

---

1   "The Biden Plan for Securing Our Values as a Nation of Immigrants," Biden/Harris campaign website, https://joebiden.com/immigration/.

Among his first acts as President, Biden issued a myriad number of executive orders rolling back Trump immigration policies.[2] Over the next two years, America saw record numbers of

---

2    Migration Policy Institute, "Biden Has Taken Nearly 300 Executive Actions on Immigration in His First Year, Outpacing Trump Wednesday" Press Release January 19,2022, https://www.migrationpolicy.org/news/biden-executive-actions-immigration-first-year#:~:text=During%20his%20first%20364%20days,journal%2C%20the%20Migration%20Information%20Source; Executive Office of the President, "Ending Discriminatory Bans on Entry to the United States," Federal Register, January 20, 2021, https://www.federalregister.gov/documents/2021/01/25/2021-01749/ending-discriminatory-bans-on-entry-to-the-united-states; Executive Office of the President, "Revision of Civil Immigration Enforcement Policies and Priorities," Federal Register, January 20, 2021, https://www.federalregister.gov/documents/2021/01/25/2021-01768/revision-of-civil-immigration-enforcement-policies-and-priorities; Executive Office of the President, "Preserving and Fortifying Deferred Action for Childhood Arrivals (DACA)," Federal Register, January 25, 2021, https://www.federalregister.gov/documents/2021/01/25/2021-01769/preserving-and-fortifying-deferred-action-for-childhood-arrivals-daca; Executive Office of the President, "On the Termination Of Emergency With Respect To The Southern Border Of The United States And Redirection Of Funds Diverted To Border Wall Construction," Federal Register, January 27, 2021, https://www.federalregister.gov/documents/2021/01/27/2021-01922/termination-of-emergency-with-respect-to-the-southern-border-of-the-united-states-and-redirection-of; Executive Office of the President, "Ensuring a Lawful and Accurate Enumeration and Apportionment Pursuant to the Decennial Census," Federal Register, January 25, 2021, https://www.federalregister.gov/documents/2021/01/25/2021-01755/ensuring-a-lawful-and-accurate-enumeration-and-apportionment-pursuant-to-the-decennial-census; "Reinstating Deferred Enforced Departure for Liberians," Center for Migration Studies, February 2, 2021, https://www.federalregister.gov/documents/2021/01/25/2021-01770/reinstating-deferred-enforced-departure-for-liberians; Executive Office of the President, "Creating a Comprehensive Regional Framework to Address the Causes of Migration, to Manage Migration Throughout North and Central America, and to Provide Safe and Orderly Processing of Asylum Seekers at the United States Border," Federal Register, February 5, 2021, https://www.federalregister.gov/documents/2021/02/05/2021-02561/creating-a-comprehensive-regional-framework-to-address-the-causes-of-migration-to-manage-migration; Executive Office of the President, "Restoring Faith in Our Legal Immigration Systems and Strengthening Integration and Inclusion Efforts for New Americans,"

illegal immigration. According to the American Immigration Council, these record numbers were a dramatic change in migration patterns.

Beginning in the mid-1970s, the U.S. Border Patrol apprehended at least a million migrants a year, primarily single adults from Mexico.[3] Depending on the time of the year, there were spikes, typically higher in the spring and lower in the winter. This

Federal Register, February 5, 2021, https://www.federalregister.gov/documents/2021/02/05/2021-02563/restoring-faith-in-our-legal-immigration-systems-and-strengthening-integration-and-inclusion-efforts; Executive Office of the President, "Establishment of Interagency Task Force on the Reunification of Families," Federal Register, February 5, 2021, https://www.federalregister.gov/documents/2021/02/05/2021-02562/establishment-of-interagency-task-force-on-the-reunification-of-families; Executive Office of the President, "Rebuilding and Enhancing Programs to Resettle Refugees and Planning for the Impact of Climate Change on Migration," Federal Register, February 4, 2021, https://www.federalregister.gov/documents/2021/02/09/2021-02804/rebuilding-and-enhancing-programs-to-resettle-refugees-and-planning-for-the-impact-of-climate-change; Executive Office of the President, "Suspension of Entry as Nonimmigrants of Certain Additional Persons Who Pose a Risk of Transmitting Coronavirus Disease 2019," Federal Register, May 6, 2021, https://www.federalregister.gov/documents/2021/05/06/2021-09711/suspension-of-entry-as-nonimmigrants-of-certain-additional-persons-who-pose-a-risk-of-transmitting; Executive Office of the President, "Emergency Presidential Determination on Refugee Admissions for Fiscal Year 2021," Federal Register, May 7, 2021, https://www.federalregister.gov/documents/2021/05/07/2021-09861/emergency-presidential-determination-on-refugee-admissions-for-fiscal-year-2021; Executive Office of the President, "Memorandum for the Secretary of State on the Emergency Presidential Determination on Refugee Admissions for Fiscal Year 2021," Federal Register, May 7, 2021, https://www.federalregister.gov/documents/2021/05/07/2021-09861/emergency-presidential-determination-on-refugee-admissions-for-fiscal-year-2021; Executive Office of the President, "Suspension of Entry as Immigrants and Non-Immigrants of Certain Additional Persons Who Pose a Risk of Transmitting Coronavirus Disease," Deferal Register, December 1, 2021, https://www.federalregister.gov/documents/2021/12/01/2021-26253/suspension-of-entry-as-immigrants-and-nonimmigrants-of-certain-additional-persons-who-pose-a-risk-of.

3    "Rising Border Encounters in 2021: An Overview and Analysis," American Immigration Council, March 4, 2022, https://www.americanimmigrationcouncil.org/rising-border-encounters-in-2021.

number included individuals whom the Border Patrol had already apprehended at least once during the same year[4]—in other words, repeat offenders—but it also intercepted many seasonal workers who returned to their home countries.

During the Great Recession of 2008 and 2009, the migrant immigration pattern changed. Under the Bush Administration immigration enforcement increased, and combined with the economic downturn in the U.S., there were significant reductions in the number of single adults attempting to come to the U.S. In fact, during this period, more unlawful migrants left the U.S. than entered.[5]

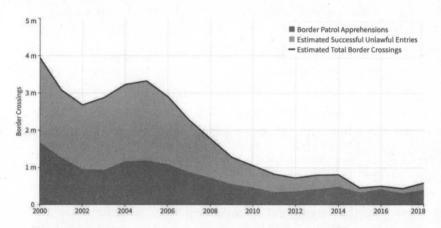

Estimated Total U.S.-Mexico Border Crossings, By Outcomes, FY 2000–2018. Source: Table 1, Model-Based Apprehension Rate, DHS Office of Immigration Statistics, "Fiscal Year 2019 Border Security Metrics Report" (August 2020); U.S. Customs and Border Protection, Annual Apprehensions FY 1925–2019.

The combination of reduced economic demand and increased immigration enforcement led to a significant reduction in the

---

4    American Immigration Council, "Rising Border Encounters."
5    American Immigration Council, "Rising Border Encounters."

number of single adults crossing the border—a trend which lasted for the next decade. As economic conditions in Mexico improved and the border became more difficult to cross, circular migration patterns were disrupted and net migration from Mexico dropped significantly, leading to more undocumented immigrants leaving the United States than entering it.

But when the Great Recession ended, higher and higher numbers of families and unaccompanied children have been attempting entry into the U.S. and frequently seeking asylum. As a Department of Homeland Security report revealed in 2017, the change has been dramatic. According to the report, in the early part of the twenty-first century, children and families made up less than 2 percent of border crossers between 2003 and 2008.[6] By the end of 2018, children and families made up more than 50 percent of border crossers.[7]

It is clear that many people are tempted to file asylum claims just so they can get into the United States. By increasing the number of applications, the review process can be burdened by abuse and fraud.

Asylum is an immigration status for foreign nationals who are already in the U.S., or who arrive at the U.S. border, while meeting the international law definition of a "refugee." Under the United Nations 1951 Convention and the 1967 Protocol, a refugee is a person who is unable to return to his home country, due either to past persecution or to a well-founded fear of being persecuted "on account of race, religion, nationality, membership

---

6    "Efforts by DHS to Estimate Southwest Border Security between Ports of Entry," Department of Homeland Security, Office Of Immigration Statistics, September 2017, https://www.dhs.gov/sites/default/files/publications/17_0914_ estimates-of-border-security.pdf.

7    Dara Lind, "What's Actually Happening at the USMexico Border, Explained," *Vox*, January 9, 2019, https://www.vox.com/2019/1/8/18173721/trump-border-facts-truth-speech-lying.

in a particular social group, or political opinion." Congress incorporated this definition into U.S. immigration law in the Refugee Act of 1980.[8]

This change had major impacts on U.S. immigration. Initially, the U.S. Citizenship and Immigration Services (USCIS) started granting more and more of these requests until, by the end of 2013, some 92 percent of asylum requests were granted.[9] As the numbers increased, the USCIS found it harder and harder to comply with the 1996 Illegal Immigration Reform and Immigrant Responsibility Act's (IIRAIRA's) requirement for mandatory detention, the purpose of which was then and still is to prevent migrants from being released inside the U.S. and then disappearing. Large numbers of aliens have never shown up for their asylum hearings once released. In fact, in 2017 some 43 percent of aliens released pending a hearing failed to ever appear in court.[10]

During the Trump Administration, an augmented effort was undertaken to warn people not to cross at a port of entry, or risk facing family separation. Ultimately, the Trump Administration was able to implement the "Remain in Mexico" policy to dramatically reduce illegal migration activity. Thousands of migrants seeking asylum were required to wait in Mexico so that the U.S. Customs and Border Protection (CBP) wouldn't be overwhelmed, and an orderly review could occur without any need to separate children from the parents.

---

8    Public Law 96-212, GovInfo, March 17, 1980, https://www.govinfo.gov/content/pkg/STATUTE-94/pdf/STATUTE-94-Pg102.pdf.

9    Rep. Bob Goodlatte, "Asylum Abuse: Is It Overwhelming Our Borders?" GovInfo, December 12, 2013, https://www.govinfo.gov/content/pkg/CHRG-113hhrg85905/html/CHRG-113hhrg85905.htm.

10   Mark Metcalf, "U.S. Immigration Courts & Aliens Who Disappear Before Trial," Center for Immigration Studies, January 24, 2019, https://cis.org/Report/Immigration-Courts-Aliens-Disappear-Trial.

But the advent of the Biden Administration meant a complete reversal of the Trump policies. What was the result? In the fall of 2021, the CPB acknowledged more than 1.6 million migrant encounters along the Southern border, more than quadruple the number of the prior fiscal year and the highest annual total on record.[11] Although much of the national focus in 2021 was on the arrival of families and unaccompanied children, headlines about "the highest number of border encounters in 20 years" were the result of trends among an entirely different group, who were responsible for more than half of all border apprehensions that year: single adults.

The Biden Administration's policies haven't been popular. Among its successes: It managed to stop construction of the border wall, and did so by *paying contractors to not complete the work.* It completely dropped the baton on the battle to end "sanctuary cities," whose municipal laws are intended to protect undocumented immigrants from deportation or prosecution, despite the existence of federal immigration law. As a consequence, they act as magnets for illegal aliens. During the 2020 campaign, Biden pledged to be an ally of "sanctuary cities," and his administration stopped the DOJ lawsuits that Trump had started to force "sanctuary cities" to comply with federal law.[12] Biden also raised the refugee cap to 62,500 migrants.[13]

---

11    John Gramlich and Alissa Scheller, "What's Happening at the U.S.–Mexico Border in 7 Charts," Pew Research Center, November 9, 2021, https://www.pewresearch.org/fact-tank/2021/11/09/whats-happening-at-the-u-s-mexico-border-in-7-charts/.

12    Caroline Kelly, "Biden DOJ Urges Supreme Court to Dismiss 'Sanctuary City' Cases," *CNN*, March 4, 2021, https://www.cnn.com/2021/03/04/politics/biden-doj-supreme-court-dismiss-sanctuary-cities/index.html.

13    Sean Sullivan, "Biden Says He Will Raise Refugee Cap From 15,000 to 62,500, After Widespread Criticism for Extending Trump-Era Levels," *Washington Post*, May 3, 2021, https://www.washingtonpost.com/politics/biden-refugee/2021/05/03/1b833126-ac4d-11eb-ab4c-986555a1c511_story.html.

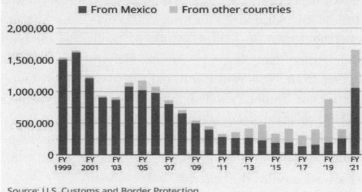

**Southern Border Apprehensions at All-Time High**

Number of apprehensions of undocumented immigrants at the U.S. Southwestern border, by national origin (1999-2021)

■ From Mexico  ■ From other countries

Source: U.S. Customs and Border Protection

In the fall of 2021, the White House created a firestorm by upbraiding Border Patrol agents in the Del Rio sector of Texas for supposedly using whips to round up Haitians at the border, based on photos of them on horses chasing the migrants. Before any investigation, Jen Psaki, then the White House press secretary, denounced the agents, calling their actions "horrific."[14] The NAACP tweeted, "These images although centuries apart still seem to represent the worst of America's capacity for humanity."[15] In the same vein, President Biden called the images "horrible," adding, "I promise you, those people will pay. There is an inves-

---

14    Dareh Gregorian, "Psaki Asked About Image Of Border Patrol Agent With Apparent Whip: 'Obviously Horrific'," *NBC News*, September 21, 2021, https://www.nbcnews.com/politics/white-house/white-house-says-images-border-patrol-whip-obviously-horrific-n1279663.

15    Bernd Debusmann Jr., "Grim Echoes of History in Images of Haitians at US-Mexico Border," BBC, September 23, 2021, https://www.bbc.com/news/world-us-canada-58654351.

tigation underway right now and there will be consequences."[16] In an appearance on the nationally syndicated TV program *The View*, Vice President Harris said that she was "outraged," claiming that the Border Patrol agents had used tactics that were "used against African Americans during times of slavery."[17] Democratic Representative Maxine Waters from California—never shy about overwrought rhetoric—called the use of "whips" by the border patrol "worse than slavery."[18] Senate Majority Leader Chuck Schumer from New York didn't want to miss out on heaping abuse on the Border Patrol, stating, "The images of inhumane treatment of Haitian migrants by Border Patrol—including the use of whips—are unacceptable."[19] At a Capitol Hill press conference, "squad" member Representative Ayanna Pressley from Massachusetts called the behavior "white supremacist."[20]

The accusations against the agents fell apart fairly quickly when it turned out that the Border Patrol were simply reining their horses, and from the angle of the photo, people looking

16    Annika Kim Constantino, "Biden Condemns Border Patrol Agents' Treatment of Haitian Migrants, Vows They Will Face Consequences," *CNBC*, September 24 2021, https://www.cnbc.com/2021/09/24/biden-condemns-border-patrol-treatment-of-haitian-migrants-in-del-rio.html.

17    Erin B. Logan, "Kamala Harris Says Footage of Border Patrol Evokes Images of Slavery," *Los Angeles Times*, September 21, 2021, https://www.latimes.com/politics/story/2021-09-24/kamala-harris-says-footage-of-border-patrol-on-horseback-evokes-images-of-american-slavery.

18    Katelyn Caralle, "'It's Worse Than Slavery': Rep. Maxine Waters Attacks Horseback-Riding Border Patrol Agents With Whips—While Ayanna Pressley Calls Them 'White Supremacists'," *Daily Mail*, September 22, 2021, https://www.dailymail.co.uk/news/article-10018685/Its-worse-slavery-Maxine-Waters-attacks-horseback-riding-Border-Patrol-agents-whips.html.

19    Chuck Schumer (@SenSchumer), Twitter, September 21, 2021, 12:40 a.m., https://twitter.com/senschumer/status/1440173960478429188?lang=en.

20    Quinn Owen, "Democrats Lash Out at Biden Administration Over Handling of Haitian Migrants," *ABC News*, September 22, 2021, https://abcnews.go.com/Politics/democrats-lash-biden-administration-handling-haitian-migrants/story?id=80174386.

for racism could convince themselves that the reins were whips. Within hours, news media began pushing back on the claims that the incident involved any type of mistreatment.[21] Even the photographer who took the controversial picture cast doubt on the claims of agent violence against the Haitians.[22] Yet the major fact-checkers suddenly went silent on whether the allegations of abuse by the Border Patrol had any merit. Neither *The Washington Post*, CNN, NBC, the Associated Press, *USA Today*, or Snopes weighed in on this issue, even as the media gave the issue almost non-stop coverage of the claims of abuse.[23]

Biden and his supporters in the media, who operated with an *Alice in Wonderland* Red Queen's "sentence first, verdict afterwards" mindset, committed a terrible injustice by falsely maligning the Border Patrol agents. The Department of Homeland Security initiated an "internal investigation" into the matter,[24] which ultimately cleared the Border Patrol agents of any wrongdoing regarding abuse of immigrants.[25] But the damage was done. A beleaguered agency that stands on the front line in the battle raging on

21    Tarik Minor, "Trust Index: Border Patrol Agents on Horseback Did Not Use Whips When Confronting Migrants," *News4Jax.com*, September 22, 2021, https://www.news4jax.com/news/local/2021/09/22/trust-index-border-patrol-agents-on-horseback-did-not-use-whips-when-confronting-migrants/.

22    Callie Patteson, "Border Patrol Pics Were 'Misconstrued' As Whipping, Photographer Says," *New York Post*, September 24, 2021, https://nypost.com/2021/09/24/border-patrol-pics-were-misconstrued-photographer-says/.

23    Joseph A. Wulfsohn, "Media's 'Fact-Checkers' Avoid False Narrative Border Patrol Agents 'Whipped' Haitian Migrants," *Fox News*, September 24, 2021, https://www.foxnews.com/media/fact-checkers-border-patrol-haitian-migrants-whip-horseback.

24    Quinn Owen and Luke Barr, "Border Agents Seen in Controversial Photos on Horseback Not Yet Questioned: Source," *ABC News*, October 26, 2021, https://abcnews.go.com/Politics/border-agents-controversial-photos-horseback-questioned-source/story?id=80801383.

25    MaryAnn Martinez, "Border Patrol Agent 'Whip' Probe Done, Produced 500-Page Report: Union," *New York Post*, April 14, 2022, https://nypost.com/2022/04/14/border-patrol-agent-whip-probe-is-a-500-page-report-union/.

America's Southern border was undermined. Where do the Border Patrol officers go to get their reputation back?

In Fiscal Year 2021, the Border Patrol "encountered" close to 2 million illegal would-be border crossers, more than 1.7 million of whom were at America's border with Mexico.[26] A September 2021 survey showed that only 38 percent of Americans support President Biden's immigration policies.[27]

President Biden's damaging behavior, however, continued. He ordered a reversal of the "Remain in Mexico" policy, and sent a comprehensive immigration reform bill—the U.S. Citizenship Act of 2021—to Capitol Hill. The attempt to end "Remain in Mexico" backfired, too. In the summer of 2022 in the White House, the Department of Homeland Security rescinded the policy after having temporarily suspending it shortly after President Biden was inaugurated.[28]

"Remain in Mexico" was a remarkably novel immigration control policy that was put in effect by the Trump Administration. Known also as Migrant Protection Protocols (MPP), the policy required asylum seekers arriving at the U.S.-Mexico border to wait in Mexico, not the U.S., for their immigration proceedings.[29]

26  "CBP Releases Operational Fiscal Year 2021 Statistics," U.S. Customs and Border Protection, January 3, 2022, https://www.cbp.gov/newsroom/national-media-release/cbp-releases-operational-fiscal-year-2021-statistics.

27  "Ipsos Poll: Core Political Data," IPSOS, September 16, 2021, https://www.ipsos.com/sites/default/files/ct/news/documents/2021-09/2021%20Ipsos%20Tracking%20-%20Core%20Political%20Presidential%20Approval%20Tracker%2009%2016%202021.pdf.

28  Alejandro N. Mayorkas, "Memorandum on Termination of the Migrant Protection Protocols Program," Department of Homeland Security, June 1, 2021, https://www.dhs.gov/sites/default/files/publications/21_0601_termination_of_mpp_program.pdf?mc_cid=304aa47fd7&mc_eid=a289e13bc1

29  Kirstjen M. Nielsen, "Memorandum on Policy Guidance for Implementation of the Migrant Protection Protocols," Department of Homeland Security, January 25, 2019, https://www.dhs.gov/sites/default/files/publications/19_0129_OPA_migrant-protection-protocols-policy-guidance.pdf.

Its purpose was to deter foreign nationals from overwhelming America's asylum process. Shortly after the "formal" repeal of the program, the state of Texas, and then Missouri, sued the Biden Administration over repeal of the "Remain in Mexico" policy.[30] A Texas Federal District judge ruled that the Biden Administration had reversed the program improperly and ordered it to be restored. Even after an emergency appeal in 2021, the Supreme Court ruled that the Biden Administration had to follow the law—either terminate the program properly or implement it.[31]

Per the Court's ruling, the Biden Administration could not simply announce the program was ended. It had to go through the formal and lengthy process of rule-making per the terms of the Administration Procedures Act (APA), and until then, the policy had to remain in effect. The proposed U.S. Citizenship Act[32]— which would legalize many illegals already in the US and expedite citizenship requests made by foreign applicants—went nowhere.

But finally, in August of 2022, the Biden administration succeed in killing the program.[33]

Another policy option the Biden White House considered, which involved offering payments to those "affected" by Trump's

30    Uriel J. García, "Texas Judge's Order to Revive 'Remain in Mexico' Policy Misinterprets Immigration Law, Migrant Advocates Say," *Texas Tribune*, August 16, 2021, https://www.texastribune.org/2021/08/16/migrant-protection-protocols-judge-ruling/.

31    Amy Howe, "Court Won't Block Order Requiring Reinstatement of 'Remain in Mexico' Policy," *SCOTUSblog*, August 24, 2021, https://www.scotusblog.com/2021/08/court-wont-block-order-requiring-reinstatement-of-remain-in-mexico-policy/.

32    Hannah Miao, "Biden's Immigration Bill Faces an Uphill Battle in Congress, But These Parts Could Find Bipartisan Support," CNBC, February 27, 2021, https://www.cnbc.com/2021/02/27/immigration-biden-bill-faces-uphill-battle-but-these-measures-could-pass.html.

33    Guardian staff and agencies, "Biden administration ends Trump-era 'Remain in Mexico' policy," *The Guardian*, August 9, 2022, https://www.theguardian.com/us-news/2022/aug/09/biden-ends-remain-in-mexico-trump-policy.

anti-immigration policies, blew up.[34] In late 2021, *The Wall Street Journal* reported that the Biden Administration was in talks to pay nearly $1 million to every immigrant family separated at the border while attempting to enter illegally.[35] According to *The Wall Street Journal*, the total payout could exceed $1 billion.[36] The plan for payments were a prime example of a White House in disarray, leading to the ongoing question of who was in charge in setting immigration policy. Once the plan became public, President Biden abruptly changed course amidst the media uproar.

Fox News White House correspondent Peter Doocy challenged the President directly on the issue:

> As you were leaving for your overseas trip, there were reports that that were surfacing that your administration is planning to pay illegal immigrants who were separated from their parents at the border up to $450,000 each, possibly a million dollars per family. Do you think that might incentivize more people to come over illegally?[37]

The President angrily declared that the report wasn't true and called it "garbage."[38] But within hours, the White House sent out

---

34  Michelle Hackman, Aruna Viswanatha, and Sadie Gurman, "U.S. in Talks to Pay Hundreds of Millions to Families Separated at Border," *Wall Street Journal*, October 28,2021, https://www.wsj.com/articles/biden-administration-in-talks-to-pay-hundreds-of-millions-to-immigrant-families-separated-at-border-11635447591?mod=article_inline.

35  Hackman, Viswanatha, Gurman, "U.S. in Talks to Pay."

36  Hackman, Viswanatha, Gurman, "U.S. in Talks to Pay."

37  Harper Lambert, "Biden Calls Report of Payments to Migrants Impacted by Trump's Family Separation Policy 'Garbage'," *The Wrap*, November 3, 2021, https://www.thewrap.com/biden-fox-news-peter-doocy-immigration-question/.

38  Myah Ward, "Biden Says $450K Payments to Families Separated at Southern Border Are 'Not Going to Happen'," *Politico*, November 3, 2021, https://www.politico.com/news/2021/11/03/biden-families-separated-southern-border-519321.

its crew to clean up the President's statement. The new statement claimed the President was only referring to the overall cost, not the idea that the federal government was in talks to make payments to immigrant families.[39] By December, *The New York Times* would report that the entire effort would be halted.[40] The program's status had gone full circle.

Meanwhile, the questions about who was setting policy in the White House picked up in earnest. Initially, the White House told the media that the President had not been appropriately briefed.[41] But after his new statement was released that came out in support of the settlement "concept," and then after the policy was abruptly halted, questions arose as to who was behind the decision. In January 2022, *The New Yorker* put the dropped policy at the feet of Ron Klain, the White House chief of staff; Susan Rice, the head of the Domestic Policy Council; and Jake Sullivan, the national security adviser.[42]

In another major misstep, President Biden issued an order ending President Trump's Title 42 COVID-19 pandemic migrant ban. Title 42 allows the federal government—especially during a pandemic—to expeditiously remove or ban al-

39    Aaron Parsley, "President Biden Clarifies That He Supports Settlements with Migrant Families Separated at Border Under Trump," *People Magazine*, November 8, 2021, https://people.com/politics/president-biden-says-paying-families-separated-at-border-up-to-450000-not-going-to-happen/.

40    Miriam Jordan, "Justice Department Halts Settlement Talks With Migrant Families," *New York Times*, December 16, 2021, https://www.nytimes.com/2021/12/16/us/biden-migrant-family-separation-settlement.html.

41    Jonathan Blitzer, "Why Biden Refused to Pay Restitution to Families Separated at the Border," *New Yorker*, December 22, 2021, https://www.newyorker.com/news/news-desk/why-biden-refused-to-pay-restitution-to-families-separated-at-the-border.

42    Jonathan Blitzer, "The Disillusionment of a Young Biden Official," *New Yorker*, January 28, 2022, https://www.newyorker.com/news/the-political-scene/the-disillusionment-of-a-young-biden-official.

together immigrants that could spread contagious diseases.[43] This authority resulted in the U.S. Border Patrol being able to stop or return hundreds of thousands of migrants in 2020 and 2021 and had the benefit of limiting the need to hold illegal migrants in crowded federal immigration facilities which could amplify the spread of the coronavirus.

According to the Centers for Disease Control (CDC), this pandemic prevention tool was no longer needed.[44] The irony in the decision is that it occurred while the Biden Administration continued to push other pandemic-mitigation policies, such as at airports, train stations, and other interstate commerce facilities. The American people had to ask themselves: if the pandemic was over and Title 42 authority was not needed at the border, why were domestic COVID-19 restrictions still in force?

The Biden Administration announced that the order would end on May 23, 2022, and almost immediately, lawsuits materialized. In a suit filed with the Fifth Circuit Court, twenty-six states brought a suit seeking to enjoin the decision.[45] National Border Patrol Council President Brandon Judd warned that ending Title 42 would lead to drug cartels gaining full control of the Southern border.[46] Additionally, there was the risk to the migrants themselves. Jon Anfinsen, vice president of the National Border Patrol

43    "42 U.S. Code § 265 - Suspension of entries and imports from designated places to prevent spread of communicable diseases," Legal Information Institute, accessed November 28, 2022, https://www.law.cornell.edu/uscode/text/42/265.

44    "CDC Public Health Determination and Termination of Title 42 Order," Centers for Disease Control and Prevention (CDC), April 1, 2022, https://www.cdc.gov/media/releases/2022/s0401-title-42.html.

45    State Of Louisiana et al v Centers For Disease Control & Prevention et al, Case No. 6:22-CV-00885, https://s3.documentcloud.org/documents/22026721/title-42-preliminary-injunction.pdf.

46    "Biden Admin Ending Title 42 'Will Give Complete Control to the Cartels,' Border Patrol Union Warns," Fox News, May 18, 2022, https://www.foxnews.com/media/biden-admin-ending-title-42-give-complete-control-cartels-border-patrol-union-warns.

Council and a Border Patrol agent working in the Del Rio area, worried at the time that many people would drown in the Rio Grande while attempting to swim to the U.S. side.[47]

Nearly a month before the scheduled expiration date, Federal District Judge Robert Summerhays issued a temporary stay and set up a schedule for hearings.[48] Almost at the same time, a bipartisan group of Senators introduced the Public Health and Border Security Act, a bill that would bar the Biden Administration from ending Title 42 protections at the border.[49] These five Democrats and six Republicans were concerned that no plan was in place to stop the expected surge in migrants at the border once the policy was overturned.[50] Even Democratic Senator Mark Warner from Virginia, a loyal backer of President Biden, explained that ending Title 42 would be a "huge mistake" that "might invite doubling, tripling, quadrupling the numbers at the border."[51]

Insisting that they wanted this measure sent to the President's desk, the bipartisan group attempted to add the provision to the President's $10 billion COVID-19 supplemental bill.[52]

47    Anastasiya Bolton, "'We Can't Sustain This' | Border Patrol Reps Say Crossings are Expected to Surge, Whether or Not Title 42 Ends This Month," *KENS5.com*, May 13, 2022, https://www.kens5.com/article/news/special-reports/at-the-border/title-42-court-update-texas-mexico-border-migrants-patrol/273-f57672cb-4b72-4d7c-8a26-3e0f9872309d.

48    Rebecca Morin, "Federal Judge Will Temporarily Block Biden Administration From Lifting Title 42," *USA Today*, April 25, 2022, https://www.usatoday.com/story/news/politics/2022/04/25/immigration-title-42-federal-judge-block-may-23/7446385001/.

49    S.4036 - Public Health and Border Security Act of 2022, 117th U.S. Congress, https://www.congress.gov/bill/117th-congress/senate-bill/4036?s=1&r=4.

50    Alayna Treene, "Scoop: Bipartisan Senate Group Bids to Block Lifting Title 42," *Axios*, April 6, 2022, https://www.axios.com/2022/04/07/bipartisan-senators-bill-prevent-biden-ending-title-42.

51    Stef W. Kight and Alayna Treene, "Biden's Border Headache to Come Whipping Back," *Axios*, March 31, 2022, https://www.axios.com/2022/04/01/bidens-border-headache-to-come-whipping-back.

52    Lindsey McPherson and Laura Weiss, "Vote On COVID-19 Spending Bill Indefinitely Delayed," *Roll Call*, April 6, 2022, https://rollcall.com/2022/04/06/vote-on-covid-19-spending-bill-indefinitely-delayed/.

Predictably, this attempt blew up the negotiations, as the White House and Democrat leaders refused to move forward on any COVID-19 bill that included a ban on ending Title 42 enforcement at the border.[53] On May 20, Judge Summerhays issued his final decision. In a 47-page ruling, the judge decided that Title 42 must stay in effect while the original lawsuit makes its way through trial and appeals.[54]

While Americans generally favor immigration and agree that it has a mostly positive effect on the economy, there is one category where Americans are critical of immigration, and that issue involves crime. Thus, it was striking that in the summer of 2021, the Biden Administration closed down the Victim of Immigration Crime Engagement (VOICE) Office, an agency that President Trump had created in 2017.[55] VOICE's purpose was to work within the Department of Homeland Security to assist crime victims and their families to ensure they would be provided information about their immigrant offender, including the offender's immigration and custody status.

But this necessary service went against the progressive narrative that immigrants never commit crimes, so it had to go. On the contrary, crimes by migrants are serious and frightening, as just a small selection of news headlines reveals:

---

53    Sahil Kapur, Frank Thorp V, and Julie Tsirkin, "Biden's Plans for Ukraine Aid, Covid Relief Jammed Up Over Immigration Dispute," *NBC News*, April 29, 2022, https://www.nbcnews.com/politics/congress/bidens-plans-ukraine-aid-covid-relief-jammed-immigration-dispute-rcna26554.

54    Louisiana v CDC.

55    Elliot Spagat, "US Closes Trump-era Office for Victims of Immigrant Crime," *AP News*, June 11, 2021, https://apnews.com/article/government-and-politics-donald-trump-joe-biden-immigration-d7369e9a81c14e02bcb1981459a6eae6; "Biden Administration Dismantles Trump-Era Office for Victims of Immigrant Crime," *CBS News*, June 12, 2021, https://www.cbsnews.com/news/biden-administration-dismantles-trump-era-office-victims-immigrant-crime/.

"Migrant Convicted of Murder Arrested in the Rio Grande Valley," December 6, 2021[56]

"Man Deported at Least Once Now Charged with Rape of Child in Tennessee," August 17, 2021[57]

"Suspect in Rape Aboard Steamship Authority Ferry Attacked Victim in Truck on Vessel, Officials Say," June 9, 2021[58]

"Fugitive Migrant Arrested at the Border in Rio Grande Valley," May 20, 2021[59]

"An Armed Child-Rape Suspect Who Left Arkansas, Where He Was Wanted on 11 Felony Counts, Was Killed in Arlington, Texas, this Week After Pointing a Gun at Police During a Traffic Stop, According to a Report," March 20, 2021[60]

56    "Criminal Migrants Arrested at the Border in the Rio Grande Valley," U.S. Customs and Border Protection, March 28, 2022, https://www.cbp.gov/ newsroom/local-media-release/migrant-convicted-murder-arrested-rio- grande-valley.

57    Andy Cordan, "Man Deported At Least Once Now Charged With Rape Of Child in Tennessee," *Border Report,* August 17, 2021, https://www.borderreport. com/hot-topics/border-crime/man-deported-at-least-once-now-charged-with- rape-of-child-in-tennessee/.

58    Travis Andersen, "Suspect in Rape Aboard Steamship Authority Ferry Attacked Victim in Truck on Vessel, Officials Say," *Boston Globe,* June 9, 2021, https://www.bostonglobe.com/2021/06/09/metro/suspect-rape-aboard- steamship-authority-ferry-attacked-victim-truck-vessel-officials-say/.

59    "Fugitive Migrant Arrested at the Border in Rio Grande Valley," U.S. Customs and Border Protection, May 20, 2021, https://www.cbp.gov/newsroom/ local-media-release/fugitive-migrant-arrested-border-rio-grande-valley.

60    Dom Calicchio, "Illegal Immigrant from Mexico Wanted for Raping 2 Young Girls is Killed by Texas Cop: Report," Fox News, March 20, 2021, https://www.foxnews.com/us/illegal-immigrant-from-mexico- wanted-for-raping-2-young-girls-is-killed-by-texas-cop-report.

"Illegal Immigrant Admits Raping Paterson Girl, 15, Taking Her Across State Lines," March 9, 2021[61]

"Man Sentenced for Raping, Killing Jogger in Random Attack at New Jersey Park," March 5, 2021[62]

During each year of the Trump Administration, violence by immigrants was lower than the year before. Now the situation is reversed: during Biden's Administration, criminal misbehavior by illegals has skyrocketed and is projected to go even higher.

## Arrests of Individuals with Criminal Convictions

The term "criminal noncitizens" refers to individuals who have been convicted of one or more crimes, whether in the United States or abroad, prior to interdiction by the U.S. Border Patrol; it does not include convictions for conduct that is not deemed criminal by the United States. Arrests of criminal noncitizens are a subset of total apprehensions by U.S. Border Patrol.

| | FY16 | FY17 | FY18 | FY 19 | FY20 | FY21 | FY22TD |
|---|---|---|---|---|---|---|---|
| U.S. Border Patrol Criminal Noncitizen Arrests | 12,842 | 8,531 | 6,698 | 4,269 | 2,438 | 10,763 | 3,662 |

*Fiscal Year 2022 runs October 01, 2021- September 30, 2022.*

US Customs and Border Protection.[63]

---

61    Jerry DeMarco, "Illegal Immigrant Admits Raping Paterson Girl, 15, Taking Her Across State Lines," *Daily Voice*, March 9, 2021, https://dailyvoice.com/new-jersey/southpassaic/news/illegal-immigrant-admits-raping-paterson-girl-15-taking-her-across-state-lines/804716/.

62    "Man Sentenced for Raping, Killing Jogger in Random Attack at New Jersey Park," *NBC New York,* March 5, 2021, https://www.nbcnewyork.com/news/local/man-sentenced-for-raping-killing-jogger-in-random-attack-in-new-jersey-park/2926400/.

63    "Criminal Noncitizen Statistics Fiscal Year 2022," U.S. Customs and Border Protection, September 14, 2022, https://www.cbp.gov/newsroom/stats/cbp-enforcement-statistics/criminal-noncitizen-statistics.

Thanks to the perception that U.S. border controls won't be enforced, in late spring of 2022, an Iraqi citizen living in Ohio set up an elaborate plan to assassinate former President George W. Bush (presumably at his Dallas residence), by smuggling in assassins across the Southern border.[64]

Is it any wonder that blacks, white, and Hispanics tell pollsters that immigration contributes to a crime problem in America?

## How do immigrants affect crime in the U.S.?

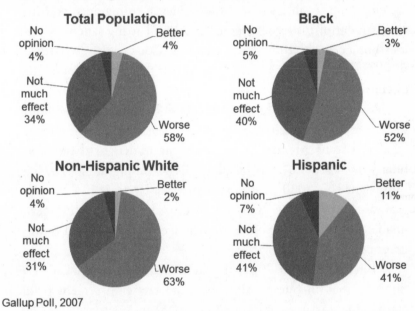

Gallup Poll, 2007

Gallup Poll.[65]

---

64    "Ohio Man Charged With Aiding and Abetting Plot to Murder Former President," Department of Justice, Southern District of Ohio, May 24, 2022, https://www.justice.gov/usao-sdoh/pr/ohio-man-charged-aiding-and-abetting-plot-murder-former-president.

65    "Immigration," Gallup, https://news.gallup.com/poll/1660/immigration.aspx.

Another issue that former President Trump tried to tackle involved so-called sanctuary cities. During the Trump Administration, more than three hundred state and local governments had laws, rules, or policies that impede federal immigration laws, and under President Biden those have expanded.[66] In fewer than ten years of the sanctuary movement, more than 10,000 criminal migrants have committed violent crimes in these "sanctuary cities."[67]

President Trump pushed legislation to restrict federal funding for cities and localities that shielded illegal immigrants, and his Department of Justice also issued an order barring sanctuary cities from receiving criminal justice funds. Courts initially blocked this order, and Biden's Justice Department formally rescinded the directive.

Now, the Biden White House has all but dropped any effort to restrict sanctuary cities or to punish illegal immigrant offenders and instead attempts to persuade the leaders of these dark-blue woke oases to stop enabling illegal immigration. Having campaigned in 2020 to protect sanctuary cities, is it a surprise that, after a year of pleading, the Biden Administration has been unable to get cities to voluntarily change their pro-illegal immigrant policies?[68]

Moreover, late in 2021, the Biden Administration issued a directive that all but prohibited federal law enforcement from conducting any immigration enforcement in sanctuary cities by

---

66    Jessica M. Vaughan and Bryan Griffith, "Map: Sanctuary Cities, Counties, and States," Center for Immigration Studies, March 22, 2021, https://cis.org/Map-Sanctuary-Cities-Counties-and-States.

67    Jessica M. Vaughan and Bryan Griffith, "Immigration Brief: Sanctuary Cities," Center for Immigration Studies, November 5, 2017, https://cis.org/Vaughan/Immigration-Brief-Sanctuary-Cities.

68    Kery Murakami, "The Biden Administration's Plea to 'Sanctuary' Cities Gets a Cool Reception," *Route Fifty*, February 8, 2022, https://www.route-fifty.com/public-safety/2022/02/sanctuary-cities-debate-grinds/361768/.

placing restrictions on the very kinds of places where law enforcement is needed most, such as schools, playgrounds, and any "place where children gather."[69] But the directive went further to cover other locations: near where a wedding might occur (like a hotel); near a vaccination site; near any place with an ongoing parade, demonstration, or a rally.[70]

Taken in totality, the Left's immigration agenda as pursued by Joe Biden isn't popular with most Americans. For blacks specifically, it's a nightmare. Illegally adding millions of people to the American workforce strains public services and puts a disproportionate burden on blacks.

Take public schools. When class sizes are expanded to accommodate a huge influx of illegal immigrants, black students lose. Blacks are overwhelmingly enrolled in public schools, and every resource provided in those schools is subdivided when greater numbers of students—in this case, illegals—are added into the mix. The increase of foreign-born students in U.S. classrooms has been explosive, and President Biden's policies have made the situation worse. According to a Kellogg School of Management Northwestern University report, nearly one-quarter of all students in public schools are immigrants.[71] This is a more than four-fold increase since 1980, when students from immigrant households made up 7 percent of the student population.[72]

---

69   Alejandro N. Mayorkas, "Guidelines for Enforcement Actions in or Near Protected Areas," Department of Homeland Security memo, October 27, 2021, https://www.dhs.gov/sites/default/files/publications/21_1027_opa_guidelines-enforcement-actions-in-near-protected-areas.pdf.

70   Vaughan and Griffith, "Immigration Brief: Sanctuary Cities."

71   David Figlio et al. "How Do Immigrant Students Affect Their Classmates' Academic Performance?," Kellogg Insight, May 3, 2021, https://insight.kellogg.northwestern.edu/article/immigrant-students-performance.

72   Steven A. Camarota, Bryan Griffith, and Karen Zeigler, "Mapping the Impact of Immigration on Public Schools," Center for Immigration Studies, January 9, 2017, https://cis.org/Report/Mapping-Impact-Immigration-Public-Schools.

Black kids are more likely than white kids to attend public schools and are more likely to be in a classroom serving immigrant populations as a consequence. Black kids, especially in the inner cities, can't easily escape to private schools.

Even within public schools there are stark differences in terms of illegal immigration's impact. Whites in public schools are more likely to attend schools where at least half the students are white with few immigrants enrolled, while 44 percent of blacks attend schools where blacks are the majority of students enrolled and where sizeable numbers of immigrants attend as well.[73] In other words, private or voluntary race-based segregation enables white households to move to public school districts with fewer minorities, and black households are stuck behind in inner city public schools with stretched resources and urban decay. In fact, in 83 out of the largest 100 cities, black students attend schools with majority non-white student populations.[74] The already beleaguered inner-city public schools are increasingly unable to fully serve their black population due to immigrant surges.

According to the Brookings Institution, only 20 percent of whites attend inner-city schools, yet all inner-city schools perform abysmally.[75] Although education is the key driver for upward mobility in the US, too many blacks are trapped in failing schools. As they are more likely to be trapped in poor performing schools

73    Abigail Geiger, "Many Minority Students Go to Schools Where at Least Half of Their Peers Are Their Race or Ethnicity," Agriculture and Natural Resources, University of California, January 30, 2018, https://ucanr.edu/blogs/blogcore/postdetail.cfm?postnum=26230.

74    Janie Boschma and Ronald Brownstein, "The Concentration of Poverty in American Schools," *Atlantic*, February 29, 2016," https://www.theatlantic.com/education/archive/2016/02/concentration-poverty-american-schools/471414/.

75    Jay P. Greene and Paul E. Peterson, "Race Relations & Central City Schools: It's Time for an Experiment with Vouchers," Brookings Institution, March 1, 1998, https://www.brookings.edu/articles/race-relations-central-city-schools-its-time-for-an-experiment-with-vouchers/.

than whites, an economic gap between life-time earnings of blacks and whites occurs.

In fact, black student graduation rates lag behind those of every other population group, and as a consequence of pandemic restrictions, those numbers will worsen. A recent McKinsey & Company study revealed that "students in majority Black schools ended the [2020-21 school] year with six months of unfinished learning."[76] In August of 2022, the US Department of Education released a report showing the devastating results of pandemic mitigation on classroom study. Average reading scores for 9-year-olds dropped at the fastest pace since 1990–landing at 215 out of a possible 500.[77]

The academic gap between blacks and whites also widened.[78] As of 2017, only 6 percent of black students who took the ACT (American College Testing) met all four requirements for college readiness. Nearly six times as many whites met the requirements.

Black students are pinned down by our failing public school systems—even if they graduate, they often don't meet high school proficiency minimums, which makes college attainment nearly impossible. Moreover, it also makes completing an employment

---

76  Emma Dorn et al. "COVID-19 and Learning Loss—Disparities Grow and Students Need Help," McKinsey & Company, December 8, 2020, https://www.mckinsey.com/industries/public-and-social-sector/our-insights/covid-19-and-learning-loss-disparities-grow-and-students-need-help.

77  Scott Calvert, "Schools Are Back and Confronting Severe Learning Losses," *Wall Street Journal*, September 6, 2022, https://www.wsj.com/articles/schools-are-back-and-confronting-devastating-learning-losses-11662472087?mod=djemalertNEWS.

78  Ben Chapman and Douglas Belkin, "Reading and Math Scores Plummeted During Pandemic, New Data Show," *Wall Street Journal*, September 1, 2022, https://www.wsj.com/articles/education-departments-first-pandemic-era-trend-data-show-worst-reading-math-declines-in-decades-11662004860.?page=1&mod=article_inline.

application challenging. What kind of employment skills can these students bring to a competitive twenty-first century marketplace?

A terrible cycle is promoted that involves limited educational attainment and diminished employment opportunities. Incarceration becomes more likely, and the high incarceration rate leads to blacks developing greater antipathy toward America and the free enterprise system.

## ILLEGALS BEFORE BLACKS

Biden's "illegals before Americans" policy preferences hurt blacks too, in their impact on Federal and state programs that assist the needy. As of 2021, 55 percent of households headed by non-citizens used at least one welfare program.[79] In fact, illegal immigrants make up the highest percentage of the uninsured in America.[80] As a result, blacks, especially those with low incomes, have to compete with people who are in the U.S. illegally for social services programs created to help Americans.

This includes hospitals and other healthcare facilities, which illegal aliens often use without bearing the costs of treatment. In 2016, *The Wall Street Journal* noted that 25 counties with large illegal-immigrant populations provided them with more than a $1 billion a year in health services, funds that could have gone to the health needs of American citizens.[81]

---

79    Steven A. Camarota, "Welfare Use for Immigrants and Native-Born Households," Center for Immigration Studies, September 1, 2021, https://cis.org/Camarota/Welfare-Use-Immigrants-and-NativeBorn-Households.

80    "Health Coverage Of Immigrants," Kaiser Family Foundation (KFF), April 6, 2022, https://www.kff.org/racial-equity-and-health-policy/fact-sheet/health-coverage-of-immigrants/.

81    Louise Radnofsky, "Illegal Immigrants Get Public Health Care, Despite Federal Policy," *Wall Street Journal*, March 24, 2016, https://www.wsj.com/articles/illegal-immigrants-get-public-health-care-despite-federal-policy-1458850082.

Illegal immigration costs American taxpayers more than $115 billion a year at the local, state, and federal level.[82] Nearly 90 billion of that is paid by state and local governments.[83]

Because most states use regressive taxes—sales and excise taxes—to fund local programs, native-born blacks who have been paying these local taxes for years are in effect subsidizing illegal immigrants who use local services, even though they haven't been in the country long enough to contribute to support these programs. School districts typically are funded by residents for years—long before or after their students attend.

The influx of illegal immigrants in just the last decade overwhelms this funding model and hurts black students in the process. School services are stretched, and attempting to quickly raise taxes to fund existing services creates "white flight." The result is that the very middle and upper-middle income families needed to finance and support the community are not available. Worse, when blacks want to use the services that they've contributed to, they have to compete with illegal aliens to wait for either stretched or reduced social assistance. Illegal Immigrants burden our social safety network.

Even legal immigrants place a burden on our social programs. In a report released in the fall of 2021, the Center for Immigration Studies found that 49 percent of immigrant households used at least one major welfare program, compared to 32 percent of households headed by the native-born.[84]

---

82    Matthew O'Brien, Spencer Raley, and Jack Martin, "The Fiscal Burden of Illegal Immigration on United States Taxpayers (2017)," Federation for American Immigration Reform (FAIR), September 2017, https://www.fairus.org/sites/default/files/2017-09/Fiscal-Burden-of-Illegal-Immigration-2017.pdf.

83    O'Brien, Raley and Martin, "Fiscal Burden."

84    Camarota, "Welfare Use for Immigrants."

Then there are the direct competitive effects of illegal immigration on black employment. Black men in particular are the biggest victims of the depressive wage effects of illegal migrant labor.[85] The overwhelming majority of U.S. immigrants are low-skilled laborers. Black men in particular are concentrated in the low-skill market and are consequently hardest hit. According to a U.S. Commission on Civil Rights report in 2008, 50 percent of the decline in black labor force participation rates over the past 30 years is attributable to illegal-migrant labor. As many as a million blacks may have lost job opportunities as a result.[86]

Within the black community, there are significant collateral effects of this job displacement. Family formation, intergenerational wealth creation, incarceration, addiction, and social service use by blacks are all affected. Poor or unemployed black men are far less likely to be seen as attractive lifelong mates. Thus, the already hemorrhaging marriage rate for blacks continues its decline. According to the US Census, more than half of black men in America are unmarried,[87] and marriage has a strong correlation with social stability and wealth creation.

These males aren't chaste. Today, a staggering 70 percent of black children are born to unwed mothers.[88] Single-parent households have the biggest challenge in getting their children to grad-

---

85  "The Impact of Illegal Immigration on the Wages and Employment Opportunities of Black Workers," United States Commission on Civil Rights, January 15, 2010, https://www.usccr.gov/files/pubs/docs/IllegImmig_10-14-10_430pm.pdf.

86  Commission, "Impact of Illegal Immigration."

87  Chanell Washington and Laquitta Walker, "Marriage Prevalence for Black Adults Varies by State—District of Columbia Had Lowest Percentage of Married Black Adults in 2015–2019," U.S. Census Bureau, July 19, 2022, https://www.census.gov/library/stories/2022/07/marriage-prevalence-for-black-adults-varies-by-state.html.

88  Submitted into the Congressional Record by the Honorable David Cicilline, "The Truth About Black Fatherhood," August 11, 2020, https://www.congress.gov/117/meeting/house/114092/documents/HMKP-117-JU00-20210929-SD012.pdf

uate and avoid addiction and incarceration. Single-parent black families have it hardest.

There is a solution that the Biden Administration could adopt that would be good for the economy and for blacks: he could separate citizenship from work visas. Instead of attempting a "cut the baby in half" immigration reform, granting citizenship to millions of people who are illegally in the country in order to halt deportations, America should separate those who might be welcomed as citizens from those only interested in temporary employment opportunities. In both cases, the decision ought to be based on what is in Americans' interests.

For purposes of citizenship, the U.S. should eliminate or dramatically reduce the immigration lottery as well as adopt new limits on so-called chain migration (an immigration advantage based on being related to someone who has already legally immigrated). The government should prioritize economically self-sufficient and highly educated applicants instead. For work visas, the U.S. should prioritize those with skills that are scarce, instead of encouraging today's shadow labor market of illegals. Employers should be required to compensate the local and state communities for any costs associated with non-citizen use of social programs, thereby ending the social-services magnet.

Visas should be both harder and easier to get. For areas where labor is truly needed, the process should work much faster, making an illegal journey to America less attractive. If you can quickly get a visa, you're less likely to cross the border illegally. On the other hand, these visas would be hard to obtain unless the type of work is in a field where there are needs in the US job market. Also, the duration of a work visa should be much shorter, regularizing the ability of migrants to return to their home country after the project ends, and then return when new opportunities arise.

America has every right—and responsibility—to determine who may become an American citizen and who may visit, for how long, under which terms. Knowing who is crossing the borders after 9/11 and the COVID-19 pandemic has taken on greater urgency. President Biden's policies reward those who enter the country illegally, thereby undermining the nation's sovereignty and hurting Americans' economic interests, especially those of black Americans. President Biden's anti-border-security policies must end; it's obvious that a country must control its own borders.

Besides the financial impact, the Biden immigration agenda provides another reason for blacks to be concerned. It represents a stark difference between the substance of policy agendas for blacks and for Hispanics. For Hispanics, Biden has absorbed the cost of abandoning the border wall by leaving it uncompleted, pushed for comprehensive immigration reform, pledged to get enacted a multi-billion dollar education training program, promised to legalize Dreamers, and agreed to review all migrants deported by Trump by the TPS (Temporary Protected Status) program. Whether Hispanic voters in America find this attractive remains to be seen. But the difference in substance between the programme offered to Latinos and blacks is significant.

In 2020, candidate Biden promised black Americans a study on reparations, a federal holiday commemorating the end of slavery, and inner-city law enforcement training reforms. Thin gruel in contrast to his plan for Hispanics—so far, he has undertaken robust executive action to limit the likelihood of deportations and even tried a legislative push for immigration reform on their behalf.

To date, the President hasn't put any muscle behind the so-called reparations commission, H.R. 40 (named for "40 acres and a mule"), and he hasn't even endorsed the bill. While reparations wouldn't actually help blacks and would definitely harm race relations, it is telling that, once in office, Biden has walked away from the issue.

The federal holiday of Juneteenth did end up being enacted, becoming the first new federal holiday since President Reagan signed the Martin Luther King, Jr. federal holiday into law. At the signing ceremony for Juneteenth, Vice President Harris said, "We have come far, and we have far to go. But today is a day of celebration."[89] But is a new holiday for federal employees to get paid without working worth celebrating? Moreover, one might wonder why December 6 wasn't chosen. That's the date that the Thirteenth Amendment, which banned slavery, was ratified.

Finally, even the more substantive police reform effort pushed by Republican Senator Tim Scott from South Carolina (mostly built on the false Black Lives Matter narrative) has gone nowhere. In fact, it is all but dead. After working months on the issue, in the fall of 2021, he announced that the negotiations had collapsed, saying that the White House and Senate Democrats insisted on the "defund the police" agenda, as well as on unduly restricting traditional law enforcement practices.[90] These issues served their purpose for Democrats—they created the impression of concern for blacks without actually doing anything.

Immigration–illegal and legal–has affected blacks for generations. Even as far back as the nineteenth century, abolitionist Frederick Douglass complained about what he called the "elbowed

---

89    Kevin Breuninger, "Biden Signs Juneteenth Bill, Creating New Federal
      Holiday Commemorating End of Slavery in U.S.," *CNBC*, June 17 2021,
      https://www.cnbc.com/2021/06/17/juneteenth-federal-holiday-biden-
      signs-bill.html.

90    Margaret Brennan and Jake Miller, "Senator Tim Scott Says Police
      Reform Talks Collapsed Because Democrats Supported 'Defunding The
      Police'," *CBS News*, September 25, 2021, https://www.cbsnews.com/news/
      senator-tim-scott-police-reform-talks-collapsed-democrats-defund-the-police/.

out of employment" effects that immigrant labor had on black Americans.[91] This phenomenon is even truer today.

To sum up, Biden's decision to abandon border controls costs blacks across the board. Blacks disproportionately bear the burden for government services provided to illegal immigrants with whom they are forced to compete for access. Except for skilled laborers, unfettered illegal immigration suppresses wage growth and makes job opportunities scarcer. Crime in black communities is elevated. And many of the safety net programs that exist for Americans are unable to fulfill their promises to black America. President Biden has done very little for the black community and has placed far more of his political muscle behind immigration policy (largely as a misguided means of appealing to Hispanic American voters) even though it would harm blacks born in the U.S. His immigration policies are anti-black and anti-American.

91    Frederick Douglass, "Speech Given by Frederick Douglass at the Anniversary of the American Anti-Slavery Society," *Liberator* 23, no. 21, May 27, 1853: 93, https://blackfreedom.proquest.com/speech-of-frederick-douglass/.

# CHAPTER FOUR

# THE KILLING FIELDS
# BIDEN'S POLICIES UNLEASH
# A CRIME WAVE IN AMERICA

## BLACKS HARMED THE MOST

Although Black Americans want and need robust law enforcement in their communities, President Biden pushes progressive schemes instead. As a result, America is experiencing a crime wave not seen since the late 1960s.

Even though the American people have paid trillions of dollars of income to alleviate poverty, homelessness, and poor education as part of the Great Society, the result has been an abject failure. Yet President Biden acts as if those approaches had never been tried before, and seeks to double down on them. He refuses to encourage the creation of stronger families, a strong work ethic, and policies that promote personal responsibility. America—and blacks in particular—suffer as a result.

Improving neighborhood safety and protecting businesses will expand the economy and give all Americans a chance. This approach is especially helpful in improving the quality of life for blacks in urban communities. Sadly, this Administration is more committed to the visions and policies of woke utopians, and he has made the country less safe.

Since the 1960s, progressives have pushed policies that greenlight crime by attempting to separate accountability from bad behavior. Today, they've largely gotten their way and a crime wave which affects every area of the country has followed.

The Chamber of Commerce reported in September 2022 that thefts for small retailers had been so extensive that nearly half of those stores had raised prices.[1] According to Neil Bradley, Executive Vice President and Chief Policy Office at the Chamber of Commerce, retail theft has increased 50 percent over the last five years, with the greatest occurring since 2021.[2] Retail theft puts employees at risk and harms already stretched household budgets.

Even the "carjacking" crisis is back. In a piece called "Carjacking: a new name for an old crime," the *New York Times* noted an explosion in car thefts in the late 1980s, the overwhelming majority occurring in urban areas, with an new twist: instead of stealing them while parked, the vehicles were being stolen while the driver was in the vehicle.[3] Then in 1991 the term "carjacking" was coined by the *Detroit News*.[4]

Carjackings became such a serious problem that Congress intervened to ban it in 1992. According to an analysis of the National Crime Victimization Survey (NCVS) conducted by the U.S. Department of Justice's Bureau of Justice Statistics, from 1993 to 2002 the rate of carjackings dropped from 49,000 to 38,000 carjackings annually Even Detroit—the carjacking capitol—saw a dramatic drop in this type of crime.[5] This modern version of highway robbery had all but been stopped in its tracks.

1    Sean Salai, "Small Retailers Raising Prices to Offset Organized Theft Surge," *Washington Times*, September 22, 2022, https://www.washingtontimes.com/news/2022/sep/22/report-small-retailers-raising-prices-offset-organ/.

2    "U.S. Chamber of Commerce Says Retail Theft a 'National Crisis'," *News Direct*, July 25, 2022, https://newsdirect.com/news/u-s-chamber-of-commerce-says-retail-theft-a-national-crisis-322730498.

3    Don Terry, "Carjacking: New Name for Old Crime," *New York Times*, December 9, 1992, https://www.nytimes.com/1992/12/09/us/carjacking-new-name-for-old-crime.html.

4    Erin Marquis, "How The Invention of 'Carjacking' May Have Spurred The Crime," *Autoblog*, December 5, 2016, https://www.autoblog.com/2016/12/05/carjacking-crime-detroit-history/.

5    Tresa Baldas, "Carjackers Losing Grip On Detroit, But Strike Daily," *Detroit Free Press*, November 30, 2014, https://www.freep.com/story/news/local/michigan/detroit/2014/11/30/detroit-police-fight-carjacking-crime/19671313/.

That trend is over. Carjacking has returned as a serious problem, with[6] 532 carjackings in 2021 in Detroit alone,[7] and increasing more than 25 percent for 2022 in Philadelphia, Chicago, Washington, DC., and Baltimore.[8]

Homicides are ballooning as well. In October of 2021, the Center for Disease Control announced that the US experienced its largest one-year increase in homicides in "modern history."[9]

## NEW YORK'S SUCCESS STORY REPUDIATED

Consider this: After New York City reached a high of 2,600 murders in 1990, the number of murders began to fall dramatically after Rudy Giuliani was elected mayor and continued to decrease to less than 600 a year by 2018.[10] Elected as the 107th Mayor of New York City, from 1994 to 2001, Guiliani tamed one of the world's most violent cities in two terms. While he is credited with implementing the so-called "broken windows" doctrine of policing[11] as a means of solving the crime problem of New

---

6    Emma Colton, "Carjackings Spike Higher than 2020 Levels in Cities Across Country: 'Perfect Storm'," *Fox News*, September 22, 2022, https://www.foxnews.com/us/cities-across-country-perfect-storm-crimes-carjackings-spike-higher-2020-levels.

7    Marquis, "Invention of 'Carjacking'."

8    Colton, "Carjackings."

9    "New CDC/NCHS Data Confirm Largest One-Year Increase in U.S. Homicide Rate in 2020," Centers for Disease Control and Prevention (CDC), National Center for Health Statistics, October 6, 2021, https://www.cdc.gov/nchs/pressroom/nchs_press_releases/2021/202110.htm.

10   John Yoo and Horace Cooper, "Reform Our Cities, Not Just the Police," *National Review,* June 17, 2020, https://www.nationalreview.com/2020/06/police-reform-refocus-law-enforcement-bolster-community-foundations/.

11   The broken windows theory posits that visible signs of crime, anti-social behavior, and civil disorder create an urban environment that encourages further crime and disorder, including serious crimes. The theory suggests that policing methods that target minor crimes such as vandalism, loitering, public drinking, jaywalking, and public transportation fare evasion help to create an atmosphere of order and lawfulness.

York, increasingly, a growing consensus has developed that a more orthodox explanation makes the most sense for the successful crime reduction in the city: arresting felons.[12]

During Giuliani's terms, the size of the city's police force grew dramatically, by more than 35 percent,[13] and the population of New Yorkers sitting behind bars ballooned by 25 percent.[14] In other words, having many more officers to investigate violent crimes and actually arresting those when they are caught lowers homicides, burglaries, vehicle thefts, assaults, and robberies.[15] Every type of crime in the city followed the same pattern. Blacks were the biggest beneficiary of this crime reduction, but the good times have ended, and the numbers show it.

In 1999, the NYPD had 40,000 officers in its department.[16] Today, the number is fewer than 36,000.[17] Arrests are on a 10-year decline, not even reaching 70,000 in 2021.[18] Today, in

12    Hope Corman and Naci H. Mocan, "Carrots, Sticks, and Broken Windows," *Journal of Law and Economics* 48 (April 1, 2005), 235-266.

13    Brian A. Reaves, Ph.D. and Matthew J. Hickman, "Police Departments in Large Cities, 1990–2000," Bureau of Justice Statistics, May 2002, https://bjs.ojp.gov/content/pub/pdf/pdlc00.pdf.

14    "What Reduced Crime in New York City," National Bureau of Economic Research, January 2003, https://www.nber.org/digest/jan03/what-reduced-crime-new-york-city. NYC residents in Prison derived from Crime Analysis Unit of the New York City Police Department and the New York City Independent Budget Office (IBO).

15    Hope Corman, Theodore Joyce, and Norman Lovitch, "Criminal Deterrence and the Business Cycle in New York City: A VAR Approach," *Review of Economics and Statistics* 69, no. 4 (November 1987): 695-700.

16    "Police Staffing Levels and Reported Crime Rates in America's Largest Cities: Results of Preliminary Analysis," New York City Independent Budget Office (IBO), March 16, 1998, https://ibo.nyc.ny.us/iboreports/crimerep.html.

17    New York City Police Department, https://www.nyc.gov/site/nypd/about/about-nypd/about-nypd-landing.page

18    Fola Akinnibi, "Arrests for Low-Level Crimes Climb Under NYC Mayor Eric Adams," Bloomberg, August 30, 2022, https://www.bloomberg.com/news/articles/2022-08-30/nyc-s-rise-of-low-level-arrests-worry-critics-of-broken-windows-era.

almost every category, crime has escalated in New York City. In 2021, the murder rate reached a ten-year high.[19] According to the *New York Post*, all major crimes topped 100,000 incidents for the first time since 2016.[20]

Blacks—especially in the urban centers of America—are suffering the most.

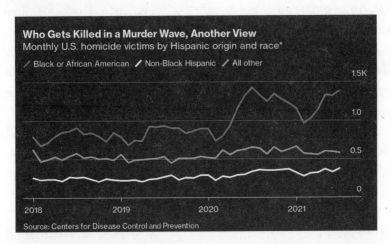

**Who Gets Killed in a Murder Wave, Another View**
Monthly U.S. homicide victims by Hispanic origin and race*

Black or African American    Non-Black Hispanic    All other

Source: Centers for Disease Control and Prevention

Early in 2022, Bloomberg ran a story with this sad headline: "Homicide Is Pandemic's Biggest Killer of Young Black Men."[21] According to the piece, the homicide rate for young black men has risen 66 percent since 2019—an increase that is nearly ten times as high as the homicide rate for the rest of Americans over

19    "Seven Major Felony Offenses," City of New York website, accessed
       October 20, 2022, https://www1.nyc.gov/assets/nypd/downloads/pdf/
       analysis_and_planning/historical-crime-data/seven-major-felony-offenses-
       2000-2020.pdf.

20    Craig McCarthy, "NYC Wiped Out Five Years of Policing Progress in 2021,"
       *New York Post,* January 3, 2022, https://nypost.com/2022/01/03/nyc-wiped-
       out-five-years-of-policing-progress-in-2021/.

21    Justin Fox, "Homicide Is Pandemic's Biggest Killer of Young Black Men,"
       Bloomberg, February 22, 2022, https://www.bloomberg.com/opinion/articles/
       2022-02-22/pandemic-murder-wave-fell-most-heavily-on-young-black-men.

that same time period.[22] Per 100,000 Americans, the homicide rate for blacks rose from 22.9 percent in 2019 to 30.7 percent in 2020. Worse, blacks—only 13.5 percent of the US population—made up 57 percent of the deaths by homicide during that time frame.[23] (Sadly, the homicide rates for all other Americans increased also, from 3.2 per 100,000 to 3.8.[24])

Among the causes are so-called criminal justice "reforms": bail reform, sentencing reform, and defunding the police.

## BAIL REFORM SCHEME

Supporters of "bail reform" argue that having to post bail prior to trial disproportionately harms the working poor and minorities because they can't afford to pay. They claim that bail isn't even needed. They couldn't be more wrong. After an arrest or arraignment, a court today has two choices: detain the defendant or release him while awaiting trial. If the defendant is released while awaiting trial, courts must determine whether a sum of money should be paid as a surety bond to guarantee that the accused will show up for trial.

Bail isn't some mechanism to punish the accused. In fact, it is a way to "split the baby"—it allows the presumption of innocence with no pretrial detention while awaiting trial. Without bail, local communities are forced to allow both the dangerous and the innocent to go free prior to trial or to detain both the innocent and the dangerous.

Bail as a concept has existed since well before the founding of the United States. There are reports of its use in ancient Rome.[25]

---

22    Fox, "Young Black Men."
23    Fox, "Young Black Men."
24    Fox, "Young Black Men."
25    Evie Lotze et al, *The Pretrial Services Reference Book*, Pretrial Services Resource Center, Department of Justice, December 1999, https://www.ojp.gov/taxonomy/term/23366.

There are examples of bail, like that used in the U.S., at least 1,000 years ago.[26] Following the Norman Conquest in 1066, England developed a system of payments to guarantee a way for disputes to be settled peacefully,[27] and the American Colonies mostly followed England's bail rules: when a defendant was arrested, he had to have someone step forward to guarantee that the defendant would appear for trial.[28] Mostly that involved a promise or pledge by a third party to be responsible, and other times it involved a cash payment.[29]

One of the earliest criminal justice laws passed in the US, the Judiciary Act of 1789, included bail for all crimes that didn't have the possibility of the death penalty.[30] Bail is also referenced in the Bill of Rights; the Eighth Amendment to the Constitution states, "Excessive bail shall not be required, nor excessive fines imposed, not cruel and unusual punishments inflicted."[31]

Chief Judge William Cranch of the U.S. Circuit Court of the District of Columbia oversaw one of the first instances of a cash bond, in a case involving would-be presidential assassin Richard

---

26   Lotze et al. *Pretrial Services*.

27   Sir Frederick Pollock and Frederic William Maitland, *The History of English Law before the Time of Edward I., 2nd ed.* (Indianapolis: Liberty Fund, 2010). Vol. 2, https://oll.libertyfund.org/page/history-of-english-law.

28   William F. Duker, "The Right to Bail: A Historical Inquiry," *Albany Law Review* 42 (1977-1978), 33, 34-36, https://heinonline.org/HOL/LandingPage?handle= hein.journals/albany42&div=12&id=&page=.

29   See generally, Paul Lermack, "The Law of Recognizances in Colonial Pennsylvania," *Temple Law Quarterly* 50, no. 475 (1976-1977).

30   "A Century of Lawmaking for a New Nation: U.S. Congressional Documents and Debates,1774–1875," Annals of Congress, 1st Congress, 1st Session, https://memory.loc.gov/cgi-bin/ampage?collId=llac&fileName=002/llac002. db&recNum=481.

31   Bryan A. Stevenson and John F. Stinneford, "The Eighth Amendment: Common Interpretation," U.S. Constitution, National Constitution Center, https://constitutioncenter.org/interactive-constitution/interpretation/ amendment-viii/clauses/103.

Lawrence.[32] In 1835, Lawrence, a house painter, attempted to shoot President Andrew Jackson not once, but twice, though remarkably, both guns he tried misfired.[33] Francis Scott Key, then the district attorney trying the case, didn't want Lawrence released prior to trial, and ultimately, Judge Cranch assessed bail at $1,500 (the equivalent of $50,000 today).[34]

In the twentieth century, much of the focus on bail involved seeing to it that defendants showed up for their trials and determining how much threat the individuals arrested posed to the local community. Two statutes were passed to address this: the D.C. Court Reform and Criminal Procedure Act of 1970, and the Federal Bail Reform Act of 1984.[35] Together, the bills set protocols for determining who should be released and who should be detained. The bills specifically authorized cases of "intentional detention" involving defendants who were a flight risk and authorized the use of a varying scale of cash bonds.

Today, President Biden has joined with the Left to completely undercut these provisions, and in the process, he has put American communities at risk.

Consider what's happened in New York City. New York State, one of the first to try out this dangerous experiment, has already seen the consequences. In the fall of 2022, the New York State Division of Criminal Justice Services finally released the data on

---

32    Peter Kumpa, "Narrow Escape From Death: The Attempt To Assassinate Andrew Jackson," *Baltimore Sun*, November 19, 1990, https://www.baltimoresun.com/news/bs-xpm-1990-11-19-1990323133-story.html.

33    "This Day In History: Andrew Jackson Narrowly Escapes Assassination," *History.com*, accessed October 18, 2022, https://www.history.com/this-day-in-history/andrew-jackson-narrowly-escapes-assassination.

34    Kumpa, "Narrow Escape From Death."

35    District of Columbia Court Reform and Criminal Procedure Act of 1970, Pus. L. No. 91-358, 84 Star. 473; Bail Reform Act of 1984, Pus. L. No. 98-473, 98 Stat. 1976.

criminal activity since bail reform began, and the results are not surprising. Bail reform led to a huge rise in crime.[36]

New York City announced in its New York Police Department (NYPD) Citywide Crime Statistics Annual report that the city experienced an overall crime spike of more than 30 percent.[37] The key takeaway is that recidivism—where criminals who are arrested and released then reoffend—increased substantially.[38] According to Charles Fain Lehman, a fellow at the Manhattan Institute, rearrests before trial alone increased nearly 7 percent for the twelve months before August 2022.[39]

Cash bail isn't just constitutional; it is essential. America will either warehouse every accused defendant prior to trial (at considerable taxpayer expense) or allow most defendants to post a bond promising to show up for trial.

Another crime control mechanism is mandatory-minimum sentencing, which requires a defendant to be sentenced to a mandatory sentence if convicted. Instead of allowing a judge or prosecutor to agree on light punishment, certain acts require a strong sentence. Americans need more mandatory minimums, not fewer. Strong sentences protect communities from violent felons and make neighborhoods safer, particularly for inner-city residents and blacks. Also, mandatory minimums reduce the likelihood

---

36  "Criminal Justice Statistics," New York State, Division of Criminal Justice Services, https://www.criminaljustice.ny.gov/crimnet/ojsa/stats.htm.

37  "NYPD Announces Citywide Crime Statistics for July 2022," New York Police Department, August 5, 2022, https://www1.nyc.gov/site/nypd/news/p00056/nypd-citywide-crime-statistics-july-2022. A comparison of July 2021 to July 2022.

38  Charles Fain Lehman, "Yes, New York's Bail Reform Has Increased Crime," *City Journal,* September 22, 2022, https://www.city-journal.org/new-yorks-bail-reform-has-increased-crime.

39  Lehman, "New York's Bail Reform." These numbers are likely higher since Lehman's report ended in October for 2022, and he suggests that if the trends occur, the rate could be a more than 10 percent higher.

that the personal bias of a judge or prosecutor will affect sentencing, which often results in under- or over-punishment. Bad actors and their bad acts would all be treated the same, regardless of their status or wealth or even their personal narrative.

Finally, mandatory minimums give society a break from the violence of jailed perpetrators by insuring that there is a longer period where violent felons are held behind bars. The logic is simple: the greater the punishment for a crime, the more likely a criminal will reconsider the behavior. The opposite is true as well: the lower the punishment threat, the more likely bad actors will continue to engage in criminal behavior.

Mandatory sentences help to reduce crime wherever they are in place. Progressives believe that punishment isn't the key to lowering crime. They argue that prison and related punishments are part of society's efforts to target blacks and other minorities.

President Biden should be working with Congress to expand mandatory sentencing for murder, rape, robbery, and arson and offer grant assistance to states that do the same. If he were serious, he'd have the Justice Department direct prosecutors to ramp up mandatory sentencing in high-crime communities to stop violent crimes in its tracks.

## SENTENCING REFORM GAMBLE

For years, the Left has pushed the false claim that America's criminal justice system unfairly targets blacks. Progressives point to "three strikes and you're out" laws, heightened penalties for violent crimes, and mandatory minimums as culprits. The effort to reform sentencing rules at both the federal and state level hasn't made much progress, certainly not in the minds of progressives. What the modern Left sees as social justice or equity, most Americans see as a license to steal, rape, and engage in mayhem. The Left has all but given up on this effort legislatively.

Rather than continuing to make the case—also known as the hard work of self-government—that the U.S. justice system is too punitive and hardhearted toward criminals, progressives have successfully short-circuited the existing criminal justice system by getting radicals elected as local prosecutors all over the county.

## DISTRICT ATTORNEYS WON'T THROW THE BOOK

Leftwing plutocrats like Laura and John Arnold have used their wealth to put in power prosecutors who refuse to prosecute. By selectively targeting district attorney races in key elections, they've turned America's criminal justice system into a criminal *in*justice system. Take Philadelphia, where the Arnolds supported the election of Larry Krasner in 2018. He Immediately stopped the use of cash bail for what he called low-level crimes: criminal mischief, prostitution, a range of drug crimes, DUI, forgery, and even resisting arrest.

Since his election, crime has ballooned in the city. He has dismissed or actually lost some 55 percent of drug-dealing-related cases in his office.[40] Similarly, his office lost, or failed to prosecute, nearly half of illegal firearm arrests. In three short years, the number of homicides in the city increased from 353 to more than 520 in 2021.[41]

In the fall of 2022, the Pennsylvania House of Representatives voted to impeach Krasner.[42] The Pennsylvania House cited

---

40    Jason C. Johnson, "Prosecutors Like Krasner Go Soft-On-Crime and It Has Consequences For Cities," Law Enforcement Legal Defense Fund, accessed December 1, 2022, https://www.policedefense.org/prosecutors-like-krasner-go-soft-on-crime-and-it-has-consequences-for-cities/.

41    Justin Sweitzer, "As Philly's Murder Rate Soars, DA Larry Krasner Plays 'Good Cop/Bad Cop'," *Pennsylvania Capital-Star*, December 18, 2021, https://www.penncapital-star.com/criminal-justice/as-phillys-murder-rate-soars-da-larry-krasner-plays-good-cop-bad-cop/.

42    Fox 29 Staff, "Pa. House votes to impeach Philadelphia DA Krasner, measure moves forward to Senate trial," *Fox29*, November 16, 2022, https://www.fox29.com/news/pennsylvania-house-krasner-impeachment-measure-philadelphia.

his failure to prosecute some crimes, his policies on bail, failing to keep victims informed of the cases he's prosecuting, and his attempts to obstruct the Pennsylvania House's investigation.[43]

Instead of aiding victims and working to keep violent criminals incarcerated, these new prosecutors are either very lenient with violent felons or refuse to charge them altogether. Instead of enforcing the laws as they exist, they wave a magic wand and (mis) enforce laws as progressives wished the laws might be.

The so-called progressive district attorneys undermine punishment in the name of their racial equity agenda and foist the consequences on America, often hurting blacks the most.

A report issued in early 2022 by the Capital Research Center showed that since 2016, more than $29 million in funding from George Soros and other progressive groups has gone specifically o back left-wing district attorney candidates.[44]

The reach of these radicals is truly remarkable, but when you have nearly $30 million in campaign support, you can truly transform the criminal justice system.

---

43    "House Resolution 420," Pennsylvania General Assembly, Regular Session 2020-2021, https://www.legis.state.pa.us/CFDOCS/Legis/PN/Public/btCheck.cfm?txtType=HTM&sessYr=2021&sessInd=0&billBody=H&billTyp=R&billNbr=0240&pn=3634.

44    Parker Thayer, "Living Room Pundit's Guide to Soros District Attorneys," Capital Research Center, January 18, 2022, https://capitalresearch.org/article/living-room-pundits-guide-to-soros-district-attorneys/.

| | | |
|---|---|---|
| Diana Becton | Contra Costa County, California. | $275,000k from Soros in 2018 |
| George Gascon | Los Angeles County, California. | Part of a $6M in 2018 |
| Monique Worrell | Ninth Judicial Circuit (Orange and Osceola Counties), Florida. | $1 Million from Soros in 2020. |
| Darius Pattillo | Henry County, Georgia. | $150k in 2016 |
| Kim Foxx | Cook County (Chicago), Illinois. | $2 Million in 2018 |
| James Stewart | Caddo Parish, Louisiana. | $1 million in radical funding |
| Scott Colom | Circuit Court District Sixteen, Mississippi. | $950k in 2015 |
| Jody Owens | Hinds County, Mississippi. | $500k in 2019. |
| Kim Gardner | St. Louis, Missouri. | $116k in Soros funds in 2021 |
| Raul Torrez | Bernalillo County (Albuquerque), New Mexico. | $107k in funding in 2016 |
| Alvin Bragg | Manhattan, New York. | $1.1M in 2021. |
| David Clegg | Ulster County, New York. | $184k in 2019. |
| Larry Krasner | Philadelphia, Pennsylvania. | $2M in 2019. |
| Jack Stollsteimer | Delaware County, Pennsylvania. | $100k in 2019. |
| Joe Gonzalez | Bexar County (San Antonio), Texas. | $1M in 2018 in Soros support. |
| John Creuzot | Dallas County, Texas. | $236k in support. |
| Brian Middleton | Fort Bend County, Texas. | 200k in 2019 |
| Kim Ogg | Harris County (Houston), Texas. | $600k In 2016 |
| José Garza | Travis County (Austin), Texas. | $400k in 2020 |
| Parisa Dehghani-Tafti | Arlington County and City of Falls Church, Virginia. | $600k in 2019 |
| Steve Descano | Fairfax County, Virginia. | $600k in 2019. |
| Buta Biberaj | Loudoun County, Virginia. | $650k in 2019 |
| Ramin Fatehi | Norfolk County, Virginia. | $220k in 2021[45] |

---

45    Thayer, "Living Room Pundit's Guide."

Not surprisingly, the result of this approach has been a huge spike in crime. According to the Council on Criminal Justice, crime data from 22 cities nationwide—including Atlanta, Detroit, Baltimore, Chicago, Denver, Memphis, San Francisco, Washington, DC, and Philadelphia—showed 218 more murders overall in 2021 than in 2020.[46]

---

### Crime Data for President Biden's First Year

▸ Aggravated and gun assault rates were higher in 2021 than in 2020. Aggravated assaults increased by 4 percent, while gun assaults went up by 8 percent.

▸ Motor vehicle theft rates were 14 percent higher in 2021 than the year before.

▸ Domestic violence incidents increased by nearly 4 percent between 2020 and 2021.

Council on Criminal Justice – January 26, 2022

---

Anti-crime efforts should focus on ending dangerous crime for all Americans. Instead of focusing on the race of criminals, protecting *all* victims should be the priority, and blacks, who are disproportionately victims, will benefit the most.

---

46  Richard Rosenfeld and Ernesto Lopez Jr., "Pandemic, Social Unrest, and Crime in U.S. Cities: Year-End 2021 Update," Council on Criminal Justice, January 24, 2022, https://counciloncj.org/crime-trends-yearend-2021-update/.

## ROAD RAGE ROLLINS

Though these faux prosecutors have been elected all across the US, President Biden (in order not to be left out) nominated a major progressive, Suffolk County, Massachusetts District Attorney Rachael Rollins to be one of his U.S. attorneys. As expected, Rollins had been quite successful as a district attorney in weaponizing her status to "transform" criminal justice in the Boston area. This made her the perfect candidate for an unelected federal role.

Elected as Suffolk County district attorney in 2018, Rollins set off almost immediately to impose a radical agenda. She single-handedly decided that her office would limit the prosecutions of certain crimes that "unfairly" targeted the dispossessed. Among her achievements was announcing wholesale that her office would ignore, dismiss, or plea out defendants arrested for at least 15 different charges.

## 15 CRIMES ROLLINS RUBBER STAMPED[47]

1. Trespassing

2. Shoplifting

3. Larceny under $250

4. Disorderly conduct

5. Disturbing the peace

6. Receiving stolen property

7. Operating with a suspended or revoked license

8. Breaking and entering

9. Wanton or malicious destruction of property

10. Threats of Violence

11. Minors in possession of alcohol.

12. Drug possession.

13. Drug possession with intent to distribute.

14. Resisting arrest alone

15. Resisting arrest for any of the other 14 crimes.

---

47    Charles "Cully" Stimson, "Meet Rachael Rollins, the Rogue Prosecutor Whose Policies Are Wreaking Havoc in Boston," *Heritage Foundation*, November 12, 2020, https://www.heritage.org/crime-and-justice/commentary/meet-rachael-rollins-the-rogue-prosecutor-whose-policies-are-wreaking.

Like her fellow radical district attorneys, Rollins never stopped to focus on whether criminals should stop committing dangerous crimes, such as resisting arrest, drug distribution, larceny, or wanton destruction of property, but focused instead on whether society had unfairly over-criminalized these actions as a way to harm these accused persons.

Rollins publicly expressed her antipathy for law enforcement at a June 1, 2020, press event about "peaceful protests" in Boston in the wake of George Floyd's death. Standing next to Boston's mayor and police commissioner, Rollins explained that she was "exhausted" because police officers "shoot us in the street as if we were animals."[48]

In early 2021, while awaiting confirmation, Rollins was investigated over a road-rage incident arising from a Christmas shopping parking-lot dispute. According to Katie Lawson, the shopper who filed the complaint, Rollins—who was using her official vehicle at the time—allegedly impersonated a police officer, including using verbal threats, to arrest Katie Lawson. Rollins reportedly even turned on her police lights to further create the impression that she was an officer of the law.[49] Progressives might not want to punish felons, but in Rollins's, case they sure are committed to get that close-in parking spot at the mall.

After the incident, Rollins took to Twitter to call Katie Lawson a "racist."[50] While the investigation closed without a recommen-

48    WBUR Newsroom, "Suffolk DA Rollins Reacts to Boston Protests in Response to George Floyd's Death," *WBUR*, June 1, 2020, https://www.wbur.org/news/2020/06/01/suffolk-da-rollins-boston-protests-george-floyd.

49    Christopher Gavin, "Mass. AG Finds No Civil Rights, Criminal Violations in Alleged 'Road Rage' Incident Involving DA Rachael Rollins," *Boston.com*, February 11, 2021, https://www.boston.com/news/local-news/2021/02/11/massachusetts-attorney-general-findings-rachael-rollins-alleged-road-rage/.

50    Tucker Carlson Tonight, "Rachael Rollins Accused of a 'Pure Abuse of Power' in Potential Road-Rage Incident," *Fox News*, December 9, 2021, video, https://video.foxnews.com/v/6286077597001.

dation, the troubling behavior pattern would appear again when Rollins was caught on video tape threatening a news crew that tried to cover her initial investigation.[51] Not surprisingly, Rollins' confirmation as U.S. Attorney to the Massachusetts District was contentious. In fact, Vice President Harris ended up casting the tie-breaking vote in order for her to be confirmed.

## BRAGG ABOUT HELPING CRIMINALS

The other DAs are just as bad.

In the summer of 2022, America recoiled upon hearing the news of the arrest of 51 year old bodega worker Jose Alba. Alba was charged with the murder of 35-year-old Austin Simon, whom he stabbed trying to defend himself at his deli. While the progressive prosecutor focused on Alba, the facts showed that it was Simon who was the aggressor, not Alba.

Video surveillance would show Simon's girlfriend berating Alba after her government issued food-stamp debit card was declined. Only moments later, Simon entered the store, walked behind the counter, and shoved Alba against the wall. Simon then stood over Alba and blocked his exit.

The *New York Post* reported that Alba had tried to defuse the situation when it started: "Papa, I don't want a problem, papa," Jose Alba, says.[52]

51    Shawn Cohen and Tommy Taylor, "EXCLUSIVE: 'People Are Scared of Her and I Understand Why': Boston Woman Threatened by Biden's New US Attorney Pick Rachael Rollins Who Pretended to be a Cop Says She's Pleased the Scandal Has Blown Up," *Daily Mail,* December 10, 2021, https://www.dailymail.co.uk/news/article-10298181/Theft-road-rage-racism-Bidens-new-Attorney-Massachusetts-filmed-threatening-reporters-charged-handling-stolen-property-called-cops-murderers-told-colleague-shut-white-man.html.

52    Melissa Klein, Georgett Roberts, and Steven Vago, "NYC bodega clerk Jose Alba tried to avoid confrontation that led to his arrest, new video reveals," *New York Post,* July 9, 2022, https://nypost.com/2022/07/09/nyc-bodega-clerk-jose-alba-tried-to-avoid-confrontation-that-led-to-his-arrest-video/.

Only by using a knife to defend himself did Alba live. Unfortunately, Simon died.

Alba's saga is just one of many instances sending the same message. It is one that Soros-backed prosecutors and the left have been pushing for years: you do not have the right to defend yourself, ever.

To add insult to injury, David Simon—whose brother Austin Simon was stabbed on July 1 by Alba in self-defense—has hired an attorney as he prepares to file suit against the Blue Moon convenience store in Hamilton Heights.

Meanwhile, after the uproar over charging Alba, Manhattan District Attorney Alvin Bragg changed course and abruptly dropped the charges.

The high-profile reversal was a rare circumstance for Bragg, who, as one of the nation's woke prosecutors in America, has made criminal justice (not victim justice) his primary focus.

A former federal prosecutor, Bragg campaigned as a reformer and convinced New Yorkers to select him to replace Cy Vance, the city's District Attorney for more than a decade. But reform doesn't appear to be his goal. Transformational justice, perhaps.

With much fanfare, Bragg's office issued a memorandum outlining his new plan for criminal justice reform.[53] Charges that in the past would have been prosecuted will no longer be processed. They include:

- ▸ Possessing marijuana
- ▸ Refusing to pay the fare for public transportation
- ▸ Trespassing

---

53    Alvin L. Bragg, Jr. to all staff, "Day One Letter," Office of the District Attorney of Manhattan website, January 3, 2022, https://www.manhattanda.org/wp-content/uploads/2022/01/Day-One-Letter-Policies-1.03.2022.pdf.

- Failing to pay fines for unlicensed operation of motor vehicle
- Committing any traffic infraction
- Resisting arrest
- Obstructing governmental administration
- Engaging in prostitution
- Most other misdemeanor offenses

That's right. The NY DA's office will simply not prosecute these cases under any circumstances.

He also announced that "non-incarceration" would be the presumption in all criminal prosecutions except in cases of:[54]

- Homicide
- A felony where the victim suffered serious physical injury from a deadly weapon
- Domestic violence felonies
- Sex offenses, such as rape and child sexual abuse
- Public corruption
- Mafia or Racketeering
- Major economic crimes

Notably not eligible for incarceration would be cases of home invasions not leading to "serious physical injury," auto theft, or distribution of narcotics to youth.

Moreover, there was nothing stopping the ability of the DA's office to take a person accused of a crime eligible for pre-trial

---

54    Alvin Bragg, "Day 1 Memo," Alvin Bragg campaign website, accessed
       December 1, 2022, https://web.archive.org/web/20220615072451/
       https://www.alvinbragg.com/day-one.

detention to have his case "reassessed"[55] and have the case charged as a non-incarceration type prosecution. In fact, the news record is replete with instances of criminals having their charges substantially reduced.

## RECIDIVISTS NEED A SECOND CHANCE TOO

Career criminal Marcus Wright, 37, was charged with grand larceny in April 2022 but was allowed to plead down to misdemeanor petty larceny. He was able to literally walk out of the courthouse without any jail time.[56] Wright, who has thirty-six busts on his rap sheet, used that freedom to punch a woman in a random attack in Chelsea.[57] Wright was released again almost immediately.

## LAW AND DISORDER

Even a massive brawl with police isn't sufficient to be eligible for pre-trial detention in Bragg's world. In an incident that started off as a noise complaint, a brawl broke out between dozens of people and the NYPD.[58] Kimberly Rivera, Felicia Davis, and several other bystanders punched officers when asked to stop blasting songs on a street corner in Harlem.[59] Despite the entire event being video-taped, Bragg's office reduced the felony assault charges of

55    Bragg, "Day 1 Memo."
56    Larry Celona and Jorge Fitz-Gibbon, "DA Alvin Bragg Cut Deals That Freed NYC Career Criminal—Who Then Punched Woman in Random Attack," *New York Post*, June 16, 2022, https://nypost.com/2022/06/16/da-bragg-cut-deal-to-free-nyc-criminal-who-then-assaulted-woman/.
57    Celona and Fitz-Gibbon, "Bragg Cut Deals."
58    Alyssa Guzman, "NYC Man and Woman Spark Mass Brawl with Cops as They Try to Arrest Woman, 32, for Blaring Music," *Daily Mail*, June 22, 2022, https://whatsnew2day.com/nyc-man-and-woman-spark-mass-brawl-with-cops-as-they-try-to-arrest-woman-32-for-blaring-music/.
59    Rocco Parascandola, "Loud Music Sparks Melee with NYPD Cops in East Harlem," *New York Daily News*, June 22, 2022, https://www.yahoo.com/news/video-loud-music-sparks-melee-220100907.html.

Rivera to a misdemeanor, and Davis—who actually had set up the outdoor speaker—got an even better deal: all charges dropped.[60]

## IS AN AXE A DEADLY WEAPON?

In another videotaped case, Michael Palacios, who pulled out a tomahawk and went on a rampage against customers and staff at a NYC McDonalds, was given a slap on the wrist.[61] Does Bragg think an axe isn't a deadly weapon, or is it that, since customers fled, no one was seriously injured? We only know that Palacios' charges were reduced to misdemeanors, thanks to Bragg.[62]

## BRAGG IGNORES RAPES TOO

In February of 2022, a teenage relative of Justin Washington reported to police that she was raped while the two were watching television together in East Harlem. Initially charged with first-degree rape, first-degree sexual abuse, and forcible touching, Washington was kept in jail with a $25,000 cash bond that he couldn't post. However, three weeks later, Bragg's office reduced Washington's charges to third-degree rape, and his bail was reduced to $12,000, which was sufficient for him to get released.

In the fall of 2022, NY DA Alvin Bragg's office promised the twenty-five-year old Washington an even sweeter deal: a thirty-day jail sentence with five years of probation and the ability to plead down to a charge of coercion. Supposedly, this was done to protect the victim.[63]

60    Celona and Fitz-Gibbon, "Bragg Cut Deals."

61    Brad Callas, "Axe-Wielding Man Arrested After Rampage in Manhattan McDonald's," *New York Post*, September 18, 2022, https://www.complex. com/life/axe-wielding-man-arrested-after-rampage-new-york-mcdonalds.

62    Jorge Fitz-Gibbon, "Madman Seen Smashing NYC McDonald's With an Ax is Released Without Bail," *New York Post*, September 18, 2022, https://nypost.com/ 2022/09/18/mcdonalds-ax-attack-suspect-michael-palacios-freed-without-bail/.

63    Alyssa Choiniere, "Justin Washington: Accused New York Rapist Goes Free, Attacks 5," *Heavy*, September 22, 2022, https://heavy.com/news/justin-washington/.

Shortly after this offer, Washington went on a sex crime spree, victimizing five more New Yorkers.

Victim 1: An 18-year-old male. Reportedly, Washington broke in through the victim's window early in the morning, reached into the young man's underwear while the young man was wearing them, and demanded a payment. After accusing the victim of not being understanding, he fled.

Victim 2: Within an hour, police say, he climbed up the fire escape of a building on Davidson Avenue. He began banging on the window of an apartment where a 26-year-old woman was home with only her 9-month-old son at the time. The startled victim says that when she pulled back the curtains, she saw Washington masturbating.

Victim 3: Incredibly, Washington actually broke into another apartment in the same building just minutes later. According to the 49-year-old female victim, he straddled her, ripped her nightgown, and once again demanded payment. Court records say the assault was only interrupted when the victim struck Washington several times with a hammer.[64] Of course, she was terrified and told the press that she was grateful that her children weren't home at the time, adding that "she can't bear to be alone in her apartment since Washington broke in and tried to sexually assault her."[65]

---

64    Minyvonne Burke, "N.Y. Man Accused of Sexually Assaulting 5 People a Week Before He Was Scheduled to Be Sentenced in Prior Rape," *NBC News*, September 23, 2022, https://www.nbcnews.com/news/us-news/ny-man-accused-sexually-assaulting-5-people-week-was-scheduled-sentenc-rcna49147.

65    Georgett Roberts and Allie Griffin, "NYC Mother Recalls Horror of Attack by Accused Sex Fiend Who Got 'Sweet' Plea Deal: 'I Can't Sleep'," *New York Post*, September 23, 2022., https://nypost.com/2022/09/23/nyc-woman-recalls-horror-attack-by-accused-sex-fiend-who-got-sweet-plea-deal/.

Victim 4: Less than half an hour later, Washington struck again. Prosecutors say he went to an apartment on Aqueduct Avenue, slipped his hand through a woman's bathroom window, stole her underwear, and then pleasured himself.

Victim 5: Moments after taking the previous victim's underwear, he was caught on surveillance footage molesting a homeless woman, including pulling down her pants and once again pleasuring himself, simultaneously. Her mistake: she had been sleeping in the lobby of the Aqueduct Building that he had just broken into. Thanks to the intervention of a passersby, she was able to escape.[66]

Only after these five incidents did Bragg's office decide to rescind the thirty-day deal. But the real question is why Washington wasn't presented with a high bail and forced to wait in Riker's Island for the rape of his cousin in the first place?

## MEET GEORGE GASCON

Gascon was elected the Los Angeles County District Attorney in 2022, unseating Jackie Lacey, the first woman and first black to serve as L.A. District Attorney since 1850. His soft-on-crime polices for Los Angeles echo Bragg's for New York City. In Gascon's case, however, even his deputies have revolted. In December of 2021, nearly 1,000 prosecutors serving under Gascon in LA accused him of refusing to take public action amid a surge in brazen smash-and-grab burglaries and robberies, which were becoming increasingly violent.[67]

---

66    Michael Ruiz, "New York Man Awaiting Soft Sentence in Rape Case Slapped with 7 New Charges," *Fox News*, September 23, 2022, https://www.foxnews.com/us/new-york-man-awaiting-soft-sentence-rape-case-slapped-7-new-charges.

67    Louis Casiano, "Los Angeles' DA Gascon still silent on crime wave, prosecutor says," *Fox News*, December 6, 2021, https://www.foxnews.com/us/la-george-gascon-crime.

In one instance, at least twenty people used sledgehammers to smash windows at a Nordstrom department store at The Grove, a popular shopping complex in Los Angeles, getting away with thousands of dollars in merchandise.[68] In another attack, in Manhattan Beach, at least eight suspects with guns shattered display cases at a jewelry store with hammers, again fleeing with thousands in merchandise.[69] In yet another case, thieves used a van to "smash" through a Chanel store.[70] Even Beverly Hills was targeted. Luxury Jewels of Beverly Hills was hit by thieves wearing masks and hoodies. They used axes, sledgehammers, and crowbars to smash the storefront window and took "several pieces of high-end jewelry."[71]

Sadly, even when more than a dozen of these "smash and grab" suspects were actually arrested, they were almost immediately released due to Gascon's zero-bail policies.[72]

Eric Siddall, the vice president of the Association of Los Angeles Deputy District Attorneys, spoke out on behalf of the Deputies DAs. He said the top prosecutor "cares more about the

---

68   Louis Casiano, "Rampant Smash-And-Grab Theft Part of Failure to Prosecute Criminals, Tolerated by Officials, Experts Say," *Fox News*, November 24, 2021, https://www.foxnews.com/us/smash-grab-theft-criminals.

69   Paul Farrell, "Moment Gang of Hammer-Wielding Robbers Wearing Ski Masks Smash Their Way into LA Jewelry Store Before Making Off in Getaway Car," *Daily Mail*, June 25, 2022, https://www.dailymail.co.uk/news/article-10953245/Shocking-moment-gang-thugs-wearing-ski-masks-smash-way-LA-jewelry-store.html.

70   Sid Garcia, "Latest Smash-and-Grab in Los Angeles Highlights Increasing Risk of Robbery, Violent Crime," *ABC7*, July 20, 2022, https://abc7.com/smash-and-grab-robbery-los-angeles-chanel/12064067/.

71   Cameron Kiszla, "Beverly Hills Police Announce Multiple Arrests in March Smash-And-Grab Robbery of Jewelry Store," *KTLA*, September 21, 2022, https://ktla.com/news/local-news/beverly-hills-police-announce-multiple-arrests-in-march-smash-and-grab-robbery-of-jewelry-store/.

72   Lee Brown, "14 Arrested for LA Smash-and-Grab Robberies All Released on Zero-Bail Policies," *New York Post*, December 3, 2021, https://nypost.com/2021/12/03/14-arrested-for-l-a-smash-and-grab-robberies-all-released-on-zero-bail-policies/."

rights of criminal suspects than crime victims, as gangs of thieves continue to loot retail stores for thousands of dollars in merchandise, often in front of customers and staff." Undaunted, Gascon has pledged that he will make an unprecedented effort to "re-evaluate and resentence" thousands of criminals.[73]

Gascon has even challenged California's holy grail—the three strikes law. Enacted in 1994 in a statewide referendum, it imposed a mandatory life sentence for a third crime, if the defendant had two prior convictions for crimes defined as serious or violent by the California Penal Code.[74] Shortly after being elected DA, Gascon announced that California's three-strike law "imposed draconian penalties" on defendants, leading them to be subjected to sentences "more than twice as long" as they would have otherwise.[75]

Voters might conclude this is exactly as it should be.

On this point, Gascon has lost twice in Court. First, Los Angeles Superior Court Judge James C. Chalfant enjoined the order and required all LA prosecutors to charge defendants for prior strikes in all new cases.[76] Gascon appealed, and in the summer of 2022, an appellate panel of state judges sided with Judge Chalfant.[77] Undaunted, in the fall of 2022 Gascon took

---

73    Emily Bazelon and Jennifer Medina, "He's Remaking Criminal Justice in L.A. But How Far is Too Far?" *New York Times*, November 17, 2021, https://www.nytimes.com/2021/11/17/magazine/george-gascon-los-angeles.html.

74    "Three Strikes Basics," Three Strikes Project, Stanford Law School, https://law.stanford.edu/stanford-justice-advocacy-project/three-strikes-basics/.

75    Marjorie Hernandez and Joshua Rhett Miller, "LA County DA George Gascón to Fight Ruling Mandating 'Three Strikes' Charges," *New York Post,* July 15, 2022, https://nypost.com/2022/07/15/la-county-da-gascon-to-fight-three-strikes-charges-ruling/.

76    Nathan Solis, "Judge Blocks Key Criminal Justice Reforms of LA District Attorney," *Courthouse News Service*, February 8, 2021, https://www.courthousenews.com/judge-blocks-key-criminal-justice-reforms-of-la-district-attorney/.

77    Eric Leonard, "Appeals Court Orders LA County DA Gascón to Enforce Three-Strikes, Special Circumstances," *NBC Los Angeles*, June 2, 2022, https://www.nbclosangeles.com/investigations/appeals-court-orders-la-county-district-attorney-george-gascon-three-strikes-special-circumstances/2908106/.

his case to the California State Supreme Court. A decision is expected in 2023.

## GASCON'S RECALL FIGHT

Unlike the state of New York, Californians have the right to recall rogue district attorneys. Article II of the California Constitution (ratified in 1911) allows citizens to recall all elected officials.[78]

Gascon has the distinction of being the subject of two separate recalls. The first began in March of 2021 but failed when supporters were not able to submit enough of the required number of signatures to get the recall on the ballot.[79] Angelenos began a second recall effort that raised more than $6 million in 2022,[80] submitting 717,000 signatures the second time around—more than 120,000 above the minimum needed. Unfortunately, the Los Angeles County Registrar Recorder determined that this time only 500,000 of the signatures were valid—missing the mark by less than 50,000.[81] Notably, though recall promoters failed to submit enough valid petitions, polling in the summer of 2022 had already shown that "recall" was running ahead of "retain" by 20 points.[82]

---

78    "Recalls," California Secretary of State website, accessed December 2, 2022, https://www.sos.ca.gov/elections/recalls.

79    James Queally, "Effort to Recall L.A. County D.A. George Gascón Fizzles Out, But a Retry is Coming," *Los Angeles Times*, September 16, 2021, https://www.latimes.com/california/story/2021-09-15/first-effort-to-recall-los-angeles-district-attorney-george-gascon-fizzles-out-but-a-retry-is-coming.

80    "Recall D.A. George Gascon," Recall Gascon campaign website, accessed December 2, 2022, https://www.recalldageorgegascon.com/.

81    Evan Symon, "LA County DA George Gascon Recall Effort Turns in 717,000 Signatures To County," *California Globe*, July 7, 2022, https://californiaglobe.com/articles/la-county-da-george-gascon-recall-effort-turns-in-717000-signatures-to-county/.

82    Lauter, "Recall Effort Had Good Chance."

The crime wave in California since 2020 has been nothing short of catastrophic. Homicides hit nearly four hundred a year in 2021, the highest in over a decade.[83] Robberies were up 50 percent year over year from 2020 to 2021, and vehicle thefts up 44 percent over the same period.[84] By the middle of 2022, the number of homicides was on track to surpass 2021.[85] Perhaps the third recall will be the charm.

## HATE THE GUN, NOT THE GUNNER

Felons using firearms are ravaging the country, yet President Biden refuses to call for their punishment unless he can claim they are acting out of anti-black animus. Without showing any link between gun control and armed violence, the White House continues to push for measures that punish the law-abiding while ignoring victims. With much fanfare, the Biden Administration announced that it was going after "ghost guns."[86] These are supposedly firearms that are made completely out of separate parts, in the process avoiding background checks or serial numbers, since

---

83    Leo Stallworth and Grace Manthey, "Homicides in Los Angeles Reach Highest Level in 15 Years During 1st Half of 2022: Report," *ABC7*, July 13, 2022, https://abc7.com/los-angeles-homicides-crime-report/12046605/.

84    Kevin Rector, Benjamin Oreskes, and Julia Wick, "How Bad is Crime in L.A.? Here Are the Numbers Behind the Mayoral Race Rhetoric," *Los Angeles Times,* March 22, 2022, https://www.latimes.com/california/story/2022-03-22/how-bad-is-crime-in-l-a-here-are-the-numbers-behind-the-mayoral-race-rhetoric.

85    Jon Regardie, "Murders in First Half of 2022 Exceed Last Year's Highs," Crosstown, July 11, 2022, https://xtown.la/2022/07/11/murder-rate-rise-los-angeles-2022/.

86    "FACT SHEET: The Biden Administration Cracks Down on Ghost Guns, Ensures That ATF Has the Leadership it Needs to Enforce Our Gun Laws," White House Briefing Room, April 11, 2022, https://www.whitehouse.gov/briefing-room/statements-releases/2022/04/11/fact-sheet-the-biden-administration-cracks-down-on-ghost-guns-ensures-that-atf-has-the-leadership-it-needs-to-enforce-our-gun-laws/.

purchases of firearm parts typically don't require background checks. The White House will require the parts sold by retailers, that are used to make "ghost guns," to be produced solely by licensed manufacturers, and that a background check will be required for the retail purchaser.[87]

But ghost guns aren't the issue. The parts are mostly purchased by collectors, and according to the anti-gun group Everytown for Gun Safety, there were only 102 federal arrests that included the use of "ghost guns" over the past decade.[88] In addition to the scarcity of their use in crimes, the anti-ghost-gun crusade is predicated on an erroneous presumption that legally-acquired firearms can always be tracked to the individual who committed the crime. A serial number can only tell law enforcement who bought the firearm—in some instances years or decades before. It can't reveal who used it to commit a crime, and criminals regularly destroy the serial numbers on firearms. It is a crime to remove the serial number, but if someone is planning on using a gun to commit a major criminal act, the lesser crime of removing a serial number is no hurdle.

In fact, the most common firearm used in a crime today is the 9 mm handgun.[89]

87    "Justice Department Announces New Rule to Modernize Firearm Definitions," Department of Justice, April 11, 2022, https://www.justice.gov/opa/pr/justice-department-announces-new-rule-modernize-firearm-definitions.

88    "Nearly 2,500 Ghost Guns Were Connected to Criminal Activity in 102 Federal Cases Over the Past Decade," Everytown for Gun Safety, accessed December 2, 2022, https://everytownresearch.org/stat/nearly-2500-ghost-guns-were-connected-to-criminal-activity-in-102-federal-cases-over-the-past-decade/.

89    Kevin D. Williamson, "The Ghost in the Machine Gun," *National Review*, April 12, 2022, https://www.nationalreview.com/the-tuesday/the-ghost-in-the-machine-gun/.

## WHEN IS AN ASSAULT WEAPON NOT AN ASSAULT WEAPON?

When he isn't decrying the mythical "ghost gun," President Biden claims that "assault weapons" are the problem. Technically, an assault rifle is a rapid-fire, magazine-fed automatic rifle designed for infantry use.[90] Actual assault rifles are highly restricted within the general population—they have been heavily regulated since 1930, and since 1986, even their manufacture or importation for the purpose of civilian access has been banned.[91]

Instead of referring to actual military rifles, gun critics often call "assault rifles" firearms that look scary, even though they have none of the lethality of actual assault rifles. They go further by declaring that firearms that have or can add "high capacity" magazines—including revolvers, most semi-automatic pistols, and rifles—constitute assault rifles that should be banned.[92]

But there's no reason to think that targeting these types of firearms will make communities safer. According to gun violence researcher Andrew Morral at the RAND Corporation, assault weapon bans aren't demonstrably effective because "mass shootings remain, at least in a statistical sense, relatively rare, and because rates of mass shootings are highly variable from year to

---

90    Jeff Daniels, "Definition of What's Actually an 'Assault Weapon' is a Highly Contentious Issue," CNBC, February 21 2018, https://www.cnbc.com/2018/02/21/definition-of-whats-an-assault-weapon-is-a-very-contentious-issue.html.

91    "Machine Guns & 50 Caliber," Giffords Law Center, accessed December 2, 2022, https://giffords.org/lawcenter/gun-laws/policy-areas/hardware-ammunition/machine-guns-50-caliber/.

92    "Assault Weapons and High-Capacity Magazines," Everytown for Gun Safety, accessed October 18, 2022, https://everytownresearch.org/wp-content/uploads/sites/4/2020/07/EFGV02_Assault-Weapons-and-High-Capacity-Magazines_Rd2_6-1.pdf.

year, there are methodological challenges to reliably detecting even fairly strong effects for these laws."[93]

President Biden claims that the number of shootings using "assault weapons" tripled after the "assault weapons" ban lapsed in 2004,[94] but the Crime Prevention Center disagrees.

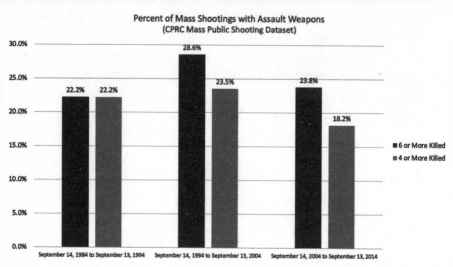

Crime Prevention Research Center.[95]

In 2018, researcher Adam Lankford released a report claiming that nearly a third of all mass shooting events have taken place in

93    Andrew R. Morral, "The Gun Laws That Work, and the Gun Laws That Don't," *The Rand Blog,* Rand Corporation, May 27, 2022, https://www.rand.org/blog/2022/05/the-gun-laws-that-work-and-the-gun-laws-that-dont.html.

94    Niels Lesniewski, "Biden Renews Calls for Congress to 'Stand Up' to Gun Lobby After Texas School Shooting," *Roll Call,* May 24, 2022, https://rollcall.com/2022/05/24/biden-renews-calls-for-congress-to-stand-up-to-gun-lobby-after-texas-school-shooting/.

95    "Biden on Assault Weapons," Crime Prevention Research Center (CPRC), May 25, 2022, https://crimeresearch.org/2022/05/biden-on-assault-weapons/.

America.[96] This sensational study was embraced by many in the mainstream media and became a talking point among progressives about the need for intensified gun control efforts.[97]

But the report was bogus. Lankford claimed that from 1966 to 2012, there were ninety mass shooters in the US and 202 shooters in the rest of the world. In fact, there were more than 3,081 mass shooters outside the U.S. in the last fifteen years alone.[98] And when the actual shootings in other countries are accurately tallied, "the US makes up less than 1.43 percent of the mass public shooters, 2.11 percent of their murders, and 2.88 percent of their attacks."[99] Mass shootings account for only 0.1 percent of all firearm related homicides.[100]

Relying on this type of data, Biden announced the day after a mass shooting event in Boulder that he was supporting a ban on

96    Adam Lankford, PhD., "Public Mass Shooters and Firearms: A Cross-National Study of 171 Countries," *Violence and Victims* 31, no. 2 (2016):187-99. doi: 10.1891/0886-6708.VV-D-15-00093.

97    Ross Pomeroy, "Study: More Guns Linked to More Mass Shootings," *Real Clear Science*, February 01, 2016, https://www.realclearscience.com/journal_club/2016/02/02/study_of_171_countries_finds_link_between_public_mass_shootings_and_gun_ownership_109526.html; Glenn Kessler, "Does the U.S. Lead the World in Mass Shootings?" *Washington Post*, September 5, 2018, https://www.washingtonpost.com/politics/2018/09/05/does-us-lead-world-mass-shootings/; Alexander Smith, "Texas School Massacre Latest 'Everyday Horror' in U.S. That Would Be Unthinkable Abroad," *NBC News*, May 25, 2022, https://www.nbcnews.com/news/world/texas-school-shooting-us-global-outlier-gun-laws-australia-dunblane-rcna30446.

98    John R. Lott, "New CPRC Research: How a Botched Study Fooled the World About the U.S. Share of Mass Public Shootings: U.S. Rate is Lower than Global Average," Crime Prevention Research Center (CPRC), August 29, 2018, https://crimeresearch.org/2018/08/new-cprc-research-how-a-botched-study-fooled-the-world-about-the-u-s-share-of-mass-public-shootings-u-s-rate-is-lower-than-global-average/.

99    Lott, "Botched Study."

100   "Mass Shootings Facts And Fiction," U.S. Concealed Carry Association, accessed October 18, 2022, https://www.usconcealedcarry.com/resources/gun-facts-and-fiction/mass-shootings/.

"assault rifles".[101] "We can ban assault weapons and high-capacity magazines in this country once again," the President said. "I got that done when I was a senator. It passed. It was the law for the longest time. And it brought down these mass killings. We should do it again."[102]

"Assault rifles," no matter how broadly defined, aren't involved. Of mass shooting incidents from 1998 to 2019, 56 percent involved handguns, and barely 13 percent of them involved any type of rifle.[103] According to the Heritage Foundation, targeting rifles with new legislation doesn't make sense since "few mass public shooters have used high-capacity magazines, and there is no evidence that the lethality of such attacks would have been affected by delays of two to four seconds to switch magazines."[104]

In fact, a 2016 Justice Research and Policy Journal study, *Large-Capacity Magazines and the Casualty Counts in Mass Shootings*, examined twenty-three mass shootings between 1994 and 2013 and determined that there was no basis for concluding that lives would have been saved if there were restrictions on the size of ammunition magazines, regardless of weapon used.[105]

101    Josh Gauntt, "Why Does The U.S. Have So Many Mass Shootings?," *WBRC*, April 14, 2021, https://www.wbrc.com/2021/04/15/why-does-us-have-so-many-mass-shootings/.

102    Quint Forgey, "Biden Calls for Federal Assault Weapons Ban After Boulder Shooting," *Politico*, March 23, 2021, https://www.politico.com/news/2021/03/23/democrats-gun-reforms-mass-shooting-477615.

103    "Breaking down Mass Public Shooting data from 1998 through June 2019: Info on weapons used; gun-free zones; racial, age, and gender demographics," Crime Prevention Research Center, July 7, 2019, https://crimeresearch.org/2019/07/breaking-down-mass-public-shooting-data-from-1998-though-june-2019-info-on-weapons-used-gun-free-zones-racial-age-and-gender-demographics/.

104    "The Current Gun Debate: Mass Shootings," *Heritage Foundation*, March 12, 2018, https://www.heritage.org/the-constitution/report/the-current-gun-debate-mass-shootings.

105    Gary Kleck, "Large-Capacity Magazines and the Casualty Counts in Mass Shootings: The Plausibility of Linkages," *Justice Research and Policy* 17, no. 1 (2016): 28-47. doi: 10.1177/152510711667492.

## IT'S NOT THE GUNS, STUPID

Rather than order the Department of Justice to target armed felons at the federal level, President Biden acts as if the guns themselves are the danger. In the summer of 2022, Biden announced that the Department of Justice would adopt a "zero tolerance" policy for federally licensed firearm dealers as a way to reduce gun violence.[106] Too bad he doesn't take a "zero tolerance" approach to violent criminals.

## FOCUS ON SHOOTERS

Criminals may be evil, but they aren't stupid. Even those who aren't felons don't typically buy a gun legally from a dealer, and felons don't, as a matter of practice, leave the gun at the scene for law enforcement to trace back to them.[107] According to author and former NYPD detective David Chianese of *Law Enforcement Today*, "stricter or additional gun laws do not reduce gun violence."[108] A recent Department of Justice review found that "43 percent of criminals had bought their firearms on the black market, 6 percent acquired them via theft, and 10 percent made a retail purchase—0.8 percent purchased a weapon from a gun show."[109]

---

106  "FACT SHEET: The Biden Administration's 21 Executive Actions to Reduce Gun Violence," White House Briefing Room, July 11, 2022, https://www.whitehouse.gov/briefing-room/statements-releases/2022/07/11/fact-sheet-the-biden-administrations-21-executive-actions-to-reduce-gun-violence/.

107  Hollie McKay, "Where Do Criminals Really Get Their Guns?" *Fox News*, February 19, 2020, https://www.foxnews.com/us/where-do-criminals-get-guns.

108  Dave Workman, "Congressional Dems Launch Big Gun Control Push," *Guns Magazine*, accessed October 19, 2022, https://gunsmagazine.com/our-experts/congressional-dems-launch-big-gun-control-push/.

109  Mariel Alper, Ph.D., and Lauren Glaze, "Source and Use of Firearms Involved in Crimes: Survey of Prison Inmates, 2016," Bureau of Justice Statistics, January 2019, https://bjs.ojp.gov/content/pub/pdf/suficspi16.pdf.

And criminals aren't limited to using guns to undertake their crimes. In fact, often times they don't use guns at all.[110]

**Percent of all state and federal prisoners who had possessed or used a firearm during their offense, 2016**

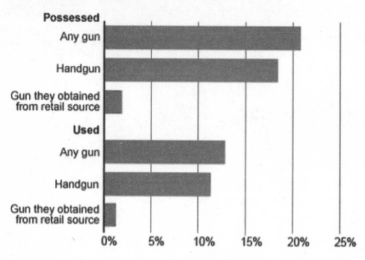

US Department of Justice.[111]

In 2012, the US Sentencing Commission issued a report on felons arrested while in possession of a firearm. At 98.2 percent, offenders were overwhelmingly male.[112] More than half were black.[113] But rather than take measures to expand criminal enforcement in urban communities where these crimes are occur-

110    Alper and Glaze, "Prison Inmates." https://bjs.ojp.gov/content/pub/pdf/suficspi16.pdf
111    Alper and Glaze, "Prison Inmates."
112    "Quick Facts—Felon in Possession of a Firearm," United States Sentencing Commission, accessed October 19, 2022, https://www.ussc.gov/sites/default/files/pdf/research-and-publications/quick-facts/Quick_Facts_Felon_in_Possession_of_a_Firearm.pdf.
113    Commission, "Possession of a Firearm."

ring, his administration would have you believe that white men in rural America are the problem.

## NOT THEIR FIRST RODEO

The overwhelming majority of murder suspects have prior criminal arrests; 90 percent of murder suspects in cities like New York and Chicago, for instance,[114] had already been arrested at least once before. According to a 2021 paper in Police Quarterly, "The Usual Suspects: Prior Criminal Record and the Probability of Arrest," a suspect with a prior criminal record is approximately twenty-nine times more likely than a suspect without a criminal record to be arrested by police.[115] In order to make the point clearly, the report further indicated that making any correlation between a criminal suspect's race and the likelihood of arrest is "spurious" if made "without controlling for the suspect's prior criminal history."[116]

Worse, progressive policy often discourages punishing felons caught in possession of a firearm. The US Sentencing Commission reported in 2018 that there had been a five-year reduction in the sentences for felons caught in possession of a firearm. [117] A 2021 report by Urban Institute found a similar result.[118] Often, gun

---

114   Rafael A. Mangual, "Second, Third, and Fourth Chances—at What Price?" *City Journal*, Winter 2018, https://www.city-journal.org/html/second-third-and-fourth-chances-at-what-price-15657.html.

115   Lisa Stolzenberg, Stewart J. D'Alessio, and Jamie L. Flexon, "The Usual Suspects: Prior Criminal Record and the Probability of Arrest," *Police Quarterly* 24, no. 1 (2020): 31-54, https://doi.org/10.1177/1098611120937304.

116   Stolzenberg, D'Alessio, and Flexon, "The Usual Suspects."

117   Commission, "Possession of a Firearm."

118   William Adams, Kelly Roberts Freeman, and Emily Tiry, "Prosecution of Federal Firearms Offenses, 2000–16," Urban Institute, October 2021, https://www.ojp.gov/pdffiles1/bjs/grants/254520.pdf. The share of defendants sentenced for a firearms offense whose sentences fell within federal sentencing guidelines decreased from 72 to 51 percent between 2000 and 2016. Most sentences that departed from the sentencing guidelines were below the applicable guideline range.

charges are dismissed. The Justice Department reported in 2015 that there has been a 10 year decline in federal convictions for firearms violations.[119]

In Philadelphia, conviction rates for being caught with an illegal gun dropped dramatically after Krasner was sworn into office in January 2018. Confirming what many had suspected, Krasner's office admitted to the Philadelphia Inquirer in January 2021, "We do not believe that arresting people and convicting them for illegal gun possession is a viable strategy to reduce shootings."[120]

*The Charlotte Observer* reported that in Charlotte, North Carolina, for the last few years half of the murder suspects have had prior gun charges dismissed.[121] In response to queries about the rate of gun charges prosecuted in Chicago, Cook County State's Attorney's Office chief data officer worried that "we might be creating a lot of people that will forever be marked as a felon."[122]

Giving violent offenders a break begets more violence. In fact, some two-thirds of people convicted of violent felonies have been arrested for a violent felony before.[123]

If prior offenders make up 90 percent of the murderers in inner cities, and "ghost guns" are involved in less than 1 percent of

119   "Ten Year Decline in Federal Weapons Convictions," Transactional Records Access Clearinghouse, October 27, 2015, https://trac.syr.edu/tracreports/crim/409/.

120   Chris Palmer, "A Philly Committee Spent 18 Months Examining the City's Gun Violence Crisis. Here's What It Found," *Philadelphia Inquirer,* January 27, 2022, https://www.inquirer.com/news/philadelphia-gun-violence-homicides-report-city-council-20220127.html.

121   Ames Alexander And Virginia Bridges, "In Durham, Where Most Gun Charges Are Dismissed, One Suspect Got Break After Break," Charlotte Observer, September 26, 2019, https://www.charlotteobserver.com/news/local/article227306114.html.

122   Frank Main, Jared Rutecki, and Casey Toner, "The Costly Toll of Dead-End Drug Arrests," Better Government Association, December 3, 2021, https://www.bettergov.org/news/the-costly-toll-of-dead-end-drug-arrests/.

123   Mangual, "Second, Third, and Fourth Chances."

murders, why is the government concentrating on the ghost guns rather than on the murderers? Because the Left has a misplaced focus on the race of the violent criminals rather than on the race of their victims, which undermines law enforcement policy. Sadly, it is this focus that the White House has embraced.

## DEFUNDING THE POLICE

President Biden offered support for the "defund the police" movement in a *Now This* interview in 2020. Before he became the Democratic presidential nominee, Joe Biden said he "absolutely" agreed that some funding should be redirected from police.[124] He walked back this position shortly afterwards, but despite publicly disclaiming any support for the "defund the police" movement, Biden's actions suggest some sympathies for this radically bad idea. He nominated progressive Rachael Rollins to be a U.S. Attorney. His Vice President, Kamala Harris, clearly has sympathies for the movement, publicly lauding Los Angeles Mayor Eric Garcetti for slashing police funding before Biden was elected.[125]

During the campaign of 2020, Biden called for the U.S. to "stop transferring weapons of war to police forces,"[126] and he hasn't been shy about using executive power to limit law enforcement. In early 2022, the White House announced that it would issue a new executive order that placed a limit on law enforcement access

124 Morgan Phillips, "Biden Says Some Funding Should 'Absolutely' Be Redirected From Police," *Fox News*, July 8, 2020, https://www.foxnews.com/politics/biden-says-some-funding-should-absolutely-be-redirected-from-police.

125 Ebony Bowden, "Sen. Kamala Harris Applauds LA Mayor's Decision to Slash Police Funding," *New York Post*, June 9, 2020, https://nypost.com/2020/06/09/kamala-harris-applauds-la-mayor-for-slashing-police-funding/.

126 Louis Jacobson and Amy Sherman, "Fact-check: Is Biden Sending More Military Equipment to Police Than Trump?," *Austin-American Statesman*, April 28, 2021, https://www.statesman.com/story/news/politics/politifact/2021/04/28/biden-military-equipment-police-black-lives-matter-fact-check/4871259001/.

to "non-lethal" and life-saving resources, such as armored vehicles and flash-bang devices, as well as placing new restrictions on local law enforcement's use of federal grants.[127] Only a loud and vigorous bipartisan pushback across the country, from the Hill and beyond, delayed the issuance of the order at the beginning of the year in 2022.

But by May of 2022, President Biden had issued an executive order all but adopting the anti-police rhetoric of politicians like Alexandria Ocasio-Cortez and groups like Black Lives Matter. It placed new "restrictions on the transfer or purchase with federal funds of military equipment that belongs on a battlefield, not on our streets."[128] However, surplus equipment being given away for local law enforcement isn't merely some bureaucratic undertaking, and it certainly isn't a way for local law enforcement to wage war on protestors. The 1033 Program is a state and local grant initiative for law enforcement specifically created by Congress and included in the 1997 National Defense Authorization Act.[129] According to the Defense Logistics Agency (DLA), more than 8,000 law enforcement agencies across the country and U.S. territories currently participate in this bi-partisan program.[130]

127  Carol E. Lee et al. "Biden plans executive action on police reform to revive stalled issue," *CNBC*, January 13 2022, https://www.cnbc.com/2022/01/14/biden-plans-executive-action-on-police-reform-to-revive-stalled-issue.html.

128  "FACT SHEET: President Biden to Sign Historic Executive Order to Advance Effective, Accountable Policing and Strengthen Public Safety," White House Briefing Room, May 25, 2022, https://www.whitehouse.gov/briefing-room/statements-releases/2022/05/25/fact-sheet-president-biden-to-sign-historic-executive-order-to-advance-effective-accountable-policing-and-strengthen-public-safety/.

129  National Defense Authorization Act For Fiscal Year 1997, https://www.congress.gov/104/plaws/publ201/PLAW-104publ201.pdf.

130  Andrew W. Lehren et al. "Floyd Protests Renew Debate About Police Use of Armored Vehicles, Other Military Gear," *NBC News*, June 20, 2020, https://www.nbcnews.com/news/us-news/floyd-protests-renew-debate-about-police-use-armored-vehicles-other-n1231288.

In 2021, progressives like Ocasio-Cortez tried to offer amendments to the Defense budget that would limit "ammunition, grenade launchers, and mine-resistant ambush-protected vehicles."[131] Rep. Nydia Velazques attempted to end the program entirely.[132] The White House didn't oppose these measures;[133] ironically, they failed to pass in a Congress in which both Houses are controlled by Democrats.

What the White House hasn't done is to champion law enforcement. On the second anniversary of the death of George Floyd, President Biden signed the aforementioned executive order, which not only places significant limits on the distribution of discarded military equipment to local law enforcement and provides grants to communities that agree to end "no knock" warrants and bar chokeholds, but it also creates a blacklist of police officers fired for misconduct.[134]

In other words, officers can be blackballed for life, their lives will be more at risk when they encounter felons that refuse to surrender, and they won't have access to the equipment needed to match the threat in their communities, in spite of the fact that, according to the latest data, more than 60,000 police officers were

---

131   Amendment to Rules Committee Print 117– 13 Offered by Ms. Ocasio-Cortez of New York, https://amendments-rules.house.gov/amendments/OCASNY_073_xml210914130023176.pdf.

132   Amendment to Rules Committee Print 117– 13 Offered by Ms. Velázquez of New York, https://amendments-rules.house.gov/amendments/VELAZQ_079_xml210914125536905.pdf.

133   Alice Speri, "Lawmakers Take on Militarization of Police in Defense Budget Talks," *Intercept*, September 20 2021, https://theintercept.com/2021/09/20/ndaa-military-equipment-police-1033/.

134   "FBI Releases 2020 Statistics for Law Enforcement Officers Assaulted in the Line of Duty," Federal Bureau of Investigation, October 18, 2021, https://www.nbcnews.com/politics/white-house/biden-signs-police-reform-executive-order-anniversary-george-floyds-de-rcna30548.

assaulted on the job in 2020, a staggering 4,000 more officers than the year before.[135]

That is not how to support police. Here's what supporting police looks like: It would include sending a bill to Capitol Hill that would impose new and stricter sentences for murder, rape, robbery, and arson, and it would include providing grants to states that do the same. It would provide more arms and training to law enforcement to counter increasingly aggressive criminal networks.

The truth is that President Biden needs to end his party's war on local law enforcement, not expand it. During the Obama Administration, the Justice Department set records for what are called "pattern and practice" (P&P) investigations, which oversee local and state law enforcement agencies to determine whether they systematically mistreat local citizens. The Obama Administration undertook twenty-five of these P&P investigations and obtained fourteen consent decrees,[136] which are voluntary legal agreements between local law enforcement and the DOJ, approved by courts, and frequently used as a way to "reform" police departments accused of civil rights violations. They aren't truly voluntary, as they are often offered as alternatives to criminal prosecutions of the law enforcement agency's staff.

Since they are approved by Courts, they can only end with a Court's agreement. In practice, they last a decade or more. In New Orleans and Detroit, news stories have highlighted the high costs of these investigations and the reform plans that have followed, including multimillion-dollar fees paid to the assigned

---

135   FBI, "Officers Assaulted."

136   Matt Vasilogambros, "The Feds Are Investigating Local Police Departments Again. Here's What to Expect," Pew Charitable Trusts, May 3, 2021, https://www.pewtrusts.org/en/research-and-analysis/blogs/stateline/2021/05/03/the-feds-are-investigating-local-police-departments-again-heres-what-to-expect.

monitors.[137] P&P policies have enriched these outside monitoring teams but have done nothing to improve safety in communities. This is the reason the Trump Administration all but stopped these investigations. Unfortunately, President Biden has brought them back. As part of his executive order to "Advance Effective, Accountable Policing and Strengthen Public Safety," issued in May of 2022, Biden directed the DOJ to expand the use of P&P investigations and pushed for the Justice Department to develop Washington, DC directed "best practices for independent investigations" of local law enforcement agencies.[138] The first police departments announced for P&P lawsuits have been Minneapolis and Louisville.[139]

## BIDEN RACIALIZES CRIMINAL JUSTICE

Rather than addressing America's crime problem in a way that separates law-abiding Americans of all stripes from the minority who are law-breakers, President Biden and his supporters seek to divide law-abiding Americans—largely along racial lines.

When the video of George Floyd's ordeal in Minneapolis of being constrained by Officer Derek Chauvin was released, Americans across the board condemned a needless act of violence, but activists, and even some in the mainstream media, insinuated that

---

137  Simone Weichselbaum, "The Problems With Policing the Police," The Marshall Project, *TIME Magazine*, https://time.com/police-shootings-justice-department-civil-rights-investigations/.

138  "FACT SHEET: President Biden to Sign Historic Executive Order to Advance Effective, Accountable Policing and Strengthen Public Safety," White House Briefing Room, May 25, 2022, https://www.whitehouse.gov/briefing-room/statements-releases/2022/05/25/fact-sheet-president-biden-to-sign-historic-executive-order-to-advance-effective-accountable-policing-and-strengthen-public-safety/.

139  Vasilogambros, "Feds Are Investigating."

there would be no investigation of his death without a public uprising.[140]

So rioters sowed destruction and death across the country.[141] Respectfully waiting for the facts to come in wasn't good enough if you wanted to be considered a good citizen. CNN's Don Lemon likened the riots to the Boston Tea Party.[142] When looters rampaged through Banana Republic, Old Navy, and Nordstrom, Seattle City Councilman Teresa Mosqueda said she "understood it."[143] MSNBC's Ali Velshi explained with a straight face, while standing in front of a burning building, that the unrest in Minneapolis was "not, generally speaking, unruly."[144]

In the midst of a pandemic that shut down the country, hitting the poor, black, and elderly hardest, when Americans across the board were told that they couldn't work, travel, or entertain guests in their own homes—they were egged on to join a mob to force a reckoning for Officer Chauvin and for law enforcement in general.

140 Jael Goldfine, "How You Can Demand Justice for George Floyd," *Paper Magazine*, May 27, 2020, https://www.papermag.com/justice-for-george-floyd-how-to-help-2646107567.html.

141 Jessica Learish and Peter Martinez, "Nationwide Protests Over George Floyd's Death," *CBS News*, June 9, 2020, https://www.cbsnews.com/pictures/protests-minnesota-george-floyd-death/.

142 "Don Lemon Compares Riots To The Boston Tea Party," *The Palmieri Report*, June 1, 2020, https://thepalmierireport.com/don-lemon-compares-riots-to-the-boston-tea-party/;https://thehill.com/opinion/white-house/505849-the-myth-of-the-boston-tea-party/.

143 Jason Rantz, "Seattle Council Member Dangerously Endorses Looting and Riots," Mynorthwest, June 2, 2020, https://mynorthwest.com/1908812/rantz-seattle-council-endorse-looting-riot/.

144 Tim Hains, "MSNBC's Ali Velshi Downplays Riot in Front of Burning Building: 'Mostly a Protest,' 'Not Generally Speaking Unruly,'" *Real Clear Politics*, May 28, 2020, https://www.realclearpolitics.com/video/2020/05/28/msnbcs_ali_velshi_downplays_riot_in_front_of_burning_building_mostly_a_protest_not_generally_speaking_unruly.html.

Then-presidential candidate Joe Biden offered his endorsement of the mob: "It's time to listen to those words, to try to understand them. To respond to them, respond with action."[145] Then-Senator Kamala Harris from California explained: "They're not going to stop…. This is a movement, I'm telling you. They're not going to stop and everyone beware, because they're not going to stop…. They're not going to let up and they should not and we should not."[146]

But this impulse to demand a prosecution is dangerous. It is predicated on the false belief that without people marching in the streets and smashing windows, law enforcement and prosecutors won't carry out their duties. Additionally, it assumes that the nation's prosecutors are so weak that they need public pressure to make an assessment of criminal behavior in their ranks and to decide which charges they will bring. Ultimately, these mob actions risk the loss of justice that all Americans are supposed to receive, because they can, in fact, affect the final decisions made in our criminal justice system.

Blacks learned a hard-earned truth during the Jim Crow era: prosecutions should never be subject to mob justice but should be solely based on the facts—and the law. Americans, particularly blacks, lose when communities succeed in pressuring prosecutors, judges, and juries. The record of mob justice in the twentieth century provides an overwhelming argument that mob justice shouldn't continue in the twenty-first.

---

145 Brendan Morrow, "Biden Hits Trump for Photo Op Holding Up the Bible: 'I Just Wish He Opened It Once in a While'," *The Week*, June 2, 2020, https://theweek.com/speedreads/917689/biden-hits-trump-photo-op-holding-bible-just-wish-opened-once.

146 Thomas Barrabi, "Flashback: Kamala Harris Said Nationwide Protests are 'Not Going to Stop'," *Fox News*, September 24, 2020, https://www.foxnews.com/politics/flashback-kamala-harris-nationwide-protests-not-going-to-stop.

Take a look at the Wilmington Race Riot of 1898 at the dawn of the twentieth century. Not surprisingly, it wasn't spontaneous. Ostensibly, this riot was about an election dispute over alleged stuffed ballots in the city of Wilmington, a thriving port city on the coast of North Carolina that had elected a black Republican majority in the previous election. On Election Day in 1898, blacks were astonished by the level of fraud. They likely were shocked when five hundred white men opened the armory and undertook a bloody assault on the black community. This chaos occurred purportedly because local law enforcement had refused to investigate claims that black men had acted disrespectfully towards white women.[147] But that was all a lie. It would take years to uncover the actual rationale for the conflict, but we now know that it was part of an orchestrated campaign involving the media, candidates, and elected officials.[148]

Even the name "Wilmington Race Riot" was a fraud designed to blame the victims. Instead of spontaneous protests, what actually happened was that hired protestors overthrew the elected government of Wilmington, confiscated land, burned houses, destroyed the black-owned newspaper, and killed more than sixty blacks in order to take over Wilmington and its government.[149]

As the comprehensive *1898 Wilmington Race Riot* report would later reveal, the rioters weren't concerned about justice. They were motivated solely by their aims to overthrow the Wilmington government and steal the property and political authority from the lawful residents. While this slaughter of blacks went on, law enforcement was nowhere to be found.

---

147   LeRae Umfleet, "1898 Wilmington Race Riot Report, North Carolina," 1898 Wilmington Race Riot Commission, North Carolina, Office of Archives and History, Research Branch, May 31, 2006, https://digital.ncdcr.gov/digital/collection/p249901coll22/id/5842.
148   Umfleet, "Wilmington Race Riot."
149   Umfleet, "Wilmington Race Riot."

Then there's the Atlanta Race Riot of 1906. Using a similar claim that law enforcement refused to arrest blacks for accosting white women, white mobs and rioters killed dozens of blacks, injured scores more, and looted and razed property and businesses owned by blacks.[150] The local paper ran extra editions of the fake assault and rape claims, including accounts "sensationalized with lurid details and inflammatory language."[151] The damage and violence would have continued if Georgia's governor hadn't ordered the National Guard to shut it down. Once again, the real aim was to take over the political structure and the assets of their political nemeses—in this case, blacks.

A dozen years later, the 1917 East St. Louis Race Riot followed the same model with even deadlier consequences. This time the rioters claimed that prosecutors failed to pursue a charge against a black man accused of killing a white man. By its conclusion, many churches and homes had been burnt and nearly a hundred blacks killed.[152] Six thousand blacks were also made homeless, all while local elected leaders and the police stood by.[153] It took Illinois Governor Frank Lowden's decision to call in the National Guard to end this racial slaughter.[154]

---

150    Clifford Kuhn and Gregory Mixon, "Atlanta Race Riot of 1906," *New Georgia Encyclopedia,* https://www.georgiaencyclopedia.org/articles/history-archaeology/atlanta-race-riot-of-1906/.

151    Kuhn and Mixon, "Atlanta Race Riot."

152    Allison Keyes, "The East St. Louis Race Riot Left Dozens Dead, Devastating a Community on the Rise," *Smithsonian Magazine,* June 30, 2017, https://www.smithsonianmag.com/smithsonian-institution/east-st-louis-race-riot-left-dozens-dead-devastating-community-on-the-rise-180963885/.

153    "East Saint Louis Race Riot of 1917," *Encyclopaedia Britannica Online,* accessed October 24, 2022, https://www.britannica.com/event/East-Saint-Louis-Race-Riot-of-1917.

154    Jared Olar, "Closing the Bicentennial Year, Remembering the Centennial," *From the History Room* (blog), November 30, 2018, https://fromthehistoryroom.wordpress.com/tag/gov-frank-orren-lowden/.

Only a few years later, the infamous Tulsa Race Massacre of 1921 occurred. Again, murderous schemers used the claim that a young black man, Dick Rowland, had acted improperly while in an elevator with a white woman named Sarah Page as their pretext for violence and looting.[155]

Crowds gathered demanding justice. Again, rather than allow any kind of investigation to go forward, one of America's most brutal race massacres would occur instead. The local paper, the *Tulsa Tribune*, was as inflammatory as possible in covering the alleged incident, leading to hordes of angry protestors charging the police station overseeing the investigation.[156] This riot involved literally thousands of whites who burned the black-owned homes and shops over a 35-city-block area. Firefighters were prevented from assisting. More than a hundred black people would be killed.[157]

Mob justice resulting in the murder and plunder of innocent blacks, in the name of outrage over a failing of our criminal justice system, is a part of America's history, one that we should never forget. Despite this history and the terrible and lasting deprivations—it would take decades or more before these communities would recover—the lesson of encouraging mob violence seems to be forgotten.

All Americans—minorities especially—benefit when prosecutors are able to do their jobs without undue efforts to influ-

---

155 "Tulsa Race Riot: A Report by the Oklahoma Commission to Study the Tulsa Race Riot of 1921," Oklahoma Commission to Study the Tulsa Race Riot of 1921, February 28, 2001, https://www.okhistory.org/research/forms/freport.pdf.

156 "1921 Tulsa Race Massacre: The Attack on Greenwood," Tulsa Historical Society & Museum, accessed October 24, 2022, https://www.tulsahistory.org/exhibit/1921-tulsa-race-massacre/.

157 Richard Warner, "Computations as to the Deaths from the 1921 Tulsa Race Riot," Tulsa Historical Society & Museum, January 10, 2000, https://www.tulsahistory.org/wp-content/uploads/2018/11/2006.126.001 Redacted_Watermarked-1.pdf.

ence them in their responsibilities. Demands by demagogues that specific charges be filed against anyone are perilous for criminal justice and are especially dangerous for blacks. Acts of violence in the name of urging an investigation should be seen for what they actually are: excuses for mayhem and an outlet for real injustice.

Instead of joining in with the mob, President Biden should take on the role of a real leader for all. He should stand up for a dispassionate role for prosecutors, instead of naming woke ones to work for him. Yes, Americans like George Floyd deserve justice, and so does everyone else—and rioting won't provide that; it hurts us all. Over $1 billion in insurance claims were made in the wake of the "mostly peaceful" Black Lives Matter protests.[158] Eleven Americans, most of them black, died during these protests.[159] Mob justice inevitably risks harming minorities most. A President looking out for blacks would seek to diminish conflict, not inflame it.

## BLACKS SUFFER MOST IN AMERICA'S CRIME WAVE

Crime in America disproportionately involves blacks. Both those who commit the drive-by shootings, robberies, and burglaries—and more importantly, their victims—are overwhelmingly black.

Blacks make up 13 percent of the population and account for 36 percent of those charged with rape, robbery, and aggravated assault.[160] According to the FBI, in absolute numbers, more blacks

---

158    Jennifer A. Kingson, "$1 Billion-Plus Riot Damage is Most Expensive in Insurance History," *Axios*, September 16, 2020, https://www.axios.com/2020/09/16/riots-cost-property-damage.

159    "At Least 11 Killed During U.S. Protests Seeking Justice for George Floyd, Many of Them African Americans," *Associated Press*, June 2, 2020, https://ktla.com/news/nationworld/at-least-11-killed-during-u-s-protests-seeking-justice-for-george-floyd-many-of-them-african-americans/.

160    Matthew Clarke, "U.S. DOJ Statistics on Race and Ethnicity of Violent Crime Perpetrators," *Prison Legal News*, June 1, 2021, https://www.prisonlegalnews.org/

are murder victims than those of any other racial group.[161] The Centers for Disease Control reports that blacks are disproportionately victims of assault.[162] Sadly, this is no anomaly. Homicide is one of the top five causes of death for black men; no other racial or ethnic group has this distinction.[163]

Leadership means responding not to the criminal actors and their circumstances but to the victims. Yet again, President Biden is missing in action. With great fanfare, he signed into law a replenishment of the federal crime victims' fund.[164] What he hasn't done is push for steps that will end or reduce the crime wave that is expanding all over America.

During President Biden's term, his supporters have sought to diminish the terrible crime news. Even though the murder rate has jumped by nearly 30 percent and aggravated assault by 12 percent, his supporters push the narrative that since other types of crime are stable or slightly dropping, there is no crime wave. Seemingly without a sense of irony, crime expert Philip Cook of Duke University explained, "There was no crime wave—there was

news/2021/jun/1/us-doj-statistics-race-and-ethnicity-violent-crime-perpetrators/.

161   "Murder Victims by Age, Sex, Race, and Ethnicity, 2019," Federal Bureau of Investigation (FBI), accessed December 4, 2022, https://ucr.fbi.gov/crime-in-the-u.s/2019/crime-in-the-u.s.-2019/tables/expanded-homicide-data-table-2.xls.

162   "WISQARS™—Web-based Injury Statistics Query and Reporting System," Centers for Disease Control and Prevention (CDC), last reviewed December 2, 2021, https://www.cdc.gov/injury/wisqars/index.html.

163   "Age-Adjusted Death Rates for Selected Causes of Death in the United States, by Race and Hispanic Origin, 2000," National Center for Health Statistics, Health, United States, 2002 With Chartbook on Trends in the Health of Americans (Hyattsville, MD: NCHS, 2002), accessed November 25, 2002, www.cdc.gov/nchs/products/pubs/pubd/hus/02tables.htm, https://www.prb.org/wp-content/uploads/2002/12/RacialethnicdifferencesinUSmortality.pdf.

164   Morgan Chalfant, "Biden Signs Bill to Bolster Crime Victims Fund," The Hill, July 22, 2021, https://thehill.com/homenews/administration/564411-biden-signs-bill-to-bolster-crime-victims-fund/.

a tsunami of lethal violence, and that's it...."[165] Noted Princeton sociologist Patrick Sharkey—a Biden sympathizer whose 2018 book *Uneasy Peace* argued that aggressive policing and incarceration policies likely reduce crime but could also "provoke a backlash among the public"[166]—joins in this sentiment. He further claims that the public's perception of a crime wave is misplaced, since the real issue is "almost entirely a rise in gun violence, rather than a more general increase in all forms of crime."[167]

## "EXCEPT FOR THE KILLINGS..."

Reminiscent of D.C. Mayor Marion Barry's appearance at a National Press Club luncheon where he explained, "Except for the killings, Washington has one of the lowest crime rates in the country,"[168] such obfuscations are an attempt at downplaying perhaps the fear of the most serious crime: murder.

Americans are increasingly afraid of being murder victims. A Gallup survey in October of 2021 asked Americans how often they worry about murder. This question has been asked since August of 2000. This time the poll yielded a twenty-year record high of Americans afraid they'll be killed, with over a fifth reporting they worry frequently or occasionally that they might get murdered.[169]

In a similar survey from Gallup, 53 percent of Americans report worrying a "great deal" about crime overall, the highest

165    David A. Graham, "America Is Having a Violence Wave, Not a Crime Wave," *Atlantic*, September 29, 2021, https://www.theatlantic.com/ideas/archive/2021/09/america-having-violence-wave-not-crime-wave/620234/.

166    Derek Thompson, "Why America's Great Crime Decline is Over," *Real Clear Policy*, March 26, 2021, https://www.realclearpolicy.com/2021/03/26/why_americas_great_crime_decline_is_over_769895.html.

167    Graham, Violence Wave."

168    Richard Keil, "Except for Murders, City is Safe, Mayor Says," *AP News*, March 23, 1989, https://apnews.com/article/28e1cc6df90065dd5237d4f1bc5c3a08.

169    "Crime," Gallup, accessed October 24, 2022, https://news.gallup.com/poll/1603/crime.aspx.

percentage in more than five years.[170] Gallup explains that this elevated level "likely reflects the record high homicide rates in many cities last year."[171] Second only to inflation and health care costs, Pew Research reported in the spring of 2022 that 54 percent of Americans list crime as the great problem facing the nation.[172]

This sentiment has shown up in elections since Biden has been in office. For instance, pro-BLM prosecutor Chesa Boudin was recalled in San Francisco.[173] Former police captain Eric Adams was elected mayor of New York City.[174] Ann Davison was elected City Attorney of Seattle, becoming the first Republican elected city-wide in decades.[175] In Maryland, voters ousted Baltimore City State's Attorney Marilyn Mosby[176] in favor of Ivan Bates, who had run on a law-and-order platform.[177] Even in Los Angeles, law-

170   Megan Brenan, "Worry About Crime in U.S. at Highest Level Since 2016," Gallup, April 7, 2022, https://news.gallup.com/poll/391610/worry-crime-highest-level-2016.aspx.

171   Claire Meyer, "Majority of Americans Strongly Worried About Crime, Poll Finds," ASIS International, April 11, 2022, https://www.asisonline.org/security-management-magazine/latest-news/today-in-security/2022/april/majority-of-americans-strongly-worried-about-crime/.

172   Doherty and Gómez, "Americans View Inflation."

173   Janie Har and Steve Peoples, "Dems Confront Criticism on Crime after San Francisco Defeat," *AP News*, June 8, 2022, https://apnews.com/article/2022-midterm-elections-california-san-francisco-government-and-politics-police-cee b67888f1c4deeb6be376a286b8be7.

174   Susan Milligan, "Eric Adams' Win Slows New York Democrats' March to the Left," *U.S. News & World Report*, July 7, 2021, https://www.usnews.com/news/politics/articles/2021-07-07/eric-adams-win-slows-new-york-democrats-march-to-the-left.

175   "Perspective: Democrats' Policies on Criminal Justice are Killing the West Coast," *Deseret News*, September 18, 2022, https://www.deseret.com/2022/9/18/23349337/criminal-justice-reimagined-george-floyd-crime-defund-police-pursuits-west-coast.

176   Josh Christenson, "As Crime Soars, Democratic Voters Turn on Left-Wing Prosecutors," *Free Beacon*, August 2, 2022, https://freebeacon.com/democrats/as-crime-soars-democratic-voters-turn-on-left-wing-prosecutors/.

177   Ivan Bates, "Ivan's Plans," Ivan Bates campaign website, accessed October 24, 2022, https://www.batesforbaltimore.com/ivansplan.

and-order candidate and former Republican Rick Caruso ended up a close second to progressive Karen Bass (who was on Biden's short list for running mates in 2020) in the nonpartisan run-off for mayor.[178]

These signs portend a blow-out for Biden's party in the 2022 midterms, but he and his team have refused to change course. Other than making a few speeches claiming to support police, he has never actually taken steps to reduce crime in America. He hasn't pushed to expand the death penalty or to add additional grants to assist local governments with exploding crime rates the way he did in 1994. Instead, he has focused on stymieing law enforcement rather than violent criminals.

Biden is the first sitting President to oppose capital punishment,[179] a position that even America's first black President didn't embrace. In July of 2021, Biden's DOJ placed a moratorium on carrying out the death penalty at the federal level.[180] However, 64 percent of Americans support capital punishment,[181] with blacks evenly split between supporting and opposing it at 49 percent [182],

---

178  Brian Eckhouse and John Gittelsohn, "Billionaire Caruso, Lawmaker Bass Advance to LA Mayor Runoff," Bloomberg, June 8, 2022, https://www.bloomberg.com/news/articles/2022-06-08/billionaire-caruso-lawmaker-bass-advance-to-la-mayor-runoff.

179  Devlin Barrett and Amy B. Wang, "Federal Executions Halted as Justice Dept. Reviews Trump-Era Policies," *Washington Post*, July 1, 2021, https://www.washingtonpost.com/national-security/federal-executions-halted-merrick-garland/2021/07/01/74dfb660-dac7-11eb-bb9e-70fda8c37057_story.html.

180  Barrett and Wang, "Federal Executions Halted."

181  Carroll Doherty et al. "Most Americans Favor the Death Penalty Despite Concerns About Its Administration," Pew Research Center, June 2, 2021, https://www.pewresearch.org/politics/2021/06/02/most-americans-favor-the-death-penalty-despite-concerns-about-its-administration/.

182  Doherty et al. "Most Americans Favor."

but note the black support is a substantially larger percentage than Democrats overall, who support it at only 34 percent.[183]

Under President Trump, thirteen executions were carried out at the federal level. There are now forty-four men on the federal death row. Examining whether mass murderer/white supremacist Dylan Roof and Boston Marathon Bomber Dzokhar Tsarnaev, along with a host of drug kingpins and murdering bank robbers, should live until their natural deaths may seem like an important area to focus on by the Biden White House. But it is a luxury that many citizens simply can't afford.

America's crime wave has costs that go beyond the victims, who are indeed very important. But failing to lower or end the crime wave not only leads to more loss of lives—especially among blacks—but also limits the economy by affecting the willingness of companies to provide services in high-crime neighborhoods. Grocery stores close or never open. Other businesses soon follow the lead. In other words, the very communities that need investment the most suffer.

The best city planners try to partner with businesses, working to attract new ones to their community and developing business-friendly policies to help grow the ones that are already there. In these places, new shops including grocery stores and fast-food chains happily reside. The residents are happier and more prosperous. But when rioting and crime is the order of the day, business flees and, along with it, the prosperity of the residents.

---

183   "2021 Gallup Poll: Public Support for Capital Punishment Remains at Half-Century Low," Death Penalty Information Center, November 19, 2021, https://deathpenaltyinfo.org/news/2021-gallup-poll-public-support-for-capital-punishment-remains-at-half-century-low.

Take the city of Baltimore. In 2015, riots broke out over the death of career felon Freddie Gray.[184] Some 380 businesses were destroyed or shut down before the protests were over—almost every one of them located in West Baltimore, the neediest part of the city.[185] In a mere seventeen days, $13 million in damages occurred. There were six officers charged in Gray's death, but three were acquitted, and the prosecutors decided not to pursue charges against the remaining three officers.[186] Obama's Justice Department investigated, but ultimately, the DOJ declined to prosecute at the federal level.

The local CVS which offered seniors prescription discounts was closed for more than a year. [187] Similarly, a senior living facility that was under construction had its opening delayed by more than a year. Sadly, even seven years later the DTLR store (a black-owned clothing and shoe chain) that started in Baltimore was never rebuilt. Today, the area is a high crime zone and there is no commercial development occurring. The overwhelmingly black residents are forced to travel out of the community for clothing, food, and employment.

184   "Freddie Gray Arrest Record, Criminal History & Rap Sheet," *Heavy*, April 27, 2015, https://heavy.com/news/2015/04/freddie-gray-arrest-record-criminal-history-rap-sheet-why-was-freddie-gray-arrested/.

185   Associated Press, "Baltimore, Business Owners Settle Over Freddie Gray Unrest," *U.S. News & World Report*, March 29, 2022, https://www.usnews.com/news/us/articles/2022-03-29/baltimore-business-owners-settle-over-freddie-gray-unrest.

186   Nick Iannelli, "$3.5M Settlement OK'd for Baltimore Businesses Damaged in Freddie Gray Riots," *WTOP News*, April 21, 2022, https://wtop.com/baltimore/2022/04/baltimore-business-owners-that-had-damage-in-freddie-gray-riots-now-getting-paid/.

187   "Now-and-Then-Pictures: Scenes from the 2015 Unrest in Baltimore," *Baltimore Sun*, April 27, 2018, https://www.baltimoresun.com/maryland/baltimore-city/bs-md-ci-riots-now-and-then-20180427-htmlstory.html.

Is it any wonder that blacks in America regularly say in polls that they support *more* law enforcement, not less, because they need it the most?[188]

President Biden's plans for the country have not made communities safer. In fact, in many cities, things have gotten substantially worse. A great goal that the country has achieved—getting Americans from all walks of life to join law enforcement—has also been undermined by a President who sounds more committed to lawbreakers than lawmen. The number of law enforcement officers nationwide[189] has dropped, as has the number of black officers.[190]

For a movement that claims to want to reform law enforcement, it uses a strange approach: attacking white police officers as racist. It's no surprise that this has created a situation where there are fewer qualified officers of any race.

Improving neighborhood safety and protecting business development in working-class communities is critically important to improving the quality of life for minorities and the poor. President Biden's polices are instead premised on the false notion that racial disparities in the criminal system are a result of anti-black bias, not of differences in behavior. Americans, blacks in particular, are harmed as a result.

Instead of tepidly opposing the defunding of police departments, President Biden should support measures to recruit more local and state police. He should replicate a successful Trump

---

188   Lydia Saad, "Black Americans Want Police to Retain Local Presence," Gallup, August 5, 2020, https://news.gallup.com/poll/316571/black-americans-police-retain-local-presence.aspx.

189   Jake Bleiberg, Kate Brumback, and Stefanie Dazio, "Law Enforcement Struggles to Recruit Since Killing of Floyd," *AP News*, June 11, 2021, https://apnews.com/article/government-and-politics-george-floyd-racial-injustice-only-on-ap-coronavirus-pandemic-d434cc8023875ddb996abb7df0a7bc44.

190   Cooper, *Making Black America Great Again*, p. 119.

crime policy, directing the Justice Department to identify communities with elevated crime levels and provide them with greater law-enforcement grants. He should push a major anti-crime measure promoting enhanced penalties for violent criminals and publicly reverse himself on capital punishment.

The Justice Department and the White House should speak out against the effort to eliminate bail, and President Biden must reverse course and pledge that he will veto any bill that comes before him that reduces "qualified immunity." Qualified immunity is a legal doctrine created by courts to shield police officers from lawsuits demanding financial payments, as long as the officers did not violate "clearly established" law.[191] Officers, as a result, can carry out their roles in the community without fear that they may lose their homes or their children's college fund, when a high-profile incident leads to an injury or worse for an accused defendant.

President Biden should buttress the efforts of local governments by offering federal assistance and expertise to fight crime. He should reverse his executive order unleashing "pattern and practice" investigations on local law enforcement and instead regularly hold White House events with officers who've served their communities in amazing ways. He should tell his party that they should end their public denunciations of law enforcement and promise Americans that his party understands their concerns and will work to ensure that they feel safe and protected in their communities.

In the 2021 State of the Union Address, President Biden announced to wide applause that he supports law enforcement. His real actions belie those words.

---

191    "Harlow et al v. Fitzgerald," 457 U.S. 800, No. 80-945 (1982), Casetext, June 24, 1982, https://casetext.com/case/harlow-v-fitzgerald.

# CONCLUSION

Leniency for violent criminals won't improve society or the criminal element. It isn't just naïve; it's dangerous.

The crime waves in the nation's urban centers should never have been allowed to take place. Furthermore, prosecutors should be committed to vindicating the livelihoods of victims. If necessary, they need to throw the book at violent offenders, especially if they are repeat offenders, who are the main problem. If they are removed from the community, crime rates will drop dramatically. But first-time rapists and car jackers should also receive severe punishments, both as a deterrent and also as a reflection of society's condemnation of their predatory behavior. Prosecutors should not reduce felony charges to misdemeanors, and, where appropriate, they should ask that criminals be sentenced for each individual conviction separately.

But too many radical district attorneys and their supporters live in enclaves of wealth and security and never face the consequences of their actions. Those who pay the price for these deluded visions of grandeur are blacks, the poor, and the other marginalized groups like the working class.

Americans must demand that government restore accountability in the criminal justice system; Americans must be able to have confidence that prosecutors will do their job and enforce the law.

# CHAPTER FIVE

# AMERICA IS RUNNING OUT OF GAS

Perhaps the most unpopular policy of Joe Biden has been his decision to prioritize climate change over abundant petroleum production.

In a Gallup survey in August of 2022, 3 percent of Americans volunteered that climate change was the most important problem facing the country.[1] There are both short-term and long-term consequences to this misplaced prioritization, but the end result is that American households have been severely harmed, blacks and the working class most of all.

President Biden's energy policies have hurt black Americans in several important ways. His extreme climate alarmism has raised energy prices, which has disrupting the nation's economy and the household budgets of blacks across the country.

These policies are in sharp contrast to the policies of the Trump Administration, when deregulation of American energy production led to annual energy-cost savings of $2,200 per household.[2] Jobs in the oil, natural-gas, and renewable-energy industries provided tremendous economic opportunities for Americans as well.[3]

---

1    "Most Important Problem," Gallup, accessed October 24, 2022, https://news.gallup.com/poll/1675/most-important-problem.aspx.

2    "How Much Does Energy Efficiency Cost?" EnergySage, July 13, 2020, https://www.energysage.com/energy-efficiency/why-conserve-energy/cost-of-ee/.

3    "Innovation-Driven Energy Dominance Is a Win for American Consumers," Trump White House Archives, November 19, 2019, https://trumpwhitehouse. archives.gov/articles/innovation-driven-energy-dominance-win-american-consumers/.

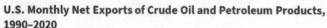

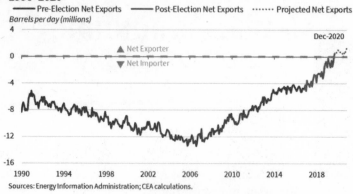

**U.S. Monthly Net Exports of Crude Oil and Petroleum Products, 1990–2020**

White House Release.[4]

The energy-cost savings benefited those at the lowest incomes the most: the bottom twentieth percentile of American households were most likely to see their budgets positively affected by the pro-energy prices under President Donald Trump.

Americans—particularly black and working-class Americans —long for those days. But the priorities of the Biden Administration are focused on "climate," not on allowing Americans to use affordable energy sources. This is ironic because Americans have struggled with energy costs for decades—what analysts in Washington refer to as "energy insecure situations." In fact, it was during President Obama's second term that the U.S. Energy Information Administration issued a report tracking this concern and discovered that more than 30 percent of households experienced "energy insecurity."

---

4    Trump, "Innovation-Driven Energy Dominance."

Paris Climate Accords, and named former Democratic Senator John Kerry from Massachusetts as his climate envoy.[11]

In one of his Administration's few bipartisan successes—the infrastructure bill—President Biden was able to get new grants for nationwide charging network for electric vehicles and a significant boost in support for clean energy projects. Biden also killed the Keystone XL Pipeline and put a freeze on oil and gas drilling on federal land. Fortunately, he was overturned in federal court on the latter issue.

## KEYSTONE PIPELINE TIMELINE

▸ February 2005—The Keystone Pipeline Extension is originally proposed by TransCanada.[12] It is to be a 3-foot diameter crude oil pipeline beginning in Alberta, Canada and extending to Nebraska in the US.[13]

March 2008—The Bush Administration issues a presidential permit to allow the $5.2 billion project to proceed.[14]

June 2010—the pipeline starts operation.[15]

August 2011—The U.S. State Department issues a final environmental impact statement determining "there would

er Milman, "John Kerry Named as Joe Biden's Special Climate Envoy," dian, November 23, 2020, https://www.theguardian.com/us-news/ /nov/23/john-kerry-biden-climate-envoy-appointment.

sa Denchak and Courtney Lindwall, "What Is Keystone XL?" Natural rces Defense Council, March 15, 2022, https://www.nrdc.org/stories/ eystone-pipeline#whatis.

ne XL Pipeline FAQs," Keystone XL website, https://www.keystonexl.com/ AQs/.

ted Press, "A Timeline of the Keystone XL Oil Pipeline," AP News, 24, 2017, https://apnews.com/article/5831ea1867454124aa4a97 48b.

at the History of the Keystone XL Pipeline Expansion," CBC News, 7, 2021, https://www.cbc.ca/news/canada/timeline-keystone-xl-1.5877117.

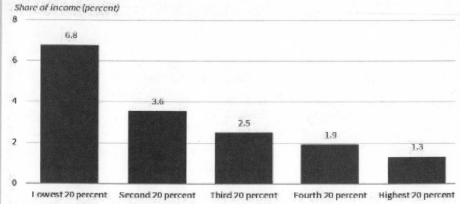

**Consumer Savings as a Share of Income by Household Income Quintile**

*Share of income (percent)*

Sources: Bureau of Labor Statistics; CEA calculations as described in the appendix.
Note: Values represent CEA's estimates of consumer savings as a share of pre-tax income in 2018.

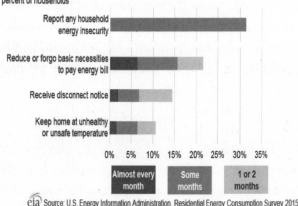

Households experiencing household energy insecure situations, 2015
percent of households

eia Source: U.S. Energy Information Administration, Residential Energy Consumption Survey 2015

The Energy Information Agency detailed the characteristics of households experiencing "energy insecurity," and the contrast between the conditions under the Obama and the Trump administrations is revealing.

In every category, Americans were better off during the Trump presidency than they were during the Obama presidency.

**U.S. household energy insecurity measures (2015 and 2020)**

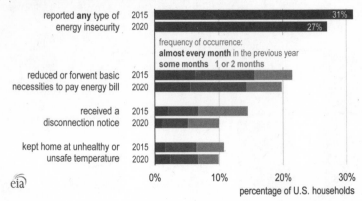

But, to quote Ronald Reagan, "You ain't seen nothing yet!" After the painstaking effort of the Trump Administration to get energy prices to the lowest in a generation, Biden pushed to reverse nearly every one of those policies. The predictable result is a government-made shortage that has driven up electricity prices, and those who can least afford to pay them are people with lower incomes, of whom black Americans comprise a disproportionate number.

## CLIMATE FIRST, BLACK INTERESTS TO THE BACK OF THE POLITICAL BUS

In 2020, candidate Biden pushed fighting climate change as one of his top priorities in a way that no President has ever done before. In the summer of 2020, shortly after receiving the Democratic nomination, he laid out an ambitious climate plan.[5] Candidate Biden insisted that environmentalism was part of "racial justice"

and promised to send Congress a "transformational pl clean energy revolution."[6] Biden pledged to spend bi R&D for clean energy technology, upgrade four million to make them more energy efficient, and make a priorit ing in public transportation for any city with more th residents.[7] In a dramatic act, at a live-streamed New townhall meeting, candidate Biden walked over to Rebecca Beaulieu and took her hands, saying, "I g I guarantee you, we are going to end fossil fuel, going to cooperate with them [the oil and gas in October 2020 presidential debate, Biden said, " is an existential threat to humanity," and promise he would move America away from oil and g paign website, he committed to net-zero emiss a 100 percent clean energy economy, as well a any financial support from the oil and gas ind elected, he created the National Climate Task

5    Marianne Lavelle, "Biden Puts Climate Change at Center of Presidential Campaign, Calling Trump a 'Climate Arsonist'," *Inside Climate News*, September 14, 2020, https://insideclimatenews.org/news/14092020/ joe-biden-climate-change-wildfires-donald-trump-2020-election/.

6    Lisa Friedman and Katie Glueck, "Biden's Big Clir He Embrace His Task Force's Goals?" *New York T* https://www.nytimes.com/2020/07/06/us/politic joe-biden-climate-change.html.

7    Timothy Gardner and Valerie Volcovici, "Factb It's Biden's Green Revolution Versus Trump's V Reuters, October 29, 2020, https://www.reut election-climate-change-factbox/factbox-on-é revolution-versus-trumps-war-on-regulation

8    Sharon Bernstein, "Trump, Biden Clash O in Final Debate," Reuters, October 23, 20; com/article/us-usa-election-debate-climat over-climate-oil-industry-in-final-debate-

9    "The Biden Plan for a Clean Energy Re Biden/Harris campaign website, https://

10   "Take Climate Action in Your Commu Task Force, January 27, 2021, https://

be no significant impacts to most resources along the proposed project corridor".[16]

▸ December 2011—President Obama delays a decision on approval for the project. Congress pushes a measure that requires the president to act on the application within sixty days, prompting Obama to deny the application. He announces that TransCanada could re-apply however.[17]

▸ May 4, 2012—TransCanada reapplies and restarts the federal review process for the Keystone pipeline.[18]

▸ March 1, 2013—The State Department issues an environmental review report that raises no major objections to the Keystone XL oil pipeline and indicates that other options to get oil from Canada to Gulf Coast refineries are worse for the climate.[19]

▸ June 25, 2013—In a speech, Obama declares that fighting climate change would be a major priority of his second term and explains that he will only approve the project if it doesn't worsen carbon pollution.[20]

---

16    "Final Environmental Impact Statement," U.S. Department of State, August 26, 2011, https://2009-2017.state.gov/r/pa/prs/ps/2011/08/171084.htm.

17    John M. Broder and Dan Frosch, "U.S. Delays Decision on Pipeline Until After Election," *New York Times*, November 11, 2011, https://www.nytimes.com/2011/11/11/us/politics/administration-to-delay-pipeline-decision-past-12-election.html.

18    Jay F. Marks, "TransCanada Re-applies for Keystone XL Permit," *Oklahoman*, May 4, 2012, https://www.oklahoman.com/story/business/energy-resource/2012/05/04/transcanada-re-applies-for-keystone-xl-permit/60939442007/.

19    Dina Cappiello and Matthew Daly, "State Department Has No Major Objections to Keystone XL Pipeline," *Christian Science Monitor*, March 2, 2013, https://www.csmonitor.com/Environment/Latest-News-Wires/2013/0302/State-Department-has-no-major-objections-to-Keystone-XL-pipeline.

20    President Barack Obama, "Remarks on Climate Change" The White House: President Barack Obama, June 25, 2013, https://obamawhitehouse.archives.gov/the-press-office/2013/06/25/remarks-president-climate-change.

▶ February 2014—A state judge in Nebraska strikes down the state law that allowed the pipeline, throwing the project into legal limbo.[21]

▶ February 2015—Congress passes fast-track legislation a second time in February of 2015. Obama vetoes the bill days later, and Congress is unable to over-ride it.[22]

▶ In a reversal, candidate Hillary Clinton announces in September 2015 that she opposes the pipeline, although when she was Secretary of State, the State Department had greenlighted the project at least three times.

▶ November 2015—President Obama denies Trans-Canada a permit.[23]

▶ June 2016—TransCanada seeks $15 billion in damages from the federal government in response to the Obama administration rejecting the Keystone XL pipeline.

▶ January 2017—Trump issues an executive order expediting the approval of the Keystone Pipeline.[24]

---

21 Associated Press, "Nebraska Judge Strikes Down Law That Allows Keystone XL Pipeline," *Denver Post*, October 25, 2022, https://www.denverpost.com/2014/02/19/nebraska-judge-strikes-down-law-that-allows-keystone-xl-pipeline/.

22 Suzanne Goldenberg, "Keystone Pipeline Passes House Vote as Republicans Defy Obama Veto Threat," *Guardian*, February 11, 2015, https://www.theguardian.com/environment/2015/feb/11/keystone-xl-pipeline-house-republican-obama.

23 Suzanne Goldenberg and Dan Roberts, "Obama Rejects Keystone XL Pipeline and Hails US as Leader on Climate Change," *Guardian*, November 6, 2015, https://www.theguardian.com/environment/2015/nov/06/obama-rejects-keystone-xl-pipeline.

24 Donald J. Trump, "Memorandum on Construction of the Keystone XL Pipeline," Administration of Donald J. Trump, January 24, 2017, https://www.govinfo.gov/content/pkg/DCPD-201700068/pdf/DCPD-201700068.pdf.

▶ January 2017—TransCanada resubmits its application for approval.[25]

▶ March 2017—State Department issues a presidential permit at the direction of President Trump.[26]

▶ November 2017—the Nebraska Public Service Commission votes three to two to approve construction of a portion of the Keystone XL pipeline in Nebraska, although the commission rejects TransCanada's preferred route for the pipeline.[27]

▶ November 2018—U.S. District Judge Brian M. Morris blocks the permit issued by the Trump administration. Morris rules that a supplemental environmental review has to be completed before the construction could proceed.[28]

▶ March 2019—President Trump attempts to over-ride the requirement for a "supplemental" environmental review by issuing an executive permit for construction, connection, operation, and maintenance to TransCanada in March of 2019.[29]

---

25  "TransCanada Says Preparing to Reapply for Keystone-XL Pipeline," *Business Insider*, January 24, 2017, https://markets.businessinsider.com/news/stocks/r-brief-transcanada-says-preparing-to-reapply-for-keystone-xl-pipeline-2017-1-1001691084.

26  Ben Lefebvre, "State Department to Approve Keystone Pipeline Permit," *Politico*, March 23, 2017, https://www.politico.com/story/2017/03/state-department-to-approve-keystone-pipeline-permit-236414.

27  Ben Lefebvre, "Keystone XL Pipeline Wins Green Light in Nebraska—But May Face New Hurdles," *Politico*, November 11, 2017, https://www.politico.com/story/2017/11/20/nebraska-approves-keystone-xl-pipeline-250341.

28  "US Judge Halts Construction of the Keystone XL Oil Pipeline," *CNBC*, November 9, 2018, https://www.cnbc.com/2018/11/09/us-judge-halts-construction-of-the-keystone-xl-oil-pipeline.html.

29  Brady Dennis and Juliet Eilperin, "Trump Signs Permit for Construction of Controversial Keystone XL Pipeline," *Washington Post*, March 29, 2019, https://www.washingtonpost.com/climate-environment/2019/03/29/trump-signs-permit-construction-controversial-keystone-xl-pipeline/.

▸ May 2020—US District Judge Morris enjoins the U.S. Corps of Engineers from undertaking necessary activities for allowing the pipeline to proceed until appellate courts determine that President Trump's executive permit order is lawful. [30]

▸ January 2021—President Biden signs an executive order that revokes the permit for the Keystone XL Pipeline, officially killing the project.[31]

The Keystone Pipeline is a desperately needed energy project. It would connect the world's third largest energy reserve (Canada) with the largest refining market (USA)[32] and generate thousands of jobs and billions in economic growth for both the US and Canada.[33] It would double the current capacity of oil transported in the U.S. per day and ensure that the US has a stable source of crude oil, while increasing employment and economic growth in the process.[34] It would contribute more than $3 billion towards our country's GDP. Additionally, taxes paid by the project would

---

30  Press Release, "Federal Court Upholds Ruling Blocking Permit Critical to Keystone XL, Other Oil and Gas Pipelines," Center for Biological Diversity, May 11, 2020, https://biologicaldiversity.org/w/news/press-releases/federal-court-upholds-ruling-blocking-permit-critical-to-keystone-xl-other-oil-and-gas-pipelines-2020-05-11/.

31  Ben Lefebvre and Lauren Gardner, "Biden Kills Keystone XL Permit, Again," *Politico*, January 20, 2021, https://www.politico.com/news/2021/01/20/joe-biden-kills-keystone-xl-pipeline-permit-460555.

32  Keystone, "Keystone XL Pipeline."

33  David Koenig, "Debate Renewed Over Economic Benefits of Keystone Pipeline," *AP News*, March 24, 2017, https://apnews.com/article/01130190be004e3fa6ce977be05291f6.

34  Mark Green, "Misunderstood Keystone XL a Reminder of the Importance of Critical Infrastructure," *American Petroleum Institute*, March 11, 2022, https://www.api.org/news-policy-and-issues/blog/2022/03/11/misunderstood-keystone-xl-a-reminder-of-the-importance-of-critical-infrastructur.

mostly benefit the towns and counties it passes through.[35] As planned, it would have been the single largest construction project happening in the U.S.[36]

It almost made it.

In other words, the 1,120-mile Keystone XL segment was on track to be completed in 2022, with operations starting in early 2023.[37] Especially during a period of elevated energy costs, having access to the pipeline would apply significant downward pressure on prices while obviating the need for President Biden to go "hat in hand" to Nicolas Maduro, the despot in Venezuela asking for assistance.

Eliminating the pipeline has done nothing to alleviate the need for it. In fact, some of the Canadian crude is now being moved by rail or truck, both of which are more expensive and require a larger carbon footprint.[38]

The White House isn't satisfied with killing the Keystone Pipeline. It's still working on a byzantine effort to make federal bank regulators stop investors and companies from promoting industries that are designated as climate threats.[39] This scheme is breathtaking. Banks would be forced to assess how their actions

---

35 Olivier Tisserand, "5 Good Reasons to Be in Favor of the Keystone XL Pipeline," Indelac Controls, March 31, 2014, https://www.indelac.com/blog/bid/339858/5-good-reasons-to-be-in-favor-of-the-keystone-xl-pipeline.

36 "Pipeline to Create Thousands of Short-Term Jobs," Bloomberg, accessed October 22, 2022, https://www.bloomberg.com/graphics/infographics/keystone-pipeline-economic-impact.html.

37 Green, "Misunderstood Keystone."

38 "Carbon Footprint: Pipelines Trump Rail on a Large Scale," Energy Matters, Enbridge, 2022, https://www.enbridge.com/energy-matters/news-and-views/carbon-footprint-pipelines-vs-rail.

39 Victoria Guida, "'Big Shift': Biden Moves to Rewrite the Rules on Climate Threat," *Politico*, January, 24, 2022, Https://Www.Politico.Com/News/2022/01/24/Biden-Climate-Banks-2103097.

affect Biden's climate change goals.[40] In other words, rather than regulate emissions and pollutants, the Biden White House would simply strangle financial access for certain types of projects like refineries. If fuel costs are high now, imagine what they'll be if this effort is allowed to go forward.

This effort wouldn't stop with banking. With significant fanfare, in the fall of 2021, the Office of Management and Budget attempted to lay out new requirements for the Federal Acquisition Regulation (FAR) to ensure that the federal supply chain minimizes the risks of climate change; created a Climate-Related Financial Risk Task Force under the Federal Credit Policy Council to "advance interagency analysis"; and established a Flood Resilience Interagency Working Group that forces the Federal Emergency Management Agency to focus federal efforts on climate change and energy-use reduction.[41]

In another disappointing move, in the spring of 2022, the White House closed off nearly half the National Petroleum Reserve in Alaska (NPR-A) to all oil and gas drilling, even as prices at the pump were rising.[42] Claiming that the policy would balance protecting "special areas and wildlife habitat with responsible resource development," the White House reversed a Trump-

40    Joe Adler and Jon Prior, "Biden's Likely Fed Pick Could Change Tone on Climate Risk, Capital Rules," *American Banker*, January 5, 2022, https://www.americanbanker.com/news/bidens-likely-fed-pick-could-change-tone-on-climate-risk-capital-rules.

41    Candace Vahlsing, "Taking Action to Address Climate-Related Fiscal Risk," White House Briefing Room, October 15, 2021, https://www.whitehouse.gov/omb/briefing-room/2021/10/15/taking-action-to-address-climate-related-fiscal-risk/.

42    Katabella Roberts, "Biden Slashes Millions of Acres Eligible for Oil Drilling," *Epoch Times*, April 26, 2022, https://www.theepochtimes.com/biden-slashes-millions-of-acres-eligible-for-oil-drilling-in-alaska_4427694.html.

era policy that would have allowed oil development on more than 80 percent of the area.[43]

Meanwhile, at the White House Conference on Hunger, Nutrition, and Health, the weekend before Hurricane Ian hit Florida, President insisted (as he has on other occasions) that he wanted to make sure that oil companies didn't "gouge" the American people due to weather related disruptions.[44] No member of the press asked how he would square that statement with his policies that clearly make fuel prices higher than necessary.

All of these policies have hurt America's energy independence and created significant pain for American households. Today, some 30 million American households face a "high" energy burden, meaning that they spend more than 6 percent of their income on energy bills.[45] Nearly a third of households skipped food or medicine to pay their energy bill in 2021.[46] According to the Energy Information Administration's "Winter Fuels Outlook" in 2021, half of American households will spend at least 30 percent *more* for natural gas heating than they did the year before.[47] Yet when asked about these pressing concerns, the official response from the

---

43    Press Release, "Following January Announcement, Bureau of Land Management Issues Record of Decision for the National Petroleum Reserve In Alaska," Bureau of Land Management, April 25, 2022, https://www.blm.gov/press-release/following-january-announcement-bureau-land-management-issues-record-decision-national.

44    Ben Lefebvre, "Don't 'Gouge the American People,' Biden Warns Oil Industry as Ian Nears," *Politico*, September 9, 2022, https://www.politico.com/news/2022/09/28/biden-gasoline-price-gouging-hurricane-ian-00059257.

45    Rozana Ayala, Ariel Drehobl, and Lauren Ross, *How High Are Household Energy Burdens?* (Washington: American Council for an Energy-Efficient Economy, 2020), https://www.aceee.org/sites/default/files/pdfs/u2006.pdf.

46    Carmen Reinicke, "20% of Americans Couldn't Pay Their Energy Bill in the Last Year. How to Keep Costs Down," *CNBC*, December 23 2021, https://www.cnbc.com/2021/12/23/20percent-of-americans-couldnt-pay-their-energy-bill-in-the-last-year.html.

47    "Short-Term Energy Outlook," U.S. Energy Information Administration (EIA), October 12, 2022, https://www.eia.gov/outlooks/steo/report/WinterFuels.php.

Biden Administration is always a variation of "Don't blame me, check the guy behind the tree."

In March 2022, Fox News' Peter Doocy challenged then-White House press secretary Jen Psaki about the harmful effects of the Biden energy policies.[48] "Why did you guys decide to rebrand the rise in gas prices as the #PutinPriceHike?" Doocy asked.[49] In a non-sequitur, Psaki claimed that no one could have predicted Russia would invade Ukraine. She added, "President Putin's buildup of military troops is leading to volatility and an increase in oil and prices, hence you have a Putin gas-price pump rise."[50]

Doocy then turned to drilling. He asked Psaki whether the Biden administration would "cut red tape" to help American oil and gas companies expand drilling in the country.[51] Psaki replied that energy companies already had the permits they needed adding, "I don't think they need an embroidered invitation to drill."[52] Everything Psaki said that day was either false or intentional double-speak. She would have Americans believe that the President's policies on oil and gas exploration and the shutdown of the Keystone pipeline have had no impact on energy prices.

---

48    Andrew Feinberg, "'Let Me Give You the Facts': Psaki Pushes Back on Fox News Reporter's Questions About Rising Gas Prices," *Independent*, March 7, 2022, https://www.independent.co.uk/news/world/americas/us-politics/gas-prices-psaki-peter-doocy-ukraine-b2030540.html.

49    Jake Lahut and Oma Seddiq, "Psaki Spars with Fox News Reporter Over Rising Gas Prices: 'We're Already Getting That Oil, Peter'," *Business Insider*, March 9, 2022, https://www.businessinsider.com/psaki-spars-with-fox-news-reporter-over-rising-gas-prices-2022-3.

50    Seddiq and Lahut, "Psaki Spars."

51    Seddiq and Lahut, "Psaki Spars."

52    Tim Hains, "Psaki and Doocy Debate Increasing U.S. Energy Production: I Don't Think Oil Companies Need an 'Embroidered Invitation' to Drill," *Real Clear Politics*, March 9, 2022, https://www.realclearpolitics.com/video/2022/03/09/psaki_vs_fncs_doocy_i_dont_think_oil_companies_need_an_embroidered_invitation_to_drill_using_existing_permits.html.

This exchange happened in March of 2022, at which point the price of gas was $4.17 a gallon, even though it had been $2.53 a gallon the day Biden was inaugurated. [53] Even if a few pennies of the increase were related to the February 24th invasion of Ukraine by Russia, there had been quite a jump in gas prices before the conflict ever occurred.

## LET THEM EAT CAKE

But it wasn't just the press secretary who ignored the concerns of the American people. While families were struggling with forty-year-high inflation and trying to figure out how to make ends meet, Biden Energy Secretary Jennifer Granholm suggested, "[i]f you are low income, you can get your home entirely weather-ized."[54] Adding insult to injury, she went on to add, "if you are moderate income, today you can get 30 percent off the price of solar panels."[55]

According to a Berkeley Lab report in 2021, Blacks communities aren't interested in solar panels.[56] Instead, solar panels are attractive to the well-heeled, highly educated, overwhelmingly

53    Dr. Nancy Yamaguchi, "EIA Gasoline and Diesel Retail Prices Update," *Fuels Market News*, January 22, 2020, https://fuelsmarketnews.com/eia-gasoline-and-diesel-retail-prices-update-january-22-2020/.

54    Jessica Chasmar, "Biden Energy Secretary Granholm Mocked for Touting 30% Tax Credit on Solar Panels for Middle-Class Americans," *Fox News*, August 21, 2022, https://www.foxnews.com/politics/biden-energy-secretary-granholm-mocked-touting-30-tax-credit-solar-panels-middle-class-americans.

55    Leah Barkoukis, "Critics Blast Granholm's Energy Advice for Poor Americans," *Townhall,* August 22, 2022, https://townhall.com/tipsheet/leahbarkoukis/2022/08/22/critics-blast-granholms-energy-advice-for-poor-americans-n2612054.

56    Emma Foehringer Merchant, "Report Finds Wide Racial and Ethnic Disparities in Rooftop Solar Installations," *Greentech Media*, January 14, 2019, https://www.greentechmedia.com/articles/read/report-finds-wide-racial-and-ethnic-disparities-in-rooftop-solar. Communities with over 50 percent black residents have 69 percent less rooftop solar installed than tracts with no racial or ethnic majority.

white wokesters that make up the backbone of the progressive movement.[57] It remains unclear how the Biden Administration expects families to make these investments or how it will offer any real help with ever increasing energy costs at a time when their official policy is to continue to depress production.

Here's the truth: this Administration has been more hostile to oil and gas exploration than any other in America's history, and it should be no surprise that American consumers have paid the price—black families most of all. Even on his campaign website, candidate Biden had promised that he would ban new oil and gas permitting on public lands and waters in pursuit of his climate agenda.[58] If enacted, the ban would affect nearly a quarter of all fossil fuels that run cars, heat homes, generate electricity, and operate factories.[59]

According to an early September 2022 *Wall Street Journal* scoop, the Biden Administration has the lowest rate of oil and gas leasing than any other administration, dating back to the end of World War II.[60]

America has felt the consequences of President Biden's energy policies prices across the board.

57    Galen Barbose et al. "Residential Solar-Adopter Income and Demographic Trends: 2021 Update," U.S. Department of Energy's Office of Energy Efficiency and Renewable Energy (EERE), April 2021, https://eta-publications.lbl.gov/sites/default/files/solar-adopter_income_trends_final.pdf. Only 9 percent of majority black neighborhoods have adopted solar.

58    Biden/Harris, "Climate Plan."

59    Matthew D. Merrill et al. *Federal Lands Greenhouse Gas Emissions and Sequestration in the United States—Estimates for 2005–14: U.S. Geological Survey Scientific Investigations Report 2018–5131,* U.S. Geological Survey (Reston, VA: Department of the Interior (DOI), 2018), https://pubs.usgs.gov/sir/2018/5131/sir20185131.pdf.

60    Anthony DeBarros and Timothy Puko, "Federal Oil Leases Slow to a Trickle Under Biden," *Wall Street Journal*, September 4, 2022, https://www.wsj.com/articles/federal-oil-leases-slow-to-a-trickle-under-biden-11662230816?st=o0nat01jktbnxbx&reflink=desktopwebshare_permalink.

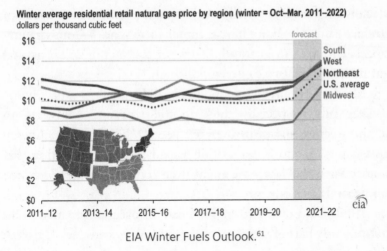

**Winter average residential retail natural gas price by region (winter = Oct–Mar, 2011–2022)**
dollars per thousand cubic feet

EIA Winter Fuels Outlook.[61]

Most natural gas is used for heating and electricity generation.[62] Roughly a third of American's energy use is from natural gas; however, production hasn't kept pace with demand.[63] Among carbon energy sources, natural gas is a cleaner-burning fuel. The International Energy Agency (IEA) says that these plants have between 45 percent and 55 percent lower greenhouse gas emissions than coal-fired plants.[64] Notwithstanding this reality, the Biden Administration has delayed issuing leasing agreements.[65] As a result, production has been lagging, and as demand has interna-

61    "Winter Fuels Outlook," U.S. Energy Information Administration, October 2021, https://www.eia.gov/outlooks/steo/special/winter/2021_Winter_Fuels.pdf.

62    "Natural gas explained," U.S. Energy Information Administration, May 24, 2022, https://www.eia.gov/energyexplained/natural-gas/use-of-natural-gas.php.

63    Gerson Freitas Jr., "Natural Gas Shortage Fears Buoy US Market as Winter Reserves Lag," *Bloomberg*, August 17, 2022, https://www.bloomberg.com/news/articles/2022-08-17/natural-gas-shortage-fears-buoy-us-market-as-winter-reserves-lag.

64    Benefits of Natural Gas," Shell, accessed October 22, 2022, https://www.shell.com/energy-and-innovation/shale-oil-and-gas/benefits-of-natural-gas.html.

65    Emma Newburger, "Biden Pauses New Oil and Gas Leases Amid Legal Battle Over Cost of Climate Change," *CNBC*, February 24 2022, https://www.cnbc.com/2022/02/24/biden-administration-pausing-new-oil-and-gas-leases-amid-legal-battle-.html.

tionally increased, especially in Europe, the U.S. market has been strained, since it didn't have a buffer to rely on.[66] Consequently prices have risen dramatically[67]—in the summer of 2022, natural gas prices spiked to a fourteen-year high.[68]

Heading into the winter of 2022–2023, analysts expect home heating bills—especially those in the East and Midwest—to see the highest prices in over ten years.[69] The National Energy Assistance Director's Association issued a report projecting that homeowners will likely see a year-over-year increase of 17 percent for natural gas alone.[70]

While a lot of the focus has been on natural gas prices, that jump is only part of the story of the pain Americans feel. Gasoline prices in March 2022 rose to the highest ever seen in the U.S.[71] The American Automobile Association reported that by the end of winter in 2023, the cost of regular gas nationwide will have

66    Leticia Gonzales, "Hefty Production Drop, Lagging Wind Generation Behind Natural Gas Futures' Huge Recovery," *Natural Gas Intelligence*, June 1, 2022, https://www.naturalgasintel.com/hefty-production-drop-lagging-wind-generation-behind-natural-gas-futures-huge-recovery/.

67    Matt Egan, "US Natural Gas Prices Spike to 14-Year High. Here's Why," *CNN Business*, August 17, 2022, https://www.cnn.com/2022/08/17/energy/natural-gas-inflation-heat-wave/index.html.

68    Myra P. Saefong, "Why Natural-Gas Prices Have Climbed to a 14-Year High," *MarketWatch*, August 19, 2022, https://www.marketwatch.com/story/why-natural-gas-prices-are-holding-near-14-year-highs-11660848405.

69    Stacey Sager, "Homeowners Could See Heating Bills Reach 10-Year High This Winter, Report Says," *Eyewitness News ABC7NY*, September 21, 2022, https://abc7ny.com/heating-bill-winter-prices-homeowners/12247650/.

70    Mark Wolfe, "Home Heating Costs Reach Highest Level in More than 10 Years. Families will Pay 17.2% More for Home Heating this Winter," National Energy Assistance Directors Association (NEADA), September 12, 2022, https://neada.org/wp-content/uploads/2022/09/winter2022-23PR.pdf.

71    "Gasoline and Diesel Fuel Update," U.S. Energy Information Administration (EIA), October 24, 2022, https://www.eia.gov/petroleum/gasdiesel/.

reached $4.25.[72] In January 2021, when President Biden took office, the price nationwide was $2.38 a gallon.[73]

In the middle of 2021, inflation jumped to 8.5 percent, the largest spike since 1981.[74] Later that year, the federal government announced that the economy contracted by 1.6 percent for the first quarter of 2022. By the time they reported the second quarter numbers, the economy had contracted again—this time by 0.6 percent.[75] As a rule of thumb, two consecutive declining quarters of GDP growth indicate that the economy is a recession.[76]

Although the Biden White House argues that the economy overall is sound, high inflation and successive quarters of GDP contractor are clear indicators of extremely poor stewardship of the economy by this Administration and signal that even more pain is in the offing.

But the White House is undaunted. In fact, then-press secretary Jen Psaki claimed, as an official position of the Biden Administration, that White House policies are not causing the spikes in energy prices.[77]

---

72   Jordan Mendoza, "Gas Prices Jump 8 Cents One Day After Breaking Record: Diesel Prices Now Highest Ever," *USA Today*, March 9, 2022, https://www.usatoday.com/story/money/2022/03/09/gas-prices-diesel-record-high/9433436002/.

73   Yamaguchi, "EIA Gasoline and Diesel."

74   Peter Butler, Marcos Cabello, and Courtney Johnston, "Inflation Hits 8.2%, Driving Down Real Earnings and Surpassing Expectations," CNET, October 13, 2022, https://www.cnet.com/personal-finance/inflation-hits-new-40-year-high-of-8-5-why-prices-keep-climbing/.

75   "Gross Domestic Product, Third Quarter 2022 (Advance Estimate)," Bureau of Economic Analysis, October 27, 2022, https://www.bea.gov/data/gdp/gross-domestic-product.

76   Maryalene LaPonsie and Emma Kerr, "Here's What 2 Quarters of Negative GDP Mean for You," US News & World Report, August 1, 2022, https://money.usnews.com/money/personal-finance/family-finance/articles/are-we-in-a-recession-heres-what-2-quarters-of-negative-gdp-mean-for-you.

77   Patricia Mcknight, "Is Biden Admin Blaming Putin for Gas Prices? Jen Psaki Sets Record Straight," *Newsweek*, March 7, 2022, https://www.newsweek.com/biden-admin-blaming-putin-gas-prices-jen-psaki-sets-record-straight-1685704.

## A NEW RUSSIA HOAX

As prices at the pump set record after record, President Biden attempted to distance himself from being the cause of discomfort for the American people. In March 2022, he explained, "It's simply not true that my administration or policies are holding back domestic energy production, that's simply not true."[78]

What's the real story?

For two years, as prices have spiked, the Biden White House has played the blame game, attempting to deflect from the real culprit: Biden's own policies. America has witnessed four of these attempts to deflect responsibility for energy price hikes.

### *Price Jump from March of 21 to March of 22*

Gasoline and Diesel Fuel Update

*Independent Statistics & Analysis*
## U.S. Energy Information Administration

|  | 03/07/22 | 03/14/22 | 03/21/22 | Change from week ago | year ago |
|---|---|---|---|---|---|
| U.S. | 4.102 | 4.315 | 4.239 | -0.076 | 1.374 |
| East Coast (PADD1) | 4.098 | 4.268 | 4.127 | -0.141 | 1.320 |
| New England (PADD1A) | 4.187 | 4.300 | 4.233 | -0.067 | 1.454 |
| Central Atlantic (PADD1B) | 4.250 | 4.351 | 4.215 | -0.136 | 1.314 |
| Lower Atlantic (PADD1C) | 3.982 | 4.208 | 4.044 | -0.164 | 1.291 |
| Midwest (PADD2) | 3.916 | 4.091 | 4.035 | -0.056 | 1.292 |
| Gulf Coast (PADD3) | 3.820 | 4.029 | 3.939 | -0.090 | 1.316 |
| Rocky Mountain (PADD4) | 3.825 | 4.137 | 4.110 | -0.027 | 1.172 |
| West Coast (PADD5) | 4.777 | 5.155 | 5.222 | 0.067 | 1.754 |
| West Coast less California | 4.325 | 4.671 | 4.675 | 0.004 | 1.532 |

Source: U.S. Energy Information Administration, Gasoline and Diesel Fuel Update

US EIA Energy Outlook March 8, 2022 Release Date: 4/4/2022.[79]

---

78    "FACT SHEET: United States Bans Imports of Russian Oil, Liquefied Natural Gas, and Coal," White House Briefing Room, March 8, 2022, https://www.whitehouse.gov/briefing-room/statements-releases/2022/03/08/fact-sheet-united-states-bans-imports-of-russian-oil-liquefied-natural-gas-and-coal/.

79    EIA, "Gasoline and Diesel."

## GAS STATION OWNERS HOAX

Biden's White House even claimed that the gas station operators were the cause of high gas prices at the pump,[80] but gas station owners aren't to blame.

> The first gasoline station opened in 1907. Owner operator John McLean purchased and operated this facility at Holgate Street and Western Avenue in Seattle, Washington. The first storage tank held only 30 gallons.[81]

Regardless of which company signs they display, most service stations are franchises. There are more than 145,000 gas stations in the US and less than 5 percent are owned by oil and gas companies.[82] The owners of these independent/franchise stations set their prices every day based on market conditions, including what it will cost to refill their storage tanks. Gas station operators don't make any money if people don't buy gas; they have every incentive to keep prices as low as possible.

Furthermore, there is evidence that dramatic price hikes hurt gas stations because—like movie theaters and ballparks—a service station proprietor makes his biggest profits from sodas, cigarettes, and other products that people buy when they're getting gas. Not surprisingly, when gas prices are high, the willingness of customers to buy soft drinks and snacks while getting gas goes down.

Prices for gasoline vary across the nation. Even in the same town, the price of gasoline isn't the same. Three factors: taxes, fuel

---

80   Joseph Clark, "White House Doubles Down on Calls for Gas Station Owners to Trim Profits," *Washington Times*, July 5, 2022, https://www.washingtontimes.com/news/2022/jul/5/white-house-doubles-down-calls-gas-station-owners-/.

81   David Wilma, "Gas Station May Have Been Invented in Seattle in 1907," History Link, January 1, 1999, https://www.historylink.org/File/2093.

82   "Service Station FAQs," American Petroleum Institute, accessed October 28, 2022, https://www.api.org/oil-and-natural-gas/consumer-information/consumer-resources/service-station-faqs.

blends, and margins ultimately determine the price at a particular station.[83]

## Taxes

The federal excise tax is 18.4 cents a gallon.[84] But there are additional fees and taxes that states assess at the pump. The average of these federal and state fees was roughly 50 cents a gallon as of January 2022.[85] Notably, in the state of California, the average tax is 86.6 cents a gallon.[86]

## Blends

There are three basic types or blends of unleaded gasoline: summer blends, winter blends and Reformulated Gasoline (RFG).[87] So-called summer blend-fuels are required by the EPA (Environmental Protection Agency) in certain parts of the country to reduce ozone levels between June 1 and Sept. 15.[88] According to GasBuddy (the service that tracks prices all across the US), summer blends have lower RVP (Reid Vapor Pressure)

---

83 "Why Gas Prices Vary Station to Station," Advancing Convenience & Fuel Retailing, February 23, 2022, https://www.convenience.org/Topics/Fuels/Why-Do-Prices-Vary-Around-the-Country-or-Around-th.

84 "Federal Gas Tax 2022: How Much Is It on A Gallon of Gas?," MARCA, March 14, 2022, https://www.marca.com/en/lifestyle/us-news/2022/03/14/622f1813268e3e976c8b4593.html.

85 "Gasoline explained: Factors affecting gasoline prices," U.S. Energy Information Administration (EIA), March 15, 2022, https://www.eia.gov/energyexplained/gasoline/factors-affecting-gasoline-prices.php.

86 Advancing Convenience, "Why Gas Prices Vary."

87 "Gasoline Blends: Answers to Frequently Asked Questions," Source North America Corporation, July/August 2018, https://www.sourcena.com/wp-content/uploads/2018/08/Source-Newsletter_Vol7-Issue4.pdf.

88 Stephanie Kelly and Jarrett Renshaw, "White House Weighs Waiving Smog Rules on Gasoline to Lower Pump Price—Sources," Reuters, May 24, 2022, https://www.reuters.com/world/us/white-house-weighing-waiving-smog-rules-gasoline-lower-pump-price-sources-2022-05-23/.

and consequently reduce the chance of gas evaporation in your car during the summer.[89] On the other hand, winter blends include fuel additives that contain oxygen, usually in the form of alcohol or ether, that when added to gasoline improve combustion efficiency during cold weather.[90] Finally, RFG may be required year-round in areas where more stringent ozone regulations are mandated. It contains fuel additives similar to summer blends that improve combustion efficiency year-round while lowering ozone levels.[91] It is currently used in sixteen states and the District of Columbia, and nearly 25 percent of gasoline sold in the U.S. is RFG.[92] California has created its own special blend (CaRFG) that includes a maximum of 10 percent ethanol.[93] More stringent for refineries than the requirements to make the federal government's RFG blend, the California RFG blend is mandated for exclusive sale in the state, and as a consequence most refineries don't produce it.[94]

While the shift from any one blend type to another can lead to cost volatility, CaRFG is perhaps the most cost-volatile. It is not only costlier to produce, but since the state also has the

89   "Summer Gas: What's Different in 2022?" GasBuddy, April 29, 2022, https://www.gasbuddy.com/go/summer-gas-2022.

90   "Gasoline Winter Oxygenates," U.S. Environmental Protection Agency, June 27, 2022, https://www.epa.gov/gasoline-standards/gasoline-winter-oxygenates.

91   "Reformulated Gasoline Program," Texas Commission on Environmental Quality, September 13, 2022, https://www.tceq.texas.gov/airquality/mobiles ource/vetech/rfgprog.html.

92   "Reformulated Gasoline," U.S. Environmental Protection Agency, October 14, 2022, https://www.epa.gov/gasoline-standards/reformulated-gasoline.

93   Gary Richards, "Roadshow: California's 'Special Blend' Gas Costs Us More, But It Saves Lives," *Mercury News*, August 11, 2016, https://www.mercurynews.com/2016/03/04/roadshow-californias-special-blend-gas-costs-us-more-but-it-saves-lives/.

94   "California Reformulated Gasoline—An Overview," California Environmental Protection Agency, Air Resources Board, accessed October 29, 2022, https://afdc.energy.gov/files/pdfs/3002.pdf.

highest state taxes in the country, Californians see prices at the pump significantly higher than residents in other states.[95] CaRFG must be kept separate from any other blends prior to reaching the service station, contributing to a higher cost.[96] This means that fewer refiners produce CaRFG, leading to a naturally tight band of production supply. Overproduction of CaRFG can't simply be offloaded to neighboring states, for example. On the other hand, any production disruptions—fires, unplanned maintenance, and so forth—can lead to significant price spikes.

## *Margins*

The profit margin on a sale of a gallon of gas varies widely. Factors include where the station is located, nearby competition from other business and fuel retailers, and the brand of fuel sold.[97] In general, the average profit margin on a gallon of gas nationwide is between three and seven cents.[98] In the U.S., gas sales at convenience stores typically account for 53 percent of revenue but only 42 percent of the profit. In other words, gas sales may generate customer traffic, but in-store sales drive the business.[99] Service stations need customers.

95  Dr. Wallace Walrod et al. "What Makes the California Fuel Environment Different in Terms of Policy, Cost, and Vulnerability?" Orange County Business Council, accessed October 29, 2022, https://cotce.ca.gov/documents/correspondence/public/documents/FUEL%20CALIFORNIA%20-%203%20-%20Fueling%20California%20FINAL%20RESEARCH%208.4.09.pdf.

96  "Gasoline Markets: Special Gasoline Blends Reduce Emissions and Improve Air Quality, but Complicate Supply and Contribute to Higher Prices," U.S. General Accounting Office, July 6, 2005, https://www.gao.gov/products/gao-05-421.

97  Advancing Convenience, "Why Gas Prices Vary."

98  Alex Kinnier, "I've Analyzed the Profit Margins of 30,000 Gas Stations. Here's the Proof Fuel Retailers Are Not to Blame for High Gas Prices," *Fortune*, August 9, 2022, https://fortune.com/2022/08/09/energy-profit-margins-gas-stations-proof-fuel-retailers-high-gas-prices-alex-kinnier/.

99  Advancing Convenience, "Why Gas Prices Vary."

Taxes, blends, and margins all impact the ability of gas stations to operate. The price of gas at the station isn't part of some cabal of gas station operators exploiting America. The price hikes are a direct consequence of White House policy. The Biden White House hasn't taken any steps to make any of these aspects more manageable for store operators.

## THE BIG OIL CON

Next, the White House claimed that it is the oil companies who are the culprits. For more than a year, the Biden Administration has claimed the oil and gas industry was withholding production to boost prices. In fact, late in 2021, the President went so far as to get the Federal Trade Commission to investigate oil and gas companies for supposedly manipulating the price at the pump.[100]

If Big Oil had conspired to collectively halt new drilling on federal lands, or refused to finish the Keystone pipeline, or end updates of other energy production infrastructure projects, the White House might have a point. But these schemes were White House policy and they have predictably resulted in boosted prices at the pump.[101]

The disruptions haven't stopped there. This Administration has regularly used its bully pulpit to condemn the oil and gas industry, sought to impose a stiffer Renewable Fuel Standard (a federal program that requires transportation fuel sold in the United States to contain a minimum volume of renewable fuels),[102] and enforced

---

100  Lorraine Woellert, "Biden Asks FTC to Investigate Oil and Gas Companies," *Politico*, November 17, 2021, https://www.politico.com/news/2021/11/17/biden-ftc-investigate-oil-gas-companies-522804.

101  Richard McKenzie, "Restarting the Keystone Pipeline TODAY Will Lower Gas Prices TODAY," Liberty Fund Network, March 22 2022, https://www.econlib.org/restarting-the-keystone-pipeline-today-will-lower-gas-prices-today/.

102  "Renewable Fuel Standard," Alternative Fuels Data Center, U.S. Department of Energy, accessed October 25, 2022, https://afdc.energy.gov/laws/RFS.

new restrictive methane emission standards.[103] The President has frequently castigated oil companies for "not making full use of existing drilling permits"[104] and claimed that oil companies were trying "to exercise excessive price increases or padding profits."[105]

What utter nonsense.

## CAPITAL IS A COWARD

The marketplace responds to incentives, and the energy sector is a marketplace just like automobile manufacturing or the high-tech industry. More investors won't put their resources into an industry that is made to feel unwelcome. As any economist can explain, capital is a coward. When you browbeat and threaten to shut down the energy sector, you lower infrastructure investment as well as reduce new research and development. This response would occur in any other sector treated this way.

And the energy sector has been besieged. Biden's anti-energy agenda has been especially painful. In 2021, more than 43 energy companies filed for bankruptcy (more than the 2005–2019 annual average of energy bankruptcy filings).[106] In 2020, in the midst of

103    Jeff Brady, "Biden Joins Global Push to Cut Climate-Warming Methane Emissions," NPR, November 2, 2021, https://www.npr.org/2021/11/02/ 1051302469/biden-proposes-new-rules-to-cut-climate-warming-methane-emissions.

104    Steven Nelson, "Biden Says He 'Can't Do Much' About Rising Gas Prices, Blames Russia," *New York Post*, March 8, 2022, https://nypost.com/2022/03/08/ biden-says-he-cant-do-much-about-gas-prices-blames-russia/.

105    President Joseph Biden, "Remarks Announcing U.S. Ban on Imports of Russian Oil, Liquefied Natural Gas, and Coal" (White House, Washington, DC, March 8, 2022), https://www.whitehouse.gov/briefing-room/ speeches-remarks/2022/03/08/remarks-by-president-biden-announcing-u-s-ban-on-imports-of-russian-oil-liquefied-natural-gas-and-coal/.

106    Allie Schwartz et al. "Trends in Large Corporate Bankruptcy and Financial Distress (Midyear 2021 Update): Energy Sector Spotlight," *National Law Review* 11, No. 237 (August 25, 2021), https://www.natlawreview.com/article/trends-large-corporate-bankruptcy-and-financial-distress-midyear-2021-update-venues.

the pandemic, a record 155 energy companies filed for bankruptcy.[107] The only time bankruptcy filings by energy companies were higher than 2020 was during the Great Recession of 2009.[108]

If you invested in these companies, you may have lost most or all of your stake. If you worked at any of these companies, you may have lost your job. In fact, the industry lost some 840,000 jobs in 2020.[109]

The oil and gas sector is often the political whipping boy for progressives. But the market for this sector is like the rest of the economy—it benefits from overall growth. But the oil and gas sector has had its ups and downs like the rest of the economy. In 2020, Exxon Mobil reported its first loss in its history, writing off a staggering $22 billion. The five largest U.S. oil refiners—Marathon Petroleum, Valero Energy, Exxon Mobil, Phillips 66, and Chevron—lost a combined $43 billion in 2020. [110] The primary reason then was that COVID-19 shutdowns worldwide yielded a dramatic plunge in oil prices and energy demand.

Would it be surprising that this sector isn't expanding and building out infrastructure after the harrowing effects of the pandemic, and even more so now when the companies can see the writing on the wall?

During the campaign, Biden promised that he would not only "transition away from oil" but also that he would end all federal

---

107    Allie Schwartz et al. "Trends in Large Corporate Bankruptcy and Financial Distress Midyear 2021 Update," Cornerstone Research, 2021, https://www.corner stone.com/wp-content/uploads/2021/12/Trends-in-Large-Corporate-Bankruptcy-and-Financial-Distress-Midyear-2021-Update.pdf.

108    Schwartz et al. "Corporate Bankruptcy."

109    *United States Energy & Employment Report 2021*, U.S. Department of Energy (Washington: 2021), https://www.energy.gov/sites/default/files/2021-07/USEER%202021%20Executive%20Summary.pdf.

110    Rick Newman, "Biden and the oil industry are talking past each other," *Yahoo Finance*, June 15, 2022, https://finance.yahoo.com/news/biden-and-the-oil-industry-are-talking-past-each-other-213916164.html.

subsidies to the industry. [111] The President has cancelled lease sales in Alaska, including reducing access to the National Petroleum Reserve, probably the most prolific basin in the world for oil and gas.[112] And in the spring of 2022, the White House's Council on Environmental Quality issued new rules sharply limiting infrastructure, permitting that reduced oil and gas exploration across the board.[113] Early in the summer, the President sent letters to the largest energy companies complaining about the profits they reported in the first quarters of 2022, without a hint of acknowledgement of the painful losses that they had recently experienced. [114]

What Biden didn't say in the letter was that he would promise to issue emergency regulations that would make it easier to refine and distribute oil and gas. He also didn't acknowledge that his permitting, leasing, and related regulatory policies act as disincentives to upgrade equipment, which leads to more frequent shutdowns for refineries. He could put these new regulations on a pause to get prices to drop.

111    Amber Phillips, "How Politically Damaging Were Biden's Comments About Closing Down the Oil Industry?" *Washington Post*, October 23, 2020, https://www.washingtonpost.com/politics/2020/10/23/how-politically-damaging-were-bidens-comments-about-closing-down-oil-industry/.

112    Senator Dan Sullivan, "Biden Admin. Shutting Down American Energy with One Exception—Interior Secretary's Home State" (U.S. Senate, Washington, DC, May 20, 2022), https://www.sullivan.senate.gov/newsroom/press-releases/sullivan-biden-admin-shutting-down-american-energy-with-one-exception-interior-secretarys-home-state.

113    "National Environmental Policy Act Implementing Regulations Revisions," Rule 87 FR 23453 by Council on Environmental Quality, April 20, 2022, https://www.federalregister.gov/documents/2022/04/20/2022-08288/national-environmental-policy-act-implementing-regulations-revisions.

114    President Biden to Darren Woods (CEO of Exxon Mobil Corporation), June 14, 2022, https://s3.documentcloud.org/documents/22060433/exxon-mobil_letter.pdf.

## VLADIMIR PUTIN'S PRICE HIKE CANARD

After more than a year of escalating prices, President Biden had the temerity to tell America that the actual reason for the price jumps was Vladimir Putin's invasion of Ukraine on February 24, 2022. The price had been increasing from the day he took the oath of office. How did the market know in 2021 that Putin would invade Ukraine in 2022?

"Seventy percent of the increase in prices in March came from Putin's price hike," President Biden explained in the spring of 2022 at North Carolina Agricultural and Technical State University.[115] Setting aside the abysmal foreign policy debacle that led to Russia's invasion of Ukraine, most Americans knew that prices had jumped from the lows of the Trump Administration well before the war started. In fact, in January of 2022, the price for a gallon of gas had already topped $3.30 some two months before Russia's 2022 Ukraine invasion and had been heading steadily upward.[116]

As media coverage of these broad increases in consumer prices including gasoline occurred throughout 2021, the White House downplayed them. Back in the fall of 2021, the White House Chief of Staff had retweeted a claim that inflation was a "high-class problem."[117] Even at that point, Americans were feeling the pain as the Consumer Price Index (CPI) hit a thirteen-year high.[118]

---

115  Glenn Kessler, "Biden's Claim That 70% of Inflation Jump is Due to 'Putin's Price Hike'," *Washington Post*, April 15, 2022, https://www.washingtonpost.com/politics/2022/04/15/bidens-claim-70-inflation-jump-was-due-putins-price-hike/.

116  "High Crude Prices Keep National Average Elevated Despite Drop in Gas Demand," American Automobile Association (AAA), January 13,2022, https://gasprices.aaa.com/high-crude-prices-keep-national-average-elevated-despite-drop-in-gas-demand/.

117  Callie Patteson, "WH Chief of Staff Slammed Over Post Calling Supply Chain Crisis 'High Class Problems'," *New York Post*, October 14, 2021, https://nypost.com/2021/10/14/ronald-klain-retweets-post-calling-supply-chain-crisis-high-class-issue/.

118  Press Release, "Consumer Price Index News," Bureau of Labor Statistics, October 13, 2021, https://www.bls.gov/news.release/archives/cpi_10132021.htm.

In March 2022, the CPI hit a forty-year high of 8.5 percent. Breathlessly, that very day, White House press secretary Jen Psaki ran to the White House press room to explain that the inflationary spiral was "Putin's price hike." It was a marvelous sight to behold, especially after spending nearly a year minimizing inflation fears by explaining that the inflation spike was only transitory.

What are the facts? During the Trump Administration, the U.S. was a net oil and gas exporter,[119] and Russian imports aren't even a significant player in the U.S. market. Now, even with the castigation of the U.S. energy sector, Russian energy imports are only 3 to 8 percent of all U.S. energy supply through the summer of 2022.[120]

Noise aside, the price hikes are President Biden's fault because the White House has strangled domestic production as part of an ambitious climate agenda. Fortunately, America doesn't buy his narrative. When Quinnipiac asked in the spring of 2022, "What is more responsible when topping off the tank hurts? A raging war from Moscow—or an economic policy constructed in D.C.?" not surprisingly, Americans say that Washington policies are responsible by nearly 20 points.[121]

119  "U.S. Energy Facts Explained: Imports and Exports," U.S. Energy Information Administration (EIA), June 10, 2022, https://www.eia.gov/energyexplained/us-energy-facts/imports-and-exports.php.

120  Monica Hersher and Joe Murphy, "Data: How Much of U.S. Oil Comes From Russia?" *NBC News*, March 9, 2022, https://www.nbcnews.com/news/us-news/data-how-much-american-oil-comes-russia-n1291369.

121  Maxwell Newman, "One-Third of Americans Cut Back on Groceries to Buy Gas," *Newsmax Finance*, April 8, 2022, https://www.newsmax.com/finance/streettalk/groceries-inflation-gas-president-biden/2022/04/08/id/1064935/.

## TESLA SKEPTICS SCHEME

> *Loosening environmental regulations or pulling back clean energy investment…will not lower energy prices for families. But transforming our economy to run on electric vehicles powered by clean energy…that will help.*

— President Joe Biden, March 8, 2022[122]

President Biden, Vice President Kamala Harris, and Secretary of Transportation Pete Buttigieg have all tried to get Americans to believe that their failure to buy expensive electric vehicles (EVs) is causing the high prices at the gas pump, and Americans who don't like or trust EVs are all but treated as flat-earthers who need to get with the program.[123]

But, like any other products in the marketplace, Americans are free to choose or to reject them, and EVs come with significant limitations that make them unattractive to most Americans. Even with federal and state rebates, they cost substantially more than conventional vehicles. EV owners typically make significantly more than the nation's median income. Only 3 percent of them are owned or leased by blacks.[124] They also have limited range and require extended recharging times. In other words, Americas need to be richer than average to own EVS, and they need to live and work in areas where the range or charging times

---

122   Shelby Talcott, "Biden Exploits Gas Pains to Push Clean Energy Agenda," *Daily Caller*, April 7, 2022, https://dailycaller.com/2022/04/07/joe-biden-gas-pain-push-clean-energy-agenda/.

123   Alex Gangitano, "White House: Biden is Invested in Electric Vehicles Because That's The Future of The Auto Industry," *The Hill*, May 18, 2021, https://thehill.com/homenews/administration/554096-white-house-biden-is-invested-in-electric-vehicles-because-thats-the/.

124   Electric Vehicle Council, *Electric Vehicle Consumer Behavior* (Alexandria, VA: Fuels Institute, June 2021), https://www.fuelsinstitute.org/Research/Reports/EV-Consumer-Behavior/EV-Consumer-Behavior-Report.pdf.

don't affect their daily lives. Additionally, what will Americans do in the midst of a major power outage, say during a hurricane or tornado? Which risks might they face if they can't leave these areas or if they find themselves stranded on the road while attempting to escape a major weather event?

By the way, the Biden climate policies that raise gas pump prices will also eventually "trickle" down to the electric grid, meaning that even the nominal price of charging cars will go up, thus eliminating what is supposed to be one of their huge advantages, and in some places, there already isn't even much of a cost savings for charging over fueling. CNBC reported in September of 2022 that in London, the price for EV charging at public stations has increased 42 percent since May of this year.[125] The report further indicated that that there was a negligible difference between the cost of driving a fuel-efficient, gas-powered vehicle on a per mile basis and a typical electrical vehicle using public chargers: twenty-one cents a mile versus twenty-two cents a mile.[126] The EV costs more, restricts your range, and it doesn't even make a significant dent in your energy cost of operation.

In order to love EV's, Americans need to be progressives: white, college-educated, and economically comfortable. Whatever the case may be, the lack of more EV usage isn't the reason gasoline prices are so high.

125   Anmar Frangoul, "EV Charge Points in Britain Are Now Nearly as Expensive as Gasoline, Research Shows," *CNBC*, September 27, 2022, https://www.cnbc.com/2022/09/27/ev-drivers-in-britain-see-jump-in-public-charging-cost-.html.

126   Frangoul, "EV Charge Points in Britain Are Now Nearly as Expensive as Gasoline, Research Shows."

## LOOK IN THE MIRROR, PRESIDENT BIDEN

No, it isn't the gas station operators, Big Oil, Vladimir Putin, or the purchase rate for electric cars that has caused this problem. It's the White House and its policies that are to blame. President Biden's policies are deeply destructive, and American families have been forced to make tough and painful choices as a consequence. In 2022, a staggering one-third (35 percent) of Americans say they spent less on groceries so they can pay for gas.[127]

This administration is completely disconnected from the priorities of the American public. In 2018, when the University of Chicago Energy Center asked Americans what they'd personally be willing to pay to fight climate change, the numbers were unsettling. Only 23 percent said they would be willing to spend $1.35 a day extra, and a staggering 57 percent said that they would only be willing to spend three cents.[128]

The evidence shows that these draconian regulations aren't even needed to accomplish the stated climate agenda objectives. According to the Environmental Protection Agency, America became a net oil and gas exporter as well as a top oil and gas producer, all while decreasing emissions, using innovation and free markets under the Trump Administration.

127  "Inflation Tops Russia-Ukraine War as Most Urgent Issue in U.S., Quinnipiac University National Poll Finds; 52% Disapprove of GOP Senators' Handling of Ketanji Brown Jackson Hearings," Quinnipiac University Poll, March 30, 2022, https://poll.qu.edu/poll-release?releaseid=3841.

128  "Is the Public Willing to Pay to Help Fix Climate Change?" AP-NORC Center, November 2018, https://apnorc.org/projects/is-the-public-willing-to-pay-to-help-fix-climate-change/.

**Annual Greenhouse Gas Emission Reductions from Shale Innovation and Major Environmental Policies**

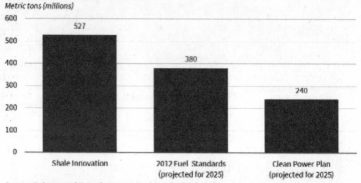

Metric tons (millions)

Sources: Environmental Protection Agency; Stock (2017); CEA calculations.
Note: The Fuel Standards refer to the 2012 Light-Duty Vehicle Greenhouse Gas Emissions and Corporate Average Fuel Economy Standards, which applied to the 2017-2025 years.

## WHO YA GONNA BELIEVE, ME OR YOUR LYING EYES?

Assuming that lowering emissions can only occur by mandates and lower economic growth is an article of faith for progressives. In 2021, Democratic Senator Elizabeth Warren from Massachusetts weighed in on energy policy, apparently under the assumption that her knowledge of the oil and gas industry was greater than that of the industry itself.

In February 2021, she demanded that the White House place new limits on the export of Liquefied Natural Gas (LNG).[129] LNG is one of the leading ways of protecting the climate. The energy industry should be encouraged to invest and maximize profits in this sector instead of having limits imposed on them.

---

129 "Warren, Colleagues Urge Biden Administration to Consider Limiting Lique-fied Natural Gas Exports As Energy Prices Rise for Americans Households," Sen. Elizabeth Warren website, February 4, 2022, https://www.warren.senate.gov/newsroom/press-releases/warren-colleagues-urge-biden-administration-to-consider-limiting-liquefied-natural-gas-exports-as-energy-prices-rise-for-americans-households.

Encouraging the wide availability of LNG to any wholesaler on the planet would not only help to promote the stated goals of the environmental movement, but it would also lower the market price for everyone. But apparently the short-term political hit against the energy industry was just too hard to resist.

However, this isn't just a push from Washington; the anti-domestic-energy advocates use every tool they have to make it harder to tap into the amazing U.S. resource of oil and gas. They use federal agency regulation, federal and state courts, and even state regulations to stymie exploration.

The Penn East and Atlantic Coast pipelines have been thwarted even though they would have had lowered energy prices for consumers significantly. The Penn East pipeline was a proposed 116-mile natural gas pipeline connecting Pennsylvania to New Jersey. But due to a lack of water and wetland permits from New Jersey, the project ground to a halt in 2021.[130] Similarly, the Atlantic Coast pipeline, a project by Duke Energy and Dominion, was a 600-mile pipeline that would have transported natural gas from West Virginia through Virginia to North Carolina. After endless litigation by opponents, it was canceled.[131]

Thousands of pages of permit requests meant there were ample opportunities for litigation and pushback. In fact, in both cases, the companies had to win before the U.S. Supreme Court to overcome the efforts of activists in order to proceed, and even that wasn't enough.

---

130   Carlos Anchondo and Niina H. Farah, "What the PennEast cancellation signals for FERC, pipelines," *E&E News*, September 28, 2021, https://www.eenews.net/articles/what-the-penneast-cancellation-signals-for-ferc-pipelines/.

131   Adam Barth et al. "The End of The Atlantic Coast Pipeline: What Does It Mean for the North American Natural Gas Industry?," *Petroleum Blog*, McKinsey & Company, September 2, 2020, https://www.mckinsey.com/industries/oil-and-gas/our-insights/petroleum-blog/the-end-of-the-atlantic-coast-pipeline-what-does-it-mean-for-the-north-american-natural-gas-industry.

The Mountain Valley pipeline, which would deliver gas from Appalachia to the Southeast, is still in the midst of litigation and may have a similar fate, even though by the fall of 2022 it was more than 94 percent complete.[132] Absent explicit congressional authority, federal courts have refused to allow it to go forward, citing environmental risks.[133]

Late in the summer of 2022, Senator Joe Manchin was able to include an agreement to fast-track environmental permitting rules in exchange for supporting the so-called Inflation Reduction Act.[134] Senator Manchin is a major backer of the Mountain Valley pipeline. Whether the pipeline gets a new life or not remains an open question.

Manchin was assured that the upcoming September 2022 Continuing Resolution (CR) would include his preferred language, to allow expedited permitting for energy projects, if he voted for the Inflation Reduction Act. However, the initial effort to include Manchin's permitting provision failed on the floor of the Senate on September 26th.[135] Adding the provision to the CR required sixty votes, and since many of his fellow Democrats like Sanders opposed the provision, and few Senate Republicans would cross over to help him, he wasn't able to get the provision included.

132    Mountain Valley Pipeline, accessed December 12, 2022, https://www.mountain valleypipeline.info/.

133    Arianna Skibell, "Pipeline fight heads to Washington," *Politico*, September 7, 2022, https://www.politico.com/newsletters/power-switch/2022/09/07/pipeline-fight-heads-to-washington-00055168.

134    Jeremy Dillon and Nick Sobczyk, "What to Expect on Permitting Reform as Congress Returns," *E&E News*, September 06, 2022, https://www.eenews.net/articles/what-to-expect-on-permitting-reform-as-congress-returns/.

135    Bryan Metzger, "Democrats Strip Manchin's Permitting Reform Bill From Must-Pass Government Funding Measure After Both Republicans and Progressives Pledged to Vote Against It," *Business Insider*, September 27, 2022, https://www.businessinsider.com/bernie-sanders-republicans-defeat-joe-manchin-permitting-reform-2022-9.

# FOOT-SOLDIERS OF THE LEFT

It is said that the progressive movement is the lifeblood of the Democrats. Where once there were Blue Dog Democrats, conservative Democrats, and moderates like Bill Clinton that dominated the party priorities, today that is no longer true. Progressives dominate the party and set its course. They believe in government action—federal over state—and public sector action over private sector action. They prefer coercion over volitional behavior. The climate issue is the perfect agenda to exploit their preferences. Progressives in the White House and across America have teamed up to stop domestic energy exploration and development.

Progressives say that the threat from climate change is real and that dramatic change must occur to avoid the consequences. These activists are not as concerned about the "great outdoors" but instead have more of an urban bias, focusing on issues like energy use, food production, and labor movements. Climate activist groups like the Natural Defense Council, the Sierra Club, and the Union of Concerned Scientists push the administration to adopt policies that have never gotten buy-ins from the American people. In the process, they've pushed Biden well out of the mainstream. He may choose to call himself a centrist, but his willingness to embrace the agenda of progressives, especially on the environment, belies this claim.

The Natural Resources Defense Council (NRDC) took the lead in litigation against the KeyStone Pipeline.[136] The Sierra Club has heavily pushed electric vehicles and the need for a multi-billion nationwide charging infrastructure, as well as a ban on oil drilling on public lands.[137] The Union of Concerned Scientists has suc-

---

136 "The Keystone XL Pipeline," Natural Resources Defense Council (NRDC), November 1, 2021, https://www.nrdc.org/court-battles/keystone-xl-pipeline.

137 "MEMO: President Biden Must Take Swift, Bold Action on Climate and Clean Energy," Sierra Club, July 19, 2022, https://www.sierraclub.org/press-releases/ 2022/07/memo-president-biden-must-take-swift-bold-action-climate-and- clean-energy.

cessfully pushed for wind and solar energy subsidies as part of its effort to achieve a 100 percent carbon free energy grid by 2035.[138]

Since 2004, Americans have reported to Gallup that the seriousness of global warming is exaggerated.[139] In fact, in 2010 the ratio of Americans saying it's exaggerated, as opposed to accurately presented, was two to one. After slightly dropping during the Obama presidency, it has almost returned to the two to one ratio.[140] And thanks to Biden's mismanagement of the economy, a spring 2022 CBS poll found that the support for action on the climate had dropped across all demographic groups.[141] A May 2022 Gallup survey found that Americans listed climate change in seventh place among seven environmental concerns, including water pollution, air pollution, and shrinking rain forests.[142] In a survey of priorities released by the Yale Program on Climate Change in 2020, blacks placed Global Warming sixteenth out of twenty-nine priorities.[143] Disaster relief, terrorism, and tax reform ranked higher. Notably, Americans respond at the highest rate in the world that climate fears are overblown.[144]

---

138  "Scientists & Experts Want Climate Action—An Open Letter to the White House," Union of Concerned Scientists USA, April 14, 2021, https://www.ucs usa.org/scientists-experts-want-climate-action-white-house.

139  "Environment," Gallup, accessed December 12, 2022, https://news.gallup.com/ poll/1615/environment.aspx.

140  Gallup, "Environment."

141  Jennifer De Pinto, "Fewer Americans See Climate Change as a Priority Than They Did a Year Ago," CBS News, April 22, 2022, https://www.cbsnews.com/ news/fewer-americans-see-climate-change-as-priority-opinion-poll-2022-04-22/.

142  Anthony Watts, "Americans Still Rank 'Climate Change' Dead Last Among Environmental Concerns, Reports Gallup," Watts Up With That? (blog), May 10, 2022, https://wattsupwiththat.com/2022/05/10/americans-still-rank-climate-change-dead-last-among-environmental-concerns-reports-gallup/.

143  Matthew Ballew et al. "Which Racial/Ethnic Groups Care Most About Climate Change?" Yale Program on Climate Change Communication, April 16, 2020, https://climatecommunication.yale.edu/publications/race-and-climate-change/.

144  Shalene Gupta, "In a Summer of Hellscape Weather, Climate Change is Top of Mind for People Around the World," Fast Company, August 25, 2022, https://www.fastcompany.com/90781968/in-a-summer-of-hellscape-weather-climate-change-is-top-of-mind-for-people-around-the-world.

## THE FISH ROTS FROM THE HEAD FIRST

John Muir, the founder of the Sierra Club, came to America from his native Scotland to explore its beauty, and in the process, he picked up some fairly negative views about blacks and native Americans.[145] He often referred to blacks as Lazy "Sambos" and savages[146] and was a close friend of Henry Fairfield Osborn, the founder of the American Eugenics Society.[147]

While the Sierra Club has attempted to make amends for its founder's provincial thinking, the broader picture of the movement is worth discussing. Today, the environmental movement is not only overwhelmingly white but is made up of elite whites.[148] Since the late nineteenth century, working-class whites have been relegated to servant-like roles in the burgeoning environmental movement.[149] The leadership after Muir also had fairly narrow views about the usefulness of blacks to the movement, most of them having either owned slaves or used former slaves as cooks,

---

145   "Sierra Club Calls Out Founder John Muir for Racist Views," *PBS News Hour*, July 22, 2020, https://www.pbs.org/newshour/nation/sierra-club-calls-out-founder-john-muir-for-racist-views.

146   Darryl Fears and Steven Mufson, "Liberal, Progressive—And Racist? The Sierra Club Faces Its White-Supremacist History," *Washington Post*, July 22, 2020, https://www.washingtonpost.com/climate-environment/2020/07/22/liberal-progressive-racist-sierra-club-faces-its-white-supremacist-history/.

147   "Redwoods and Hitler: The Link Between Nature Conservation and the Eugenics Movement," *From the Stacks* (blog), New York Historical Society, September 25, 2013, https://www.nyhistory.org/blogs/redwoods-and-hitler-the-link-between-nature-conservation-and-the-eugenics-movement.

148   "Environmentalist Demographics and Statistics In the US," Zippia, accessed October 29, 2022, https://www.zippia.com/environmentalist-jobs/demographics/ . 51% of environmentalists have a bachelor degree while only 32% of the general population has a bachelor's degree.

149   Dorceta E. Taylor, "Race, Diversity, and Transparency in Environmental Organizations," *American Sociological Association* 49, no. 3 (Summer 2021), https://www.asanet.org/race-diversity-and-transparency-environmental-organizations.

launderers, porters, and as basic labor resources.[150] Blacks were barred from being members of groups like the Sierra Club even into the twentieth century;[151] until the 1950s, the Sierra Club actively voted to bar blacks from local clubs.[152] In fact, the movement didn't begin to welcome blacks until the civil rights era.[153]

Not surprisingly, black Americans haven't flocked to this movement. In 1990, less than 2 percent of the environmental movement was not white. When its leaders were called out about this, they claimed that blacks weren't interested in the environment.[154] Meanwhile, the leadership and supervisors of the green movement are overwhelmingly high income and white.

A 2014 report on the racial make-up of the Sierra Club revealed that less than 5 percent of the 3.2 million rank and file members were black.[155] Today the non-white membership of the green movement is only 16 percent, even as the non-white population of the U.S. exceeds 38 percent.[156]

Working-class people, including most blacks, may not feel welcome in the environmental movement, but they can't afford

---

150 Dorceta E. Taylor, *The Rise of the American Conservation Movement* (Durham: Duke University Press, 2016), https://www.dukeupress.edu/the-rise-of-the-american-conservation-movement.

151 Michael P. Cohen, "History: Origins and Early Outings," in *The History of the Sierra Club: 1892-1970* (Sierra Club Books, 1988), https://vault.sierraclub.org/history/origins/.

152 Stephen R. Fox, *American Conservation Movement: John Muir and His Legacy* (New York: Little Brown & Co, 1981).

153 Taylor, "Race, Diversity, and Transparency."

154 "Lifestyle; Earth Issues Lure a New Breed of Young Worker," *New York Times*, July 29, 1990, https://www.nytimes.com/1990/07/29/style/lifestyle-earth-issues-lure-a-new-breed-of-young-worker.html.

155 Dorceta Taylor, *The State of Diversity in Environmental Organizations: Mainstream NGOs, Foundations, Government Agencies*," GREEN 2.0 (Ann Arbor, Michigan: University of Michigan, School of Natural Resources & Environment, July 2014), doi:10.13140/RG.2.2.34512.40962. By 2020, that number increased to nearly 10 percent.

156 Zippia, "Environmentalist Demographics."

to ignore it because it has an outsized influence over the lives of all Americans, including theirs. In fact, the green program is especially costly to groups lower on the income scale. Many activists blame free enterprise for the environmental concerns they identify with, but free enterprise could be the actual solution to their problems. Sadly, they aim to empower themselves to make decisions for their fellow citizens, rather than trusting Americans armed with information to act with care.

By rejecting free markets, they also open themselves to the charge of being socialists or worse.

Here's the truth: open competitive markets lead to innovation and increases in the standard of living. Progressives, like the Puritans of yore, would rather use mandates, a decline in the standard of living, and government subsidies to achieve their goals.

## PROGRESSIVES BELIEVE YOU CAN DO ANYTHING YOU WANT AS LONG AS IT'S MANDATORY

Over the last few decades, progressives have made environmentalism one of their chief concerns. This despite the reality that America's water[157], air,[158] and lead levels[159] are in better shape than any time since the creation of the Environmental Protection Agency.

The primacy of environmentalism on the Left has pushed the issue to the political forefront, significantly moving it ahead of issues they've traditionally been associated with, such as assisting

157   "Water Quality and Protection," U.S. Government Accountability Office, accessed October 29, 2022, https://www.gao.gov/water-quality-and-protection.

158   *Our Nation's Air: Trends Through 2021* (Washington: U.S. Environmental Protection Agency (EPA), 2021), https://gispub.epa.gov/air/trendsreport/2022/#air_trends.

159   "Lead Trends," U.S. Environmental Protection Agency (EPA), August 1, 2022, https://www.epa.gov/air-trends/lead-trends.

the working class and promoting integration, women's rights, and education. In fact, only the LGBT agenda remains as prominent for today's Left as the green agenda. As a consequence, blacks—a core constituency for Biden and the Democrats—increasingly find their concerns are pushed to the back of the political bus.

A balanced and well-rounded environmental movement would keep the concerns of the working class in mind when assessing costs. Rather than pursue policies that raise the cost of housing and energy beyond their reach, incorporating the concerns of the dispossessed would likely make their program more popular with the public, especially with blacks.

Today's green activists include animal rights supporters, climate alarmists, and environmentalists who seek a more expansive level of federal government authority to achieve their ends. In all three groups, there is a socialist element. Though Americans of all races and background support a balanced approach to environmentalism—one that doesn't kill jobs or destroy the energy sector—the "greenies" advocate radical solutions that will ultimately cripple America's economy and her people along the way.

## BLACKS HARDEST HIT

While rising energy costs are a real hardship for many Americans, and all of America is suffering from President Biden's restrictive energy policies, black Americans are harmed the most. UC Berkeley's Energy Institute at Haas released a white paper in the summer of 2020 finding that black households pay "significantly" more of their income for energy than whites,[160] the gap persisting even when controlling for income, household size, and

---

160   Eva Lyubich, *The Race Gap in Residential Energy Expenditures*, Energy Institute (Berkeley, CA: Haas School of Business at the University of California, June 2020), https://haas.berkeley.edu/wp-content/uploads/WP306.pdf.

homeowner status—black homeowners pay $408 more annually for energy.[161] (Several earlier studies had also reached this conclusion.[162]) The study concludes that this energy affordability gap exacerbates wealth and housing disparities.[163]

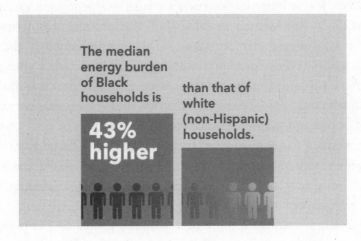

The American Council for an Energy-Efficient Economy (ACEEE).[164]

A few weeks later, the American Council for an Energy-Efficient Economy (ACEEE) issued a report with a similar finding. According to its September 2020 report *How High Are Household*

161    Rachel Frazin, "Black Households Pay More for Energy than White Households: Analysis," *The Hill*, June 23, 2020, https://thehill.com/policy/energy-environment/504138-black-households-pay-more-for-energy-than-white-households-analysis/.

162    American Council for an Energy-Efficient Economy (ACEEE), "'Energy Burden' on Low-Income, African American, & Latino Households up to Three Times as High as Other Homes…" April 20, 2016, https://www.aceee.org/press/2016/04/report-energy-burden-low-income; Jeniffer Solis, "Study Examines How People of Color Get Stuck with Higher Energy Bills," *Nevada Current*, November 26, 2019, https://www.nevadacurrent.com/blog/study-examines-how-people-of-color-get-stuck-with-higher-energy-bills/.

163    Frazin, "Black Households Pay More."

164    Drehobl, *"Face High Energy Burdens."*

*Energy Burdens?*,[165] the median energy burden for black households is 43 percent higher than for non-Hispanic white households (4.2 percent versus 2.9 percent, respectively).[166]

Tragically, black, Hispanic, and Native American households all face dramatically higher energy burdens—spending a greater portion of their income on energy bills than the rest of America.

Blacks should pay attention when environmentalists chant that natural gas exploration must be ended, because when climate activists succeed, blacks pay more. After record progress was made in lowering the cost of energy in America, the progressive's renewed war on oil and gas has resulted in record numbers of Americans experiencing "energy poverty" meaning "the lack of access to sustainable modern energy services and products," which Habitat for Humanity recasts as "a lack of adequate, affordable, reliable, quality, safe and environmentally sound energy services...."[167]

By some estimates, more than a billion people on the planet suffer from "energy poverty."[168] Thanks to President Biden's domestic policies, it isn't just a problem for third world countries. The U.S. has programs in place to ameliorate these concerns, such as the Low Income Housing Energy Assistance Program (LIHEAP). Created in 1981, LIHEAP is one of many programs that offers grants to needy families to offset energy costs.[169] Due to the Biden policies, energy assistance is needed more than ever.[170]

---

165  Ayala, Drehobl, and Ross, *"Household Energy Burdens."*

166  Ayala, Drehobl, and Ross, *"Household Energy Burdens."*

167  Habitat for Humanity, *Energy Poverty: Effects on Development, Society, and Environment/Europe, Middle East And Africa* (Georgia: Habitat for Humanity), https://www.habitat.org/emea/about/what-we-do/residential-energy-efficiency-households/energy-poverty.

168  "What is Energy Poverty?" Energy Matters, Enbridge, accessed October 20, 2022, https://www.enbridge.com/energy-matters/energy-school/what-is-energy-poverty.

169  Title XXVI of the Omnibus Budget Reconciliation Act of 1981 (Public Law 97-35), as amended, 42 U.S.C. § 8621 et seq., https://www.congress.gov/bill/97th-congress/house-bill/3982

170  "Low Income Home Energy Assistance Program (LIHEAP)," Benefits.gov, https://www.benefits.gov/benefit/623.

In a recent CNN Online op-ed, executive director of the National Energy Assistance Directors Association (NEADA) Mark Wolfe said that households across the U.S. are drowning in household-energy-bill debt. At one point during the pandemic, he explained, thirty-three states had policies in place to assist families who can't pay their utility bills, but by the middle of 2022, all those programs had expired.[171]

Ironically, as more funds are devoted to assisting poor households, President Biden's climate policies continue to make the problem worse and, at least according to Professor Tony Reames, head of the Urban Energy Justice Lab at the University of Michigan, they have benefited higher-income communities more than the needy.[172]

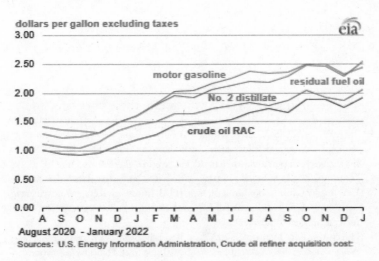

August 2020 - January 2022
Sources: U.S. Energy Information Administration, Crude oil refiner acquisition cost:

---

171  Mark Wolfe, "Struggling US families face a wave of power shutoffs if Congress doesn't act," *CNN*, April 28, 2022, https://www.cnn.com/2022/04/28/perspectives/utility-bills-power-shutoffs/index.html.

172  Tony Reames interviewed by Andy Stone, "Combating Energy Poverty in the U.S.," April 20, 2021, in *Energy Policy Now* (podcast), produced by Kleinman Center for Energy Policy, https://kleinmanenergy.upenn.edu/podcast/combating-energy-poverty-in-the-u-s/.

The Energy Information Agency forecast that heating bills would jump by 30 percent for the average household before 2021 closed.[173] By the spring of 2022, electricity bills for the first year of Biden's presidency had been increasing at the fastest rate since 2008.[174] Year over year, the rate across America rose 4.3 percent in 2021. For 2022, the rate was projected to increase another 4.3 percent,[175] but by the beginning of autumn of 2022, that estimate was revised upwards to 7.5 percent, with some locations like New York and New England experiencing price increases well over 50 percent.[176] As this book goes to press, the numbers are projected to get much worse through the winter of 2022-23.[177]

173  "EIA Forecasts U.S. Winter Natural Gas Bills Will Be 30% Higher Than Last Winter," U.S. Energy Information Administration (EIA), October 25, 2021, https://www.eia.gov/todayinenergy/detail.php?id=50076.

174  "During 2021, U.S. Retail Electricity Prices Rose at Fastest Rate Since 2008," U.S. Energy Information Administration (EIA), https://www.eia.gov/todayinenergy/detail.php?id=51438. By the fall EIA projected that in 2022, energy costs would increase another 7.5 percent.

175  "Electricity Rate Increases in 2022 and Beyond," *Solar Power and Clean Energy | News, Resources, and Updates* (blog), Palmetto, June 6, 2022, https://palmetto.com/learning-center/blog/electricity-rate-increases-in-2022-and-beyond. 4.3 percent is the highest growth rate since 2008.

176  "Short-Term Energy Outlook," U.S. Energy Information Administration (EIA), October 12, 2022, https://www.eia.gov/outlooks/steo/.

177  Press Release, "Home Heating Costs Reach Highest Level in More than 10 Years—Families will Pay 17.2% More for Home Heating this Winter," National Energy Assistance Directors Association (NEADA), September 12, 2022, https://neada.org/wp-content/uploads/2022/09/winter2022-23PR.pdf.

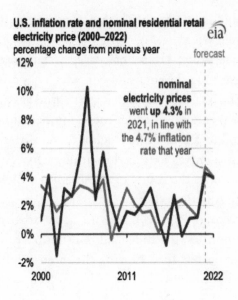

US EIA Energy Outlook March 8, 2022.

## CONCLUSION

Energy access is essential for all American households. When families are threatened with having their power shut off, they cut back on food and even medicine. An estimated 3.5 million people were disconnected in 2020 and 2021, in thirty-two states and the District of Columbia.[178]

Statistically, blacks households are more vulnerable than white and Asian households when it comes to energy affordability. In two short years, the Biden Administration has managed to turn America from an energy powerhouse where Americans of all backgrounds had ready access to low-cost fuel to one in which

---

178  Tami Luhby, "Utility Shutoffs Loom as Energy Prices Soar and Moratoriums End. But Help is Available," *CNN*, April 24, 2022, https://www.cnn.com/2022/04/24/politics/us-gas-electric-moratoriums-end-liheap/index.html.

many households struggle with the staggering costs of gasoline and utility bills.

The Biden White House has caved to progressives when it comes to energy and the environment, which has caused repercussions across the board: families that can't afford gas or the light bill won't spend the funds needed for tutors for their children, nor can they afford to buy a house in a neighborhood with better schools. An extreme anti-energy agenda doesn't just starve America's economy, it undermines the ability of all Americans, including blacks, to achieve the American dream.

While making vigorous claims to be an advocate for blacks and other minorities, the Biden Administration continues to put its climate supporters first, moving the interests of blacks to the back of the political bus.

# CHAPTER SIX

# KILLING BLACKS BETTER: THE BIDEN APPROACH TO ABORTION

*Martin Luther King, Jr. spoke of a Beloved Community
where all are treated with respect and dignity…. Today, we
are compelled to continue Uncle Martin's fight by standing up
for those who are treated as less than human because of their
helplessness and inconvenience. The unborn are as much a part
of the Beloved Community as are newborns, infants, teenagers,
adults, and the elderly. Too many of us speak of tolerance and
inclusion, yet refuse to tolerate or include the weakest and most
innocent among us in the human family. As we celebrate the
life of Uncle Martin, let us renew our hearts and commit our
lives to treating each other, whatever our race, status, or stage of
life, as we would want to be treated. Let us let each other live.*

— ALVEDA C. KING[1]

Alveda King, the niece of Dr. Martin Luther King, Jr., tells her
story about the abortion culture in the late 1960s and early 1970s,
including personally having two abortions, and how she came to

---

1    Press Release, "Dr. Alveda King on King Day: The Dream Includes Us All,
     Born and Unborn," Priests For Life, January 18, 2010, https://web.archive.
     org/web/20150906101038/https://www.priestsforlife.org/library/3011-dr-
     alveda-king-on-king-day-the-dream-includes-us-all-born-and-unborn.

realize the error of her ways.[2] It was MLK's father, Martin Luther King, Sr., who taught her that abortion was a terrible crime, against blacks in particular, and helped her turn her life around. She would eventually have six living babies and go on to be a great pro-life champion.[3] Indeed, to this day, she is one of the leading advocates of the unborn, not just in the U.S., but around the world.

Alveda King explains that abortion was an issue in America well before *Roe v. Wade* was decided in 1973. In 1950, when she was born, her mother (Naomi Ruth King) considered an abortion, fearing that childbirth would prevent her from going to college.[4] Even then, when abortion was illegal, there were groups promoting it, often within black neighborhoods.

## A GRANDFATHER'S DREAM

Alveda recounts, "There was an organization in town called the Birth Control League. Right around that time, they changed their name to Planned Parenthood. They passed out fliers, especially in African-American schools, saying, 'A woman has the right to choose what she does with her body, and we can help you not have a lot of babies.'"[5]

---

2  Benjamin Craft, "Dr. Alveda King, Niece of Martin Luther King Jr., Shares Stories About Her Uncle and Her Involvement in the Pro-Life Movement at Convocation," *Liberty Champion*, January 20, 2020, https://www.liberty.edu/champion/2020/01/dr-alveda-king-niece-of-martin-luther-king-jr-shares-stories-about-her-uncle-and-her-involvement-in-the-pro-life-movement-at-convocation/.

3  Cooper, *Making Black America Great Again*; Suzanne McLaughlin, "Alveda King, niece of Martin Luther King Jr.: Abortion a human rights violation," Masslive Media, May 6, 2011, https://www.masslive.com/news/2011/05/alveda_king_martin_luther_king_jr_niece_abortion_a_human_rights_violation.html.

4  Benjamin Craft, "Dr. Alveda King."

5  Natalie Hoefer, "Alveda King: From Abortion Recipient to Pro-Life Advocate," *The Criterion*, October 16, 2015, https://www.archindy.org/criterion/local/2015/10-16/king.html.

Naomi King took the flyer to her pastor and father-in-law Martin Luther King Sr. (father of MLK), who successfully swayed Naomi to keep the child. He told her, "That's not a lump of flesh. That's my granddaughter. I saw her in a dream three years ago. She has bright skin and bright red hair, and she's going to bless many people."[6] Alveda King was born, bright red hair and all, and has proven to be a blessing to many people.

But it didn't seem that she'd be a champion for life in the beginning. Prior to the *Roe v. Wade* ruling legalizing abortion, Alveda King had what she called an "involuntary" abortion. It was performed "without my consent," she said. "The doctor said, 'You don't need to be pregnant.'"[7] He then performed what he called a "local D and C," she explained. "He gave me an illegal abortion with no anesthesia."[8] She would end up having to have surgery to repair her cervix.[9]

In 1973, Alveda became pregnant again, and at age 22, she walked into a Planned Parenthood clinic, where the doctors explained, "Don't talk to your family. Don't talk to your church. We're your friends, and we're going to give you this procedure," and Alveda underwent a second abortion.[10] It would be nearly 10 years before Alveda King would become one of the champions of the pro-life movement.

---

6    "In Pursuit Of The American Dream, Evangelist Alveda C. King," Alveda King Ministries, October 2021, https://www.alvedaking.com/in-pursuit-of-the-american-dream.

7    "Alveda King: A Voice for the Voiceless," Christian Broadcasting Network, Inc., https://www1.cbn.com/700club/alveda-king-voice-voiceless.

8    Amanda Whitesell, "Alveda King: Prayer is most effective strategy for pro-life change," Priests for Life, Livingston Daily, May 4, 2012, https://www.priestsforlife.org/columns/4192-alveda-king-prayer-is-most-effective-strategy-for-pro-life-change.

9    Aprille Hanson, "Alveda King Says Abortion Movement Rooted in Racism," *Arkansas Catholic*, February 26, 2015, https://www.arkansas-catholic.org/news/article/4151/Alveda-King-says-abortion-movement-rooted-in-racism.

10   Hoefer, "Alveda King."

Today she recalls her grandfather's perspective on the perils of abortion: "Injustice anywhere is a threat to justice everywhere. Ripping babies apart is a very unjust act. It is very violent."[11]

Abortion has been a plague on the black community for decades, but this is no accident. The abortion movement at its founding shared many of the goals of the eugenics movement of the early twentieth century.

## MARGARET SANGER: NO FRIEND OF BLACK AMERICA

The leading group promoting abortion today is Planned Parenthood. Founded as the American Birth Control League in 1921, it changed its name to Planned Parenthood in 1942.[12] Its founder Margaret Sanger was a eugenicist who targeted blacks. In 1921, she explained, "The most urgent problem today is how to limit and discourage the over-fertility of the mentally and physically defective."[13] "Mentally and physically defective" was her code for black people.

Sanger was the main organizer of the first World Population Conference in Geneva, Switzerland in 1927, whose purpose was to deal with the global threat of overpopulation. In her writings afterwards, she acknowledged her disappointment that birth-rate control was not allowed to take the main stage at the event.[14]

---

11    "Alveda King on the impact of abortion on minorities," EWTN Global Catholic Network, January 17, 2019, YouTube video, https://www.youtube.com/watch?v=iy_8qeo7HX0.

12    Kathryn Cullen-DuPont, *Encyclopedia of Women's History in America*, 2nd ed. (Facts on File; August, 2000), p. 11, https://www.amazon.com/Encyclopedia-History-America-Kathryn-Cullen-Dupont-dp-0816041008/dp/0816041008/ref=dp_ob_title_bk.

13    Carlie Porterfield, "Planned Parenthood Drops Margaret Sanger's Name From Manhattan Clinic Over Ties To Eugenics Movement," *Forbes*, July 21, 2020, https://www.forbes.com/sites/carlieporterfield/2020/07/21/planned-parenthood-drops-margaret-sangers-name-from-manhattan-clinic-over-ties-to-eugenics-movement/?sh=22ad448290a.

14    Miriam Reed, *Margaret Sanger: Her Life in Her Words* (New York: Barricade Books, April 2004), https://churchandstate.org.uk/2016/06/margaret-sanger-her-life-in-her-words/.

In 1939, she started "The Negro Project" with the aim of expanding birth control services for Black communities in the south, according to a report by New York University.[15] Sanger's agenda was largely hidden, especially from blacks. She explained her objectives in a letter to a staff member in 1939: "We do not want word to go out that we want to exterminate the Negro population."[16] In order to achieve her goals, she needed to hire black doctors and ministers.[17]

## DENOUNCE THE PLANNER, NOT THE PLANS

Today Planned Parenthood has a budget of over $1.7 billion and assets exceeding $2.1 billion.[18] In 2022, Planned Parenthood received more than half a billion dollars in federal taxpayer support.[19] Besides ending the life of the unborn, it turns out abortion is a huge business, and like any other business, Planned Parenthood strives to achieve a regulatory environment that has little to no

---

15   "Birth Control or Race Control? Sanger and the Negro Project," *Newsletter* 28 (Fall 2001), Margaret Sanger Papers Project, New York University, https://sanger.hosting.nyu.edu/articles/bc_or_race_control/.

16   Margaret Sanger to Dr. C.J. Gamble, December 10, 1939, Margaret Sanger Papers, Sophia Smith Collection, Smith College Library, https://libex.smith.edu/omeka/files/original/d6358bc3053c93183295bf2df1c0c931.pdf.

17   "Fact Check—Planned Parenthood Founder Margaret Sanger's 1939 Quote on Exterminating Black Population Taken Out of Context," Reuters, May 9, 2022, https://www.reuters.com/article/factcheck-pp-exterminating/fact-check-planned-parenthood-founder-margaret-sangers-1939-quote-on-exterminating-black-population-taken-out-of-context-idUSL2N2X11YN.

18   *2020-21 Annual Report* (Washington: Planned Parenthood Federation of America, 2022): 30, https://www.plannedparenthood.org/uploads/filer_public/40/8f/408fc2ad-c8c2-48da-ad87-be5cc257d370/211214-ppfa-annualreport-20-21-c3-digital.pdf.

19   Caroline Wharton, "Biden Gives Planned Parenthood Even MORE Money But Their Total Take Is Still Secret," *Students for Life of America* (blog), June 16, 2022, https://studentsforlife.org/2022/06/16/biden-gives-planned-parenthood-even-more-money-but-their-total-take-is-still-secret/.

limits. Is it any wonder that Planned Parenthood has pledged to spend $50 million in political activity for the November 2022 midterm elections?[20] Walmart, Apple, and Exxon Mobil—companies that are nearly 10 times larger[21]—have committed collectively less than 7 percent of the audacious political funding level promised by Planned Parenthood.[22] It's clear that for Planned Parenthood, a lot is at stake.

## A PROTECTED INDUSTRY NO MORE

In 1973, the abortion industry received a gift that any business might want. The U.S. Constitution severely limited the ability of federal, state and local governments to interfere with its practices. Imagine what Wal-Mart or General Motors could accomplish if they had limits on government interference removed.

There once was a time when the Supreme Court sided with business. Historians note that from about 1897 to 1937, the Supreme Court used a strained interpretation of the "due process" clause of the Fourteenth Amendment to strike down all manner of business regulations. It was called the Lochner era, named after a case in which the Supreme Court struck down a New York State law, which placed a maximum ten-hour day and sixty-hour work week on employment in a bakery to protect employees from workplace hazards.[23] Under what is now referred to an action

---

20    Colin Lodewick, "Planned Parenthood is Spending $50 Million—the Most Ever—on Midterm Elections," *Fortune*, August 17, 2022, https://fortune.com/2022/08/17/planned-parenthood-50-million-midterm-elections-abortion/.

21    Prof. Dr. Amarendra Bhushan Dhiraj, "These Are America's Top 10 Largest Companies By Revenue, 2019," *CEO World*, July 26, 2019, https://ceoworld.biz/2019/07/26/these-are-americas-top-10-largest-companies-by-revenue-2019/.

22    Open Secrets, "Organization Profiles," https://www.opensecrets.org/orgs/. A tally of all three companies political activities is $3.2M.

23    Lochner v. New York, 198 U.S. 45, No. 292 (1906), U.S. Supreme Court, https://supreme.justia.com/cases/federal/us/198/45/.

relying on "substantive due process," the Supreme Court regularly countermanded the ability of Congress and the several states to enact measures that the Court said "interfered with the freedom of contract."[24] It also struck down laws passed by Congress to prevent firings over union membership,[25] laws making it illegal for movie theater companies to enter into agreements to set ticket prices, and laws also preventing gas station operators from engaging in "price-fixing."[26]

After a threat by President Roosevelt to pack the Supreme Court with justices more sympathetic to business regulation, the Lochner era ended. In a case often referred to as the "switch in time that saved nine", Justice Owen Roberts abandoned "freedom of contract" in a minimum wage case and joined with four other Justices to allow the law to go into effect.[27]

Today, legal commentators mock this doctrine, saying that it was merely a mechanism for the Court to impose its economic and business judgements on America. Many of the mockers of substantive due process are progressives. Yet substantive due process undergirds much of their abortion jurisprudence.

## SUBSTANTIVE DUE PROCESS STRIKES BACK

For more than 40 years, progressives relied upon a "made up" right of abortion that wasn't tied to the language or history of the actual Constitution. Like "freedom of contract" at the start of the

---

24  "Freedom of Contract: Everything You Need to Know," Upcounsel, accessed October 19, 2022, https://www.upcounsel.com/freedom-of-contract; "Lochner v. New York."

25  Adair v. United States, 208 U.S. 161, No. 293 (1908), https://supreme.justia.com/cases/federal/us/208/161/.

26  Williams v. Standard Oil Co., 278 U.S. 235, 239-45 (1929) (retail sale of gasoline); Tyson & Bro., 273 U.S. at 429-45 (resale of theater tickets).

27  West Coast Hotel Co. v. Parrish, 300 U.S. 379, No. 293, (1937), https://supreme.justia.com/cases/federal/us/300/379/.

20th century, the progressive movement used the "women's right to choose" power as a tool to bludgeon federal, state, and local government, and the abortion industry—Planned Parenthood in particular—welcomed these changes.

After *Roe v. Wade*, not only did the industry demand to be able to operate in any jurisdiction whether or not a particular state welcomed them, Planned Parenthood pushed back against all manner of restrictions, including those affecting the regulation of its actual facilities. Whereas General Motors has to accept OSHA oversight and submit compliance reports for a byzantine number of regulations regarding its business of car manufacturing, Planned Parenthood has regularly claimed over the last forty years that any state or local regulations it didn't like—such as medical licensing, requirements that clients be legally old enough to give consent, and minimum staffing requirements—were unconstitutional. When it comes to business regulations, Planned Parenthood sounds more like nineteenth century laissez-faire advocate Spencer Herbert[28] than a social justice organization. It has pushed to keep its industry all but immune from government interference.

Initially, Planned Parenthood was remarkably successful, able to use constitutional protections to overcome not only spousal but most parental consent laws, thus ensuring its customer base could expand.[29] It also successfully pushed to have the Medicaid program cover its services.[30] Imagine if the American Psychological Association could claim the Constitution requires that its services

---

28    William Sweet, "Herbert Spencer (1820–1903)," *Internet Encyclopedia of Philosophy* (IEP), https://iep.utm.edu/spencer/.

29    Akron v. Akron Ctr. for Reprod. Health, 462 U.S. 416, No. 81-746, (1983), https://supreme.justia.com/cases/federal/us/462/416/.

30    McRae v. Mathews, 421 F. Supp. 533 (E.D.N.Y. 1976), **US District Court for the Eastern District of New York—421 F. Supp. 533 (E.D.N.Y. 1976) October 22, 1976,** https://law.justia.com/cases/federal/district-courts/FSupp/421/533/1769889/.

should be paid for by Medicaid. Planned Parenthood was even able to tap into taxpayer-financed international funding.[31]

In a surprising win for the industry, it even overturned a state law banning abortion advertisements.[32] Imagine if Big Tobacco could have such protections. It also succeeded in overturning regulations requiring doctors to use abortion techniques that "maximized the chance of fetal survival."[33] For years, the abortion industry was able to have their federally funded facilities refer patients for abortion.[34] In a victory that many businesses would envy, the industry even prevailed in its claim that protestors interfered with its business and should be limited in their ability to protest.[35] Today, school teachers, bus drivers, and welfare recipients have to comply with drug testing requirements,[36] but Planned Parenthood was able to avoid even this.[37] Apparently, it's never heard of the "drug free workplace."

In contrast to rules mandating a "cooling off" period for guns (whose ownership is expressly protected by the Second Amendment), the abortion industry successfully claimed that the Constitution forbade a 48-hour waiting period for a minor.[38] Most

---

31    "Title X 'Gag Rule' Is Formally Repealed," Guttmacher Institute, August 1, 2000, https://www.guttmacher.org/gpr/2000/08/title-x-gag-rule-formally-repealed.

32    Bolger v. Youngs Drug Products Corp., 463 U.S. 60, No. 81–1590 (1983), https://supreme.justia.com/cases/federal/us/463/60/.

33    Thornburgh v. Amer. Coll. of Obstetricians, 476 U.S. 747, No. 84-495, (1986), https://supreme.justia.com/cases/federal/us/476/747/.

34    "Timeline of Important Reproductive Freedom Cases Decided by The Supreme Court," American Civil Liberties Union (ACLU), https://www.aclu.org/other/timeline-important-reproductive-freedom-cases-decided-supreme-court.

35    Schenck v. Pro-Choice Network of Western N. Y., 519 U.S. 357, No. 95-1065. (1997), https://supreme.justia.com/cases/federal/us/519/357/.

36    "States that Drug Test for Welfare 2022," World Population Review, https://worldpopulationreview.com/state-rankings/states-that-drug-test-for-welfare.

37    Ferguson v. Charleston, 532 U.S. 67, No. 99-936. (2001), https://supreme.justia.com/cases/federal/us/532/67/.

38    Ayotte v. Planned Parenthood of Northern New Eng., 546 U.S. 320, No. 04–1144 (2006), https://supreme.justia.com/cases/federal/us/546/320/.

recently, it successfully pushed to overturn a decision by state governments to ban Planned Parenthood from receiving grants.[39]

But all of this came to an end with the Supreme Court ruling on *Dobbs v. Jackson Women's Health*. Once the abortion industry's constitutional claims were stripped away, it has been forced to defend its business activities—albeit more gruesome than most—the same way every other business does. Post-*Dobbs*, Planned Parenthood can have any and all business impositions placed on it, including minimum-wage requirements, industry-specific taxes, safety requirements, and environment and hazardous waste regulations.

In the past, and without irony, Planned Parenthood had claimed that these types of rules would run it out of business and prevent a "woman's right to choose." Yet, when these rules were applied against Plymouth and Saturn, progressives never argued about anyone's right to travel or "freedom of contract." Maybe those car companies would still be around if they had.

Sadly, forty years of misguided abortion jurisprudence have been destructive to black America. The Guttmacher Institute reports that the abortion rate for black women is almost five times that for white women.[40] Blacks account for 38 percent of all abortions,[41]

---

39    "Federal Judge Temporarily Keeps Planned Parenthood on State Funding List," *Lubbock Avalanche-Journal*, April 30, 2012, https://www.lubbockonline.com/story/news/local/2012/04/30/federal-judge-temporarily-keeps-planned-parenthood-state-funding-list/15160222007/.

40    Susan A. Cohen, "Abortion and Women of Color: The Bigger Picture," *Guttmacher Policy Review* 11, no. 3 (2008), https://www.guttmacher.org/gpr/2008/08/abortion-and-women-color-bigger-picture.

41    "Reported Legal Abortions by Race of Women Who Obtained Abortion by the State of Occurrence," Kaiser Family Foundation (KFF), accessed October 29, 2022, https://www.kff.org/womens-health-policy/state-indicator/abortions-by-race/?currentTimeframe=0&sortModel=%7B%22colId%22:%22Location%22,%22sort%22:%22asc%22%7D. No other racial group received more abortions than black women.

even though they are only 11.2 percent of the U.S. female population.[42]

Is it a coincidence that an organization founded by a eugenicist who specifically targeted blacks would continue its deadly program in the black community today? The truth is that this industry preys on blacks, and Joe Biden as President has worked to empower it in ways no previous President ever had.

It is to America's great shame that the Fourteenth Amendment to the U.S. Constitution—which sought to guarantee, first and foremost, liberty and equality for newly freed slaves after the bloody U.S. Civil War—was twisted in this way by the U.S. Supreme Court. The Court's majority created out of whole cloth a so-called constitutional right to abortion in the infamous 1973 *Roe v. Wade* ruling that lasted nearly fifty years until the 2022 decision in *Dobbs v. Jackson Women's Health*.

The legal straightjacket of *Roe v. Wade* inhibited states from preventing more than 62 million abortions—murders of defenseless human beings—in the nearly five decades since the ruling.[43] More than one third of these lives snuffed out, "the weakest and most innocent among us in the human family," as Alveda King said, were black babies,[44] descendants of the very freedmen the Fourteenth Amendment sought to protect. This is a terrible tragedy.

---

42    "Women of Color in the United States: Quick Take," Catalyst, January 31, 2022, https://www.catalyst.org/research/women-of-color-in-the-united-states/.

43    Data compiled from the CDC and Guttmacher Institute, National Right to Life Committee (NRLC), https://www.nrlc.org/abortion/.

44    *Policy Report: The Effects of Abortion on the Black Community* (Washington: Center for Urban Renewal and Education, 2015), https://www.congress.gov/115/meeting/house/106562/witnesses/HHRG-115-JU10-Wstate-ParkerS-20171101-SD001.pdf; NRLC, abortion data.

# JOE BIDEN, THE MOST PRO-ABORTION PRESIDENT IN U.S. HISTORY

Abortion is a top priority for the Biden White House. Sadly, the team there has demonstrated an absolute commitment to promoting it in a number of ways. Senator Joe Biden, and later Vice President Joe Biden, said for decades that he supported the Hyde Amendment, which restricts funding for abortion across many federal programs. However, he abandoned this position when he started his run for President in 2019, and his Administration has been fighting to kill the Hyde Amendment since he entered the White House.

In a twist that would have been comical if it wasn't so sad, then-Representative Cedric Richmond, a Democrat from Louisiana and one of candidate Biden's top advisors, went on TV to defend Joe Biden's allegedly deeply-held views on the Hyde Amendment. This was on June 5, 2019. On June 6, less than 24 hours later, Biden flip-flopped on the issue, just as the campaign was starting in earnest. Richmond would eventually get a job in the Biden White House, where he lasted for just over a year before being shunted off to the Democratic National Committee.

Abortion and the Hyde Amendment is one of a string of issues on which Biden originally posed as a moderate, and then shifted towards the far Left when he came under pressure. It's not clear whether Biden was lying in his earlier position, or is simply a weak, unprincipled politician. Very possibly, it's both. Either way, it's not good news for the country to have such a person in a position of great power.

Upon entering the White House, President Biden stuck to his new extreme pro-abortion position. One of the more wearisome aspects of the Republican-to-Democrat, Democrat-to-Republican presidential transfers in recent decades is the way certain executive actions simply switch on and off like a light switch. Abortion is perhaps the starkest area where this is true. On every abortion-related issue, where the light switch flipped when Joe Biden entered the White House, life got worse for blacks in America.

On January 28, 2021, President Biden issued an executive action—formally a "Memorandum on Protecting Women's Health at Home and Abroad"[45]—to restore funding to abortion providers like Planned Parenthood by:

▸ Directing the Secretary of Health and Human Services to review and undo the Trump Administration's Title X Rule and other Trump-era restrictions on the Title X program;

▸ Revoking the Trump Administration's Mexico City Policy denying U.S. taxpayer funds for family planning organizations advocating abortion in foreign countries, and directing the Secretaries of State, Defense, and Health and Human Services, and the USAID Administrator to rescind any related actions; and

▸ Directing the Secretary of State to resume funding to the United Nations Population Fund even though critics charge the UNFPA "supports, or participates in the management of, a program of coercive abortion or involuntary sterilization."[46]

---

45 President Biden to The Secretaries of State, Defense, Health and Human Services, and the Administrator of The United States Agency for International Development, "Memorandum on Protecting Women's Health at Home and Abroad," Office of the President, January 28, 2021, https://www.whitehouse.gov/briefing-room/presidential-actions/2021/01/28/memorandum-on-protecting-womens-health-at-home-and-abroad.

46 Liz Ford and Nadia Khomami, "Trump administration halts money to UN population fund over abortion rules," *Guardian*, April 4, 2017, https://www.theguardian.com/global-development/2017/apr/04/trump-administration-un-population-fund-abortion.

Biden's campaign decision in 2019 to cave to the far Left telegraphed his assault on the Hyde Amendment. When Administration budget requests were developed, the White House formally requested that the Hyde Amendment come to an end.[47]

Named for the late Republican Representative Henry Hyde from Illinois, the amendment had barred federal funds for the performance of abortions. It became so ingrained as a budget and appropriations rider that it has become perfunctory to include the language in money bills authored by both parties since its 1977 introduction.[48] The Biden Administration, however, rejected the Hyde Amendment in its budgets for both fiscal years 2022[49] and 2023.[50] It also fought against the Hyde Amendment being included in both the so-called American Rescue Plan[51] in early 2021 and the so-called Build Back Better bill.[52]

The $1.9 trillion American Rescue Plan has become law. Most of this money has been wasted on bailing out state and city governments that have been spending like drunken sailors for years.

47    "Biden's Budget Proposal Reverses A Decades-Long Ban On Abortion Funding," NPR, May 31, 2021, https://www.npr.org/2021/05/31/1001881788/bidens-budget-proposal-reverses-a-decades-long-ban-on-abortion-funding.

48    Jon O. Shimabukuro, *Abortion: Judicial History and Legislative Response* (Washington: Congressional Research Service, updated February 25, 2022), https://crsreports.congress.gov/product/pdf/RL/RL33467.

49    "Biden budget drops Hyde Amendment to allow public funding of abortion," Reuters, May 28, 2021, https://www.reuters.com/world/us/biden-budget-drops-hyde-amendment-allow-public-funding-abortion-2021-05-28/.

50    Alanna Vagianos, "Biden's Budget Would Scrap Decades-Old Rule And Permit Federal Funding Of Abortions," *Huffington Post*, March 29, 2022, https://www.huffpost.com/entry/biden-budget-federal-funding-of-abortions-hyde-amendment_n_62434342e4b0e44de9ba42c1.

51    Press Secretary Jen Psaki, "Press Briefing," White House Briefing Room, February 16, 2021, https://www.whitehouse.gov/briefing-room/press-briefings/2021/02/16/press-briefing-by-press-secretary-jen-psaki-february-16-2021/.

52    Press Secretary Jen Psaki, "Press Briefing," White House Briefing Room, October 6, 2021, https://www.whitehouse.gov/briefing-room/press-briefings/2021/10/06/press-briefing-by-press-secretary-jen-psaki-october-6-2021/.

This spending bill has also been a major contributor to the current inflation surge; the federal government could only hit the trillion-dollar-debt button so many times in the short space of two years before making a hash of monetary policy. The nation is now suffering through forty-year inflation highs. But alas, abortion funding was greenlighted.

On the "good news" side, however, the Build Back Better plan—named for Biden's transparent attempt to mirror Donald Trump's Make America Great Again slogan—has so far failed to make it across the finish line in Congress. As introduced, it would allow more funding for abortion. A much more truncated version finally did pass, dubiously named the "Inflation Reduction Act."[53]

## ABORTION IS BAD

It must be said: abortion is a bad, terrible thing. For all the droning on about "science" from the Left, the science on abortion is entirely straightforward: abortion ends a human life—or, to quote the bumper sticker, abortion stops a beating heart. For all the pro and con discussion about this issue, it can be boiled down to this terrible fact: it ends a baby's life.

This is not a partisan or ideological observation. Large majorities of the American public believe that abortion is a bad thing[54] that should be avoided if at all possible. This is true even for millions of people who don't believe that abortion should be illegal but who also understand that there's something wrong here.

---

53    "FACT SHEET: The Inflation Reduction Act Supports Workers and Families," White House Briefing Room, August 19, 2022, https://www.whitehouse.gov/briefing-room/statements-releases/2022/08/19/fact-sheet-the-inflation-reduction-act-supports-workers-and-families.

54    "Knights of Columbus/Marist Poll," *Real Clear Politics*, January 2017, https://www.realclearpolitics.com/docs/20171023_Knights_of_Columbus_Marist_Poll_Abortion_Tables_January_2017_(2).pdf.

Think of it this way: every human—indeed, every living creature on planet Earth—has its own distinct DNA. Frederick Douglass had Frederick Douglass's DNA, and no one else will ever have that. Harriet Tubman, Winston Churchill, Clarence Thomas, Tom Brady—each has had his or her own DNA, and no one else ever will have it. The one partial exception is with identical twins, but even they typically accumulate differences in their DNA.[55] And in no case is the baby ever simply a lump of tissue with the same DNA as the mother. The baby is a whole, unique, distinct individual from the beginning.

When a mother conceives a baby in her womb, a new human being is formed. Is this a religious belief? An ideological belief? For many people, surely, it is those things. But it's also scientific fact: the DNA of a new human being, distinct from mother and father, has been created. The science is settled, as liberals love to (usually falsely) assert about their pet issues. In this case, however, it's actually true.[56]

For many decades, there was a political consensus that, whatever the laws should be, abortion should be treated as an activity to avoid, not celebrate. Bill Clinton won the presidency twice on the platform that abortion should be "safe, legal, and rare." Without speculating on whether Clinton has any kind of moral hesitancy about abortion, the more important fact was his correct read of the political environment. Keeping abortion rare was a winner.

And why should abortion be rare? Because abortion isn't a good thing.

---

55    Theresa Machemer, "Many Identical Twins Actually Have Slightly Different DNA," *Smithsonian Institution*, January 13, 2021, https://www.smithsonianmag.com/smart-news/identical-twins-can-have-slightly-different-dna-180976736/.

56    "When Human Life Begins," American College of Pediatricians, March 2017, https://acpeds.org/position-statements/when-human-life-begins.

However, this strategic positioning changed in 2008, when the Democratic platform replaced "rare" with "regardless of ability to pay," and then in 2016, when the platform was changed to "advocate that abortion be essentially available at all times and for any reason.[57]" The shift to a Brave New World mindset was almost totally complete. Did the Democratic Party make this change because of a sincere evolution in belief on abortion? Probably not. More likely, it was made because of a strategic ideological calculation to capitulate to the ascendant progressive forces of the Left.[58]

The simple fact is that if abortion should be rare because it's a bad thing, then it follows that we as a society should look for ways to reduce it and make it rarer, even if not illegal. That perspective puts pro-abortion ideologues on the defensive. Conceding that abortion is bad was an invaluable advantage to pro-life advocates. Progressives pushed to drop this approach; it's no wonder the loudest voices on the Left have resorted to ever-more-bizarre slogans in recent years, such as "Shout Your Abortion."[59] It's their goal, they say, to "destigmatize" abortion; in other words, there is no moral dimension whatsoever to aborting a child.

---

57    Gerhard Peters and John T. Woolley, "2004 Democratic Party Platform,"
      American Presidency Project, University of California, Santa Barbara,
      https://www.presidency.ucsb.edu/documents/2004-democratic-party-platform;
      Gerhard Peters and John T. Woolley, "2008 Democratic Party Platform:
      RENEWING AMERICA'S PROMISE," The American Presidency Project, August
      25, 2008, https://www.presidency.ucsb.edu/documents/2008-democratic-party-
      platform; Gerhard Peters and John T. Woolley, "2016 Democratic Party Platform,"
      The American Presidency Project, July 21, 2016, https://www.presidency.ucsb.edu/
      documents/2016-democratic-party-platform.

58    Evie Stone, "Dems' New Abortion Language Courts Pro-Life Moderates,"
      NPR, August 12, 2008, https://www.npr.org/sections/vox-politics/2008/08/
      dems_new_abortion_language_cou.html.

59    Michael Pearson, "Women embrace, criticize #ShoutYourAbortion," CNN,
      September 29, 2015, https://www.cnn.com/2015/09/22/living/shout-your-
      abortion-feat/index.html.

Indeed, in just the past year, after years of calling itself "pro-choice," Planned Parenthood has embraced the term "pro-abortion" to describe itself![60] As *The Washington Post* reported, "[Alexis] McGill Johnson [the president of Planned Parenthood] said the group would now use a term like 'pro-abortion,' a drastic change from the group's rhetoric even a few years ago. 'Planned Parenthood would stay away from any language that would stigmatize abortion as a procedure,' she said." This wasn't *The Babylon Bee*—this was *The Washington Post*.

OK, then. The good news for pro-lifers is that this approach may be even worse for the pro-abortion side than the nuanced idea that "abortion is bad, but we shouldn't do anything about it." When progressives admit what a horror abortion is, normal people conclude that it not only shouldn't be normalized but that it should be actively discouraged.

Presenting abortion as a positive good, as establishment abortion groups now do, is positively repellent to most people, making those activists look creepy and strange even to people who have no strong views about abortion. The simple fact is that not only is abortion bad, but enthusiasm for abortion *is in fact* creepy and strange. The good news is that this will, over time, strengthen the opposition to abortion and those parts of society that are looking to help women find alternatives to abortion.

If the science says that abortion is the ending of a human life, and it does, then how should we feel about it, morally and ethically? For thousands of years, every significant enduring society has condemned the taking of innocent human life. The Ten

---

60    Caroline Kitchener, "With Roe Endangered, Democrats Divide on Saying the Word 'Abortion'," *Washington Post*, April 2, 2022, https://www.washingtonpost.com/politics/2022/04/02/abortion-rhetoric-roe/.

Commandments can be summarized as "God is God, and don't you forget it; and don't kill or hurt each other.[61]"

The Code of Hammurabi, the teachings of Buddha and Mohammed, and the ancient Greeks and Romans have all, to varying degrees, promoted protections for innocent human life and condemnation of murder.[62] Many things have changed over the centuries, but even very brutal societies have always drawn a distinction between those guilty of crime and those innocent of crime.

## ABORTION IS PARTICULARLY BAD FOR BLACKS

Blacks are disproportionately victimized by abortion, meaning that they should benefit particularly if abortion can be reduced or eliminated. The numbers are staggering: while blacks make up 13 percent of the population,[63] they account for 30 to 40 percent of abortions performed nationwide in America, a strikingly consistent range over the past fifty years.[64] If Joe Biden has his way,

---

61  Ex. 20:1–14 (JPS), https://biblehub.com/jps/exodus/20.htm.

62  "The Code of Hammurabi," translated by L. W. King, https://avalon.law.yale.edu/ancient/hamframe.asp; Surat Al-Māʾidah, Qurʾan, accessed December 13, 2022, https://legacy.quran.com/5/32-33; "The Homicide Courts Of Ancient Athens," accessed December 13, 2022, https://scholarship.law.upenn.edu/cgi/viewcontent.cgi?article=7670&context=penn_law_review; Andrew Bartles-Smith et al. "Reducing Suffering During Conflict: The Interface Between Buddhism And International Humanitarian Law," 2021, https://eprints.soas.ac.uk/36219/1/14639947.2021.pdf; R A Bauman, "Crime and Punishment in Ancient Rome," 1996, https://www.ojp.gov/ncjrs/virtual-library/abstracts/crime-and-punishment-ancient-rome.

63  U.S. Census Bureau, accessed December 13, 2022, https://www.census.gov/quickfacts/fact/table/US/PST045221

64  KFF, "Abortions by Race"; Abortion Surveillance, United States, 1984–1985, Morbidity and Mortality Weekly Report (MMWR) Series (Washington: Centers for Disease Control and Prevention, September 1, 1989), https://www.cdc.gov/mmwr/preview/mmwrhtml/00001467.htm.

more black babies will be killed by abortion than ever before. "Put y'all back in chains" indeed.

The Trump Administration undertook various measures to try to reduce taxpayer funds going to abortion and to put in place judges who would understand the historical value given to the inalienable right to life in America's founding documents.[65] Happily, many important steps were taken, including the effort to work with twenty-three nations to oppose abortion,[66] creating a federal right of conscientious objection for doctors and medical care givers opposed to abortion[67] and repealing an Obama-era federal regulation that mandated state governments fund some abortion clinics in their state.[68]

Americans may hope that over the coming decades, many of these judges will author legal decisions like the *Dobbs v. Jackson Women's Health*[69] ruling that overturned *Roe V. Wade* and continue to promote a culture of life—not to mention issuing many other important pro-liberty and pro-common sense rulings.

---

65 "President Trump's Record on Life," March 9, 2020, National Right to Life Committee, https://www.nrlc.org/uncategorized/president-trumps-record-on-life/.

66 Grégor Puppinck, "An alliance Against Abortion," European Centre for Law and Justice, https://eclj.org/abortion/un/onu-une-alliance-pour-contrer-lavortement?lng=en.

67 Press Release, "HHS Issues Notice of Violation to California for its Abortion Coverage Mandate," U.S. Department of Health & Human Services, January 24, 2020, https://public3.pagefreezer.com/content/HHS.gov/31-12-2020T08:51/https://www.hhs.gov/about/news/2020/01/24/hhs-issues-notice-of-violation-to-california-for-its-abortion-coverage-mandate.html.

68 Press Release, "President Donald J. Trump Signs H.J.Res. 43 into Law," White House Archive, April 13, 2017, www.whitehouse.gov/briefings-statements/president-donald-j-trump-signs-h-j-res-43-law/.

69 Dobbs, State Health Officer of The Mississippi Department of Health, et al. v. Jackson Women's Health Organization et al. June 24, 2022, https://www.supremecourt.gov/opinions/21pdf/19-1392_6j37.pdf.

A big part of America's prospects for the twenty-first century include continuing to be a beacon for the rule of law and a place where everyone receives justice under a consistently functioning system. The judges appointed by Trump will hopefully play an important role in getting us there.

However, the Biden Administration has dedicated itself from day one to reversing all these gains.[70] In particular, it is restoring Title X funding to Planned Parenthood, meaning that some $60 million in funding[71] will be added to Planned Parenthood's budget. And that's *annual* funding, meaning that every single year Planned Parenthood gets another check for $60 million. Unfortunately, Planned Parenthood gets even more taxpayer money than that: roughly $500 million[72] every year—more than a third of its total operating budget.[73]

Another statistic that shows the terrible toll on blacks in America is comparing the total lives lost every year to accidents,

70  Sarah Mccammon, "Biden Administration Prepares To Overturn Trump Abortion Rule," NPR, January 21, 2021, https://www.npr.org/sections/president-biden-takes-office/2021/01/21/959170860/biden-administration-prepares-to-overturn-trump-abortion-rule; Mairead McArdle, "Biden to Sign New Round of Executive Orders on Abortion, Immigration," *National Review*, January 24, 2021, https://www.yahoo.com/video/biden-sign-round-executive-orders-145736834.html.

71  Grace Panetta, "Planned Parenthood Just Forfeited $60 Million in Federal Funding So They Don't Have to Comply With a Rule That Bans Abortions," *Business Insider*, August 19, 2019, uhttps://www.businessinsider.com/trump-gag-rule-limits-abortion-2018-5.

72  "Fact Check: Does Planned Parenthood Get Over $500 Million a Year in Government Funding?" *Tennessee Star*, May 21, 2018, https://tennesseestar.com/2018/05/21/fact-check-does-planned-parenthood-get-over-500-million-a-year-in-government-funding/.

73  *2019–20 Annual Report* (Washington: Planned Parenthood Federation of America, 2021), https://www.plannedparenthood.org/uploads/filer_public/67/30/67305ea1-8da2-4cee-9191-19228c1d6f70/210219-annual-report-2019-2020-web-final.pdf.

disease, and violent crime. Abortion is by far the leading cause of death for blacks, about half of all deaths every year.[74]

In New York City, this is provably the case: not only are more black babies aborted than born alive annually, but also about twice as many black babies die in abortions than already-born blacks die of any cause.[75] This is an incredibly sad set of facts. Black babies, like all babies, deserve a chance at life, whether with both parents, one parent, a grandparent or grandparents, or through adoption. The rest of America should not settle for the New York approach.

Planned Parenthood's defenders tend to suggest that economic reasons drive abortions among blacks and other minorities. But the fact is that most of the organization's abortion clinics are located near black and Hispanic communities. Planned Parenthood essentially markets itself disproportionately to blacks and other minorities.[76] It's the old joke that three things matter in real estate: location, location, and location. Planned Parenthood has actively decided to finance operations in black neighborhoods and to encourage and subsidize the abortions of black babies.

---

74    "U.S. Abortion Patients" (infographic), Guttmacher Institute, May 9, 2016, https://www.guttmacher.org/infographic/2016/us-abortion-patients; "Induced Abortion in the United States," Guttmacher Institute, September 2019, https://www.guttmacher.org/fact-sheet/induced-abortion-united-states; "Leading Causes of Death–Males–Non-Hispanic black–United States, 2016," Centers for Disease Control and Prevention (CDC), accessed December 13, 2022, https://www.cdc.gov/healthequity/lcod/men/2016/nonhispanic-black/index.htm.

75    Lauren Caruba, "Cynthia Meyer says more black babies are aborted in New York City than born," PolitiFact, November 25, 2015, https://www.politifact.com/factchecks/2015/nov/25/cynthia-meyer/cynthia-meyer-says-more-black-babies-are-aborted-n/; "Table 31c : Death Summary Information by Race/Ethnicity New York City–2013," New York State Department of Health, accessed December 13, 2022, https://www.health.ny.gov/statistics/vital_statistics/2013/table31c.htm.

76    Carol M. Swain, "Systemic Racism At Planned Parenthood," *First Things*, February 5, 2021, https://www.firstthings.com/web-exclusives/2021/02/systemic-racism-at-planned-parenthood.

Is this a coincidence? An accident of real estate pricing and other subtle economic factors? It is not. Planned Parenthood's founder, Margaret Sanger, was keenly aware of the pro-eugenics arguments being made about certain ethnic groups. She was high in the councils of the eugenics movement in the 1920s and 1930s; not only was she familiar with the Ku Klux Klan's anti-black agenda, but she was also a guest speaker at one of the KKK's auxiliary groups.[77] She shared the KKK's beliefs that the world, particularly America, would be better off without blacks. Never did she work to take a public stand against this view—she simply regarded the Ku Klux Klan as an ally in the fight for abortion.

In July 2020, Planned Parenthood finally acknowledged founder Margaret Sanger's ties to the eugenics movement by the token action of removing her name from a New York City facility,[78] and even disavowing Margaret Sanger as a racist in a *New York Times* op-ed.[79] But Planned Parenthood's "clinics" remain where they are situated, substantially targeting black and other nonwhite women, and there's no sign that this will end anytime soon.

However, the consequences are significant. The outsized amount of abortion within the black population has political consequences. It isn't simply the case that the next Ben Carson or Barack Obama may never be born—the overall size of the black population is significantly smaller than what it might have been otherwise, and

---

77  Alexis McGill Johnson, "I'm the Head of Planned Parenthood. We're Done Making Excuses for Our Founder," *New York Times,* April 17, 2021, https://www.nytimes.com/2021/04/17/opinion/planned-parenthood-margaret-sanger.html.

78  Press Release, "Planned Parenthood of Greater New York Announces Intent to Remove Margaret Sanger's Name from NYC Health Center," Planned Parenthood of Greater New York, July 21, 2020, https://www.plannedparenthood.org/planned-parenthood-greater-new-york/about/news/planned-parenthood-of-greater-new-york-announces-intent-to-remove-margaret-sangers-name-from-nyc-health-center.

79  Johnson, "Head of Planned Parenthood."

along with that reduction in numbers has come a reduction in influence. Consider this: without racially targeted abortion, the voting power of the black community would now be at 16 percent nationally rather than the current 13 percent.[80]

## WHAT AMERICANS SHOULD DO ABOUT ABORTION

Abortion advocates argue that women should have "choice," and certainly freedom is an important part of the American Dream. This is a serious question that deserves a serious answer. There are fair-minded people in the political middle who may ask the same question.

Because abortion is the taking of innocent human life, abortion should be restricted as much as possible. If that means that abortion is prohibited after viability, or after some number of months in the womb, that would be a step forward. Even though the Court has ruled that there is no constitutionally protected right to an abortion, it remains largely unrestricted across the country. State legislatures should act with dispatch to impose limits or an outright ban. Certainly there should be no taxpayer funding of abortion. There are many things that Americans can do to impede the economics of abortion, to make the process of abortion less efficient, less available, and less desirable. They must offer love and compassion to those women who find themselves in a situation where they think abortion is their best option, including financially supporting women's shelters as well as even taking these women into their own homes.

But that is not the end of this issue, which is unlikely to go away completely, and Americans have to think about how to undo the Biden Administration's damage to the self-image of Americans, very much including black Americans.

---

80   CURE, *Effects of Abortion on the Black Community.*

When the lives of our fellow unborn humans are considered unworthy of protection, we undermine our ability to value and appreciate the lives of those who are born. The disproportionate killing of black babies overwhelms any argument that "Black Lives Matter"—why should nonblack Americans care about blacks in the midst of slaughter of black babies by black adults in abortion clinics?

There are many subtle actions the government can take to try to end abortion. Taxpayer funding, for one example, is more than dollars that flow to Planned Parenthood for its grisly activities. It's also a stamp of approval from the federal government: when the U.S. government gives you a check, it's a positive endorsement for what you're doing. Ending taxpayer funding of Planned Parenthood probably won't gut the organization financially—there are many pro-abortion millionaires and billionaires who could replace that money tomorrow. Indeed, many liberal politicians and wealthy liberal donors have said that they want to be ready to jump in and fund abortion if any new restrictions or reductions in funding are approved. What can't be replaced is the message the federal government sends when it spends millions of dollars to support a certain kind of activity. If the federal government ends taxpayer subsidies for abortion, it will be a subtle shift in the culture that could save thousands or millions of lives.

However, there are other important policy inputs as well. Liberals often argue that if pro-lifers were *really* pro-life, they'd support all sorts of crazy new spending programs to hand out welfare to various favored groups. To some extent, this may be understood as the way the liberal brain works: "If I love you, I'll loot the federal treasury for you!" It's yet another reason why Americans shouldn't allow liberals to take charge of public policy. However, Americans should try to understand the mentality of people on different sides of an issue, especially on issues as important as abortion.

It would also be fair to ask the reverse question: are pro-abortion advocates proposing a compromise to end abortion in exchange for new social support programs? They are not. In addition, the spending programs liberals support for new mothers do not, in fact, work very well. Welfare programs are mostly just jobs programs for Democrat-voting federal workers, who create dependence by able-bodied adults who really would be better off working in the private sector. Dependence on welfare programs is a bad thing. It weakens the initiative to be independent among those it allegedly helps. These programs typically don't work well, are poorly administered, and end up spending most of the funds on implementation instead of the designated beneficiaries. Even worse, poor performance by these programs often creates a vicious cycle of politicians coming back for more money the next year and blaming poor performance on insufficient funds—but it's not lack of funding, it's lack of a good idea and a functioning model.

Sometimes funding for contraception is offered as the answer to abortion. But this is a red herring. States with the highest rates of contraception use, such as New York, also feature the highest abortion rates. States with low rates of contraception use, such as South Dakota, also have low abortion rates.

The policies that Joe Biden has been supporting for fifty years in public office have corresponded with—and helped to cause—the catastrophic collapse of black families in America. In 1960, only 24 percent of black babies were born out of wedlock.[81] By 2020, 70 percent of black babies were born out of wedlock.[82]

---

81    George A. Akerlof and Janet L. Yellen, *An Analysis of Out-Of-Wedlock Births in the United States* (Brookings Institution, August, 1996), https://www.brookings.edu/research/an-analysis-of-out-of-wedlock-births-in-the-united-states/.

82    Michelle J.K. Osterman, M.H.S. et al. *Births: Final Data for 2020*, National Vital Statistics Reports (Washington: Centers for Disease Control and Prevention, 2022), https://www.cdc.gov/nchs/data/nvsr/nvsr70/nvsr70-17.pdf.

However, that doesn't mean that nothing can be done. During the Obama Administration, Joe Biden's former boss at least acknowledged the social problem of fatherless homes by paying lip service to a Fatherhood Initiative.[83] President Obama gave occasional, poignant remarks on the issue, but fundamental public policies driving the problem didn't change.

President Biden has failed to make even token gestures in the direction of assessing the impact of social welfare programs and their harmful effects on blacks. To some extent, this is yet another example of President Biden kowtowing to the new woke hierarchy of the Democratic Party. Most Democratic leaders are so obsessed with new definitions of gender identity and "modern families" that to even talk about the need for fathers is triggering for them.

To say that a child should have a father is a "cisgender heteronormative expression of reactionary patriarchal privilege-mongering." (If you didn't understand that previous sentence, congratulations! You just tested negative for the woke virus.)

Even more triggering for fruity Leftists on college campuses is the staggering correlation between the marital status of women who become pregnant and their likelihood of choosing abortion. Planned Parenthood's own research arm, the Alan Guttmacher Institute, reports that 86 percent of women seeking abortions are not married at the time of the procedure.[84] This is not to say

---

83    President Barack Obama, "Responsible Fatherhood—No Excuses," The White House: President Barack Obama, June 21, 2010, https://obamawhitehouse. archives.gov/blog/2010/06/21/president-obama-promotes-responsible-fatherhood-no-excuses.

84    "Percentage distribution of U.S. women obtaining abortions in nonhospital settings and of all U.S. women aged 15-44, and abortion index, by selected characteristics, 2014 and 2008," Guttmacher Institute, table 1, accessed December 14, 2022, https://www.guttmacher.org/sites/default/files/report_downloads/us-abortion-patients-table1.pdf.

that there aren't married women getting pregnant who also have financial difficulties that make giving birth seem like a hardship.

However, clearly we should do what we can to help encourage those unmarried women—who are overwhelmingly open to having an abortion—to include the father in the picture, preferably by marriage, to help provide a supportive environment to raise that child. Americans can and must support policies that help women to increase their chances of having a stable family situation, as well as support that will persuade them to not have an abortion. Welfare programs and the tax code often discriminate against married people,[85] which is an incentive for people not to get married. That must be fixed.

We need to do more education about the health risk of abortion unrelated to the welfare of the baby. Abortion can do severe psychological and physiological harm to women. Numerous studies have suggested a link between having an abortion and an increased risk of breast cancer.[86] Girls should be told about these things in school, certainly by high school. The Left, of course, wants detailed sex education and every form of "alternative lifestyle" taught to even very young children. However, to the extent that any of this type of classroom instruction takes place, it should certainly include the truth about the risks of abortion for the mother.

Another issue that deserves serious focus at both the public policy and cultural level is adoption. Pro-lifers should promote

85    Angela Rachidi, "Do Welfare Programs Discourage Marriage?" American Enterprise Institute, July 27, 2016, https://www.aei.org/economics/do-welfare-programs-discourage-marriage/; Alicia Tuovila, "What Is the Marriage Penalty?" Investopedia, updated October 28, 2022, https://www.investopedia.com/terms/m/marriage-penalty.asp.

86    T Parkins, "Does Abortion Increase Breast Cancer Risk?" National Institutes of Health (NIH), December 15, 1993, https://pubmed.ncbi.nlm.nih.gov/8246284/.

adoption services, an entire ecosystem, to ensure that pregnant women know that if they choose to have a baby and give it up for adoption, there is a reliable system in place.

Most important, perhaps, are crisis pregnancy centers. If the federal government is spending money in this area, rather than sending it to abortion factories like Planned Parenthood, it should send it to clinics with the mission of providing women alternatives to abortion.

## ROE V. WADE AS A DRED SCOTT REDUX

The U.S. Supreme Court's 1973 *Roe v. Wade* ruling chillingly mimicked the kind of reasoning embedded in the Court's infamous 1856 *Dred Scott* decision, in which Chief Justice Taney declared that blacks are "so far inferior, that they had no rights which the white man was bound to respect."[87] How far off is this sentiment conceptually from "no case could be cited that holds that a fetus is a person"—which was Justice Harry Blackmun's contention in *Roe*?[88] The perspective of U.S. jurisprudence remained fundamentally off-kilter on this issue all the way until 2022, when the court rendered its decision in *Dobbs v. Jackson Women's Health*. Every member of the human family deserves respect and protection under the law.

## GOOD NEWS FROM JUDGES, NO THANKS TO BIDEN

The decision on *Dobbs* by the U.S. Supreme Court turned on challenges to abortion-related laws in several states that ended

---

87    "Dred Scott, Plaintiff in Error, v. John F. A. Sandford," Legal Information Institute, accessed December 14, 2022, https://www.law.cornell.edu/supremecourt/text/60/393

88    "Jane Roe, et al., Appellants, v. Henry Wade," Legal Information Institute, accessed December 14, 2022, https://www.law.cornell.edu/supremecourt/text/410/113.

in the reversal of the landmark rulings in *Roe v. Wade* (1973), *Planned Parenthood v. Casey* (1992), and others.

The Left has claimed for years that state legislators across America kept pushing restrictions on abortion access because they want to undermine women.[89] Repeating this mantra over and over has been effective as it has promoted what analysts refer to as the gender gap: the common differences between men's and women's views on social, political, and cultural matters. Although typically used to explain the differences between how men and women vote, ironically, the pro-life movement is overwhelmingly made up of female leaders: Julie Brown, Alveda King, Penny Nance, Charmaine Yoest, Mildred Jefferson, Phyllis Schlafly, Marjorie Danensfelser, Beverly LaHaye, and Andrea Sheldon, among many other women, have been steadfastly promoting life as the best choice and working to influence state and federal legislators to end abortion. They've been effective not because they are women but because they put an effort into making strong arguments. They haven't bullied legislators; instead, they have persuaded them.

Progressives often forget that America as a country operates on the principle of self-government, which requires consent. We as a country aren't controlled by external forces or political authorities. We the citizens use the ballot as a means by which we express our views and concerns. That's where persuasion comes in. The most enduring way to achieve change in America is to persuade Americans that change is needed.

The civil rights movement is a great example of persuasion. Racists and bigots weren't forced to stop mistreating blacks be-

---

89    Osub Ahmed, Bela Salas-Betsch, and Lauren Hoffman, *State Abortion Bans Will Harm Women and Families' Economic Security Across the US* (Washington: Center for American Progress, August 2022), https://www.americanprogress.org/article/state-abortion-bans-will-harm-women-and-families-economic-security-across-the-us/.

cause some exogenous political authority forced them to. It was actually the decisions of people who lived all across America, including many in the very neighborhoods where the bigots lived, that caused the change.

Consider the Twenty-fourth Amendment, which banned poll taxes or special fees that had to be paid in order to vote. Adopting a Constitutional Amendment is hard. One faction or energized minority can't get one passed. The Twenty-fourth Amendment took less than two years to be ratified.[90] That meant that the legislatures of thirty-eight states had to act in favor. Its passage is an example of an argument that was persuasive.

The effectiveness of the pro-life movement has been a result of persuasion. It didn't have more money, it didn't have cultural elites on its side, and it wasn't supported by the mainstream media. But its arguments were taken to legislature after legislature for more than forty years. The Left—relying on money, cultural elites, and the media—haven't achieved nearly the same impact, as measured by the willingness of state legislatures to push their agenda.

Progressives are just over a quarter of all Americans, whereas more than a third of all Americans identify as conservative.[91] The remainder—so-called moderates—end up ultimately deciding elections. This disparity does make changing opinion in an enduring way much harder for the Left; it is far easier to get to 50 percent of the population when you start at one-third than if you start at one-fourth.

---

90    "The Twenty-fourth Amendment, August 27, 1962," History, Art & Archives, U.S. House of Representatives, accessed October 23, 2022, https://history.house.gov/HistoricalHighlight/Detail/37045.

91    Michael Lind, "Progressives are a minority in America. To win, they need to compromise," *Guardian*, December 19, 2020, https://www.theguardian.com/us-news/commentisfree/2020/dec/19/progressives-us-democrats-power-new-deal.

## SOMETIMES IT'S THE DOG FOOD

In advertising, there is a saying that all the best ad campaigns and product endorsements won't make owners buy more of a particular brand of dog food if the dogs don't actually like the taste. When it comes to abortion and the American people, it's the dog food. America simply doesn't buy the slick campaign and endorsements pushed by the pro-abortion industry. The right has been far more successful, despite being underfunded and contrary to the cultural leitmotif. In fact, progressives know this, which is precisely why the Left resorts to the Federal Courts.

Winning in Court is not the same as winning the hearts and minds of a people. All of the essential elements of the civil rights movement were won in legislatures: the Civil Rights Act, the Voting Rights Act, and the Fair Housing Act.[92] These hard-fought gains will continue for centuries—as long as America does—because they represent the views of the American people.

*Roe v. Wade* was never accepted by the American people. It was simply imposed on them by courts. When progressives say that the ruling had popular support, they can't explain why so many states around the country consistently took steps to undermine it. The Left never understood that the key to enduring policy is to persuade the American people, not five robed judges.

Critics of *Roe v. Wade*—including former Justice Ruth Bader Ginsburg, scholar and professor John Hart Ely (an Earl Warren clerk), constitutional scholar and Yale University Professor Alexander Bickel, Nixon Special Prosecutor Archibold Cox, and even scholar and Harvard Law Professor Lawrence Tribe—were never

---

92    Mehrunnisa Wani, "8 Key Laws That Advanced Civil Rights," History Channel, January 26, 2022, https://www.history.com/news/civil-rights-legislation.

persuaded of the merits of the ruling under the law.[93] To this date, there is no consensus by *Roe* proponents as to what specific provision of the Constitution the right to abortion rests upon. But to call *Roe v. Wade* merely incoherent is to imply that when Marie Antoinette told starving peasants in France that they were should "eat cake," she was being compassionate and logical. *Roe* was not coherent, compassionate, or logical. Relying on a "penumbra formed by emanations"[94] to create a generalized right of privacy, it was bound to collapse under repeated challenges in Court. Progressives hoped that its incoherence would be ignored by those enthralled by the benefit of abortion rights.

## THE TEXAS HEARTBEAT ACT

In the leadup to *Dobbs*, the Lone Star State's innovative Heartbeat Act took effect on September 1, 2021, after becoming law in May of that year.[95] The U.S. Supreme Court allowed the law, which prohibits abortions when a fetal heartbeat can be detected—typically at the six-week point of a pregnancy—due to the law's reliance on private citizens to enforce it by way of civil lawsuits.[96] The high court left the law in place a second time in December

---

93    Clarke D. Forsythe, "A Survey of Judicial and Scholarly Criticism of Roe v. Wade Since 1973, Legal Criticism and Unsettled Precedent," Americans United for Life, January 2022, https://aul.org/wp-content/uploads/2022/01/A-Survey-of-Judicial-and-Scholarly-Criticism-of-Roe-v.-Wade-Since-1973.pdf.

94    Griswold v. Connecticut, 381 U.S. 479, No. 496, (1965), https://supreme.justia.com/cases/federal/us/381/479/.

95    Shannon Najmabadi, "Gov. Greg Abbott Signs Into Law One of Nation's Strictest Abortion Measures, banning procedure as early as six weeks into a pregnancy," *Texas Tribune*, May 19, 2022, https://www.texastribune.org/2021/05/18/texas-heartbeat-bill-abortions-law/.

96    Amy Howe, "Supreme Court Leaves Texas Abortion Ban in Place," *SCOTUSblog*, September 2, 2021, https://www.scotusblog.com/2021/09/supreme-court-leaves-texas-abortion-ban-in-place/.

2021,[97] before the sweeping opinion in *Dobbs* was issued in June 2022.

Anyone paying attention could predict what was happening. Here again, what the media said to America wasn't an accurate depiction of the dispute. Tellingly, what progressives argued in Court revealed the truth.

Elected in 2016, State Senator Bryan Hughes (R-TX) introduced the Texas Heartbeat Bill.[98] The measure banned abortions in the state after 6 weeks, or when a fetal heartbeat could be detected. But rather than empower prosecutors, or even the state Attorney General, to enforce the ban, it used a novel approach: it authorized private citizens to sue civilly anyone that performs or aids in an abortion procedure involving an unborn child with a heartbeat.[99]

The bill became law.

The media reported that Texas had contravened *Roe v. Wade* by putting a "bounty" on abortion providers.[100] Breathlessly, CBS reported that the "Texas abortion ban turns citizens into 'bounty hunters.'"[101] Such reporting attempted to conjure up fears of rov-

---

97    Amy Howe, "Court leaves Texas' six-week abortion ban in effect and narrows abortion providers' challenge, *SCOTUSblog*, December 10, 2021, https://www.scotusblog.com/2021/12/court-leaves-texas-six-week-abortion-ban-in-effect-and-narrows-abortion-providers-challenge/.

98    Patrick Svitek, "The Texas GOP Lawmaker Behind the Abortion Ban, Voting Restrictions Bill and More," *Texas Tribune*, September 17, 2021, https://www.texastribune.org/2021/09/17/texas-abortion-ban-voting-bryan-hughes/.

99    Texas Heartbeat Act (S.B. 8), accessed December 14, 2022, https://capitol.texas.gov/tlodocs/87R/billtext/pdf/SB00008F.pdf.

100    Ross Ramsey, "Analysis: Intentional Loopholes in Texas Abortion Law Draw a J udge's Rebuke," *Texas Tribune*, October 11, 2021, https://www.texastribune.org/2021/10/11/texas-abortion-bounty-hunters/.

101    Aimee Picchi, "Texas Abortion Ban Turns Citizens Into 'Bounty Hunters'," *CBS News*, September 3, 2021, https://www.cbsnews.com/news/texas-abortion-law-bounty-hunters-citizens/.

ing vigilantes traveling across the state to injure or do worse to women exercising their legal right.

But progressives made a far different argument to the Court. They argued that the state of Texas was simply dodging the review of federal court oversight,[102] and because the state was "contriving" to avoid federal court review (and in the process, stripping Americans of constitutional rights), it should be stopped by a federal court.[103] Not nearly the apocalyptic charges being made in the media.

## SUING ON BEHALF OF THE KING

But all Texas did was adopt a *Qui Tam* measure. *Qui Tam* is the abbreviation for the Latin phrase "qui tam pro domino rege quam pro se ipso in hac parte sequitur," meaning "Who sues on behalf of the King." This idea that regular citizens can sue in place of the government predates the U.S. to at least 725 AD.[104] In America, it was a tool broadly adopted by Abraham Lincoln during the Civil War. Often referred to as the "Lincoln Law," it allowed any citizen to sue any individual or company that was defrauding the war effort, and if successful, enabled those citizens the right to recover damages and penalties on the government's behalf.[105]

Such laws exist today at the federal level, and successful litigants can keep up to 30 percent of the fraud they're able to prove.

---

102   Ramsey, "Intentional Loopholes."

103   "W.D. Tex. - Whole Woman's Health V. Jackson – Complaint," ACLU, September 13, 2021, https://www.aclu.org/legal-document/wd-tex-whole-womans-health-v-jackson-complaint?redirect=legal-document/whole-womans-health-v-jackson-complaint.

104   "History of Whistleblower 'Qui Tam' Lawsuits," The Cochran Firm, accessed December 14, 2022, https://cochranfirm.com/washington-dc/history-whistle blower-qui-tam-lawsuits/.

105   "False Claims Act," Phillips & Cohen, accessed December 14, 2022, https://www.phillipsandcohen.com/false-claims-act-history/.

Some thirty states have adopted similar laws.[106] Far from being un-American, it is central to the operation of good government.

In the case of the Texas Heartbeat Law, progressives wanted the law struck down. They argued that the law itself was somehow unusual or that that the law was still an action by the government of Texas that restricted abortions. Regardless of which argument was accepted, the problem was who should the Court order to stop enforcing the law?

Although they found a liberal federal judge to buy into one or both of these arguments, neither the Fifth Circuit Court nor the Supreme Court would ultimately agree. U.S. Federal District Court Judge Robert Pitman, an Obama appointee, had tried to "cut the baby in half" and ordered all of the state courthouse clerks and state judges to refuse to assist in the implementation of the law.

But both the Fifth Circuit and Supreme Court understood that a federal judge should never order a state court to take an action.[107] There are a host of federalism and state-rights issues that occur. Instead of targeting state judges, the principle is that federal judges should direct their actions toward prosecutors, governors, or even state legislatures. The efforts in court failed, even if their claims in public proved persuasive. Ironically, the very concept they denounced when used to limit abortions, they publicly promoted when California set up a bounty and civil suits for gun-control purposes.[108]

---

106 "Whistleblower Laws by State—False Claims," Phillips & Cohen, accessed December 14, 2022, https://www.phillipsandcohen.com/state-false-claims-statutes/.

107 "Conflicts of Jurisdiction: Federal Court Interference with State Courts," US Law, Justia, https://law.justia.com/constitution/us/article-3/40-conflicts-of-jurisdiction-federal-court-interference-with-state-courts.html

108 "California Enacts Gun Control Law Inspired by Texas Abortion Ban," *VOA*, July 22, 2022, https://www.voanews.com/a/california-enacts-gun-control-law-inspired-by-texas-abortion-ban-/6670667.html.

Judge Pittman was overruled, and the Texas Heartbeat law was allowed to stand. Once again, the Left was willing to overturn existing jurisprudence to achieve their pro-abortion goals. The irony must be noted of the Left accusing the Supreme Court of being unprincipled when it simply applies the Constitution, rather than twist the law and jurisprudence to achieve a given outcome.

## THE END OF *ROE V. WADE*

In the end, the right to abortion was overturned.[109] Progressives called the decision "political" and "judicial activism," while never acknowledging that at its inception, it was *Roe v. Wade* itself that was a political and activist decision. The abortion movement had been trying since the 1920s to liberalize abortion laws, only succeeding with *Roe v. Wade*. But when the same Court that granted their win took it away, they were caught flat-footed.

## PRO-LIFE VICTORY

This victory is incredible news for the country and for the culture in general. However, it comes in the teeth of resistance from the Biden Administration, which has been fighting to load the federal courts up with far-left pro-abortion activists. Perhaps that's only fair, because *Dobbs* is the culmination of decades of work by the pro-life movement—on culture, politics, and the law—to roll back abortion. However, without the Supreme Court's assistance, pro-abortion judges won't succeed, and without being able to persuade a majority of Americans, abortion on demand is largely a policy doomed for failure. As a reminder, it isn't because the abortion promoters are operating without assistance.

---

109    Dobbs v. Jackson Women's Health Organization, 597 U.S. ___ (June 23, 2022), No. 19–1392, Justia, https://supreme.justia.com/cases/federal/us/597/19-1392/.

## PRO-ABORTION MEDIA

The establishment media is even more left-wing on abortion than on other issues. This probably owes something to the social backgrounds of most reporters and other members of the media. They tend to be from upper-middle-class backgrounds, have little or no religious faith, are over-credentialed (too much time being brainwashed by left-wing college professors), and reside almost entirely inside deep-blue urban liberal enclaves.

The media has spent decades falsely implying that if the Supreme Court reverses *Roe v. Wade*, abortion will suddenly be illegal in America. This has had the effect of helping Democrats politically, since it makes Supreme Court action seem like a radical change. The truth, as everyone can now see, is that reversing *Roe* has not in and of itself banned abortion. In fact, it was *Roe* that imposed itself on state laws. What *Roe* (and associated decisions) did is in fact quite radical in the opposite direction, in that it stopped all levels of government from restricting abortion in any significant way. *Dobbs* merely lets the legislative process go forward in whatever way it chooses. Any careful read demonstrates that nowhere in *Dobbs* did the Court announce a ban on abortions or even recommend new restrictions on abortion. The ruling merely reversed *Roe v. Wade* and its successor *Planned Parenthood v. Casey*.[110]

Reversing these rulings defers action to the states. This is important because it "allows" states inclined to do so—such as Texas, Mississippi, and others—to restrict abortion, and several of them have. But many states have seen no change whatsoever

---

110    Planned Parenthood of Southeastern Pa. v. Casey, 510 U.S. 1309, No. A-655 (1994), Justia, https://supreme.justia.com/cases/federal/us/510/1309/.

to their laws, and at least five states post-*Dobbs* have worked to expand abortion access.[111]

Americans can expect the Biden Administration, however, to not only fight tooth and nail for more abortions all across the country, and in as many legislative efforts as he can, but to also lie about what's going on. Consider this: the DOJ has sued the state of Idaho over its abortion regulations that are nearly identical to those in Texas, Louisiana, and Mississippi. But those states are in the jurisdiction of the Fifth Circuit Court of Appeals, one of the most conservative in the nation. Idaho is in the jurisdiction of the Ninth Circuit, one of the most liberal. Surely this is no accident.

The Department of Justice may win in the Ninth Circuit, but ultimately, Idaho will take the case to the Supreme Court, where the prospects of success are not good for the DOJ. The Administration will say that the reversal of *Roe* is the end of democracy, a holocaust, and even worse than Donald Trump tweets. But remember that even this sweeping action by the Supreme Court has left roughly half the country with abortion laws more permissive than in Europe[112] or almost any country in the world, save China. For the pro-life movement, there is more work to be done.

The Biden Administration went in an even creepier direction in the leadup to the Supreme Court's *Dobbs* announcement. There was a leak of an early draft of the ruling that would eventually overturn *Roe v. Wade*. When the draft ruling was reported in May 2022—an event that constitutes an unprecedented and criminal betrayal of the judicial system—the Biden Administration

---

111  "State Legislation Tracker—Major Developments in Sexual & Reproductive Health," Guttmacher Institute, updated October 15, 2022, https://www.guttmacher.org/state-policy.

112  "European Abortion Laws: Where Do They Stand?" Center for Reproductive Rights, October 21, 2022, https://reproductiverights. org/center-reproductive-rights-european-abortion-laws/.

made excuses for the ensuing violent protests. One group listed the home addresses of Supreme Court justices. In an effort reminiscent of the "mostly peaceful" media euphemism for the 2020 riots, the Biden White House claimed that protesting outside of judges' homes, harassment, and publicizing personal information was perfectly legitimate.[113] This went too far for pro-choice Senator Dick Durbin (D-IL) who called these protests "reprehensible," saying, "Stay away from the homes and families of election officials and members of the court."[114] Even when Nicholas Roske was arrested for attempting to assassinate Justice Brett Kavanaugh (over the *Dobbs* ruling), the President initially refused to take questions about the matter, and days later only obliquely condemned threats against the Supreme Court.[115]

Additionally, over one hundred pro-life crisis pregnancy centers have been attacked, some with firebombs.[116] Biden and the DOJ have sat back mute.

---

113　Caroline Downey, "Psaki Refuses to Condemn Protests outside Justices' Homes, Accuses GOP of Hypocrisy for Calling Out Intimidation," *National Review*, May 10, 2022, https://www.nationalreview.com/news/psaki-refuses-to-condemn-protests-outside-justices-homes-accuses-gop-of-hypocrisy-for-calling-out-intimidation/.

114　Zack Smith, "'Stay Away From Homes and Families' of Justices,' Sen. Dick Durbin Tells Supreme Court Protesters. He's Right," *Daily Signal*, May 12, 2022, https://www.dailysignal.com/2022/05/12/stay-away-from-homes-and-families-of-justices-durbin-tells-supreme-court-protesters-hes-right/?.

115　Houston Keene, "Biden Yet To Speak On Alleged Kavanaugh Assassination Attempt, 2 Days After Arrest," *Fox News*, June 10, 2022, https://www.foxnews.com/politics/biden-kavanaugh-assassination-attempt-arrest.

116　Jessica Chasmar, "More Than 100 Pro-Life Orgs, Churches Attacked Since Dobbs Leak," *Fox News*, October 20, 2022, https://www.foxnews.com/politics/100-pro-life-orgs-churches-attacked-dobbs-leak.

## NEXT STEPS ON ABORTION AND THE BLACK COMMUNITY

President Biden, during the first two years of his presidency, has given a total commitment to abortion across the U.S., with a particular focus on black women, under the guise of "equity." However, a disproportionately large share of abortions is hardly equity.

With luck, most of President Biden's plans will continue to get bogged down in Congress or in the courts over the next several years, until finally he and they can be replaced with better options. (The good news is that many of his nominees are self-evidently radical or simply too goofy to take seriously. True story: for a senior financial regulatory position that requires Senate confirmation, Joe Biden in 2021 nominated a literal communist from the Soviet Union. Thankfully, even a few Senate Democrats found this too half-baked a gambit, and the nominee was withdrawn.)

President Biden's judges, his executive orders, his personnel appointments, and his Build Back Better plans for seemingly an abortion clinic on every street corner are to persuade even more black women than ever before to terminate their pregnancies before their babies even get a chance to compete for the American dream.

# CHAPTER SEVEN

# PUT Y'ALL BACK IN CHAINS

*I mean, you got the first mainstream African-American who*
*is articulate and bright and clean and a nice-looking guy.*

— *Joe Biden, about Barack Obama, 2007*

In 2007, on the day he would officially file his Federal Election Commission paperwork to launch his presidential campaign, Joe Biden gave an infamous interview to *The New York Observer* in which he offered this dubious compliment to Senator Barack Obama.

While not attacking Biden, Obama explained that the remarks were "historically inaccurate" and explained that "African-American presidential candidates like Jesse Jackson, Shirley Chisholm, Carol Moseley Braun, and Al Sharpton gave a voice to many important issues through their campaigns, and no one would call them inarticulate." Biden was forced to call a press conference to explain that his remarks were taken out of context.[1]

A few years later, he spoke at Senator Robert Byrd's funeral, calling the West Virginia Democrat a mentor, and went so far as to claim that "the Senate is a lesser place for his going."[2] Senator Byrd, a former "exalted cyclops" of the Ku Klux Klan, who had the

1    Thai and Barrett, "Biden's description of Obama."
2    President Barack Obama and Vice-President Joseph Biden, "Remarks at a Memorial Service for Senator Robert C. Byrd," The White House: President Barack Obama, July 2, 2010, https://obamawhitehouse.archives.gov/reality check/the-press-office/remarks-president-and-vice-president-a-memorial-service-senator-robert-c-byrd.

odious distinction of being the only Senator to have voted against both blacks named to the Supreme Court at that time,[3] who also managed to complain during a Fox News Sunday interview that Americans talks too much about race, and even complained that there are "white N******".[4]

Enough about Robert Byrd.

Early in his career, Joe Biden was anything but a racial moderate. While it is true that two of his great-great-grandfathers were slaveowners, Joe Biden can't be blamed for that.[5] He can be blamed, however, for his use of dog whistles for his own political advantage. In Biden's first U.S. Senate campaign against moderate Republican Senator Cale Boggs, he had ads printed in local papers that mocked Boggs, saying, "To Cale Boggs an unfair tax was the 1948 poll tax."[6] Boggs, a two-term Senator and former Delaware governor, was highly regarded as a civil rights supporter, having voted for the Twenty-fourth Amendment to the U.S. Constitution, which banned poll taxes.[7] Boggs had also voted in favor of the Civil Rights Acts of 1964,[8] the Voting

---

3    Theo Lippman, Jr., "One Senator Who in 1997 Voted Against…," *Baltimore Sun*, October 19, 1991, https://www.baltimoresun.com/news/bs-xpm-1991-10-19-1991292020-story.html. Robert Byrd cast no votes for Clarence Thomas and Thurgood Marshall when they were nominated to the Supreme Court.

4    "Top Senate Democrat Apologizes for Slur," CNN, March 4, 2001, https://edition.cnn.com/2001/ALLPOLITICS/03/04/byrd.slur/.

5    Celine Castronuovo, "Biden Ancestors Owned Enslaved People, Genealogist Says," *The Hill*, September 14, 2021, https://thehill.com/homenews/administration/572125-biden-ancestors-owned-enslaved-people-genealogist-says/. Jesse Robinett and Thomas Randle were listed in the 1800 census as s lave holders.

6    Bo Erickson, "When a Young Joe Biden Used His Opponent's Age Against Him," *CBS News*, June 4, 2019, https://www.cbsnews.com/news/when-a-young-joe-biden-used-his-opponents-age-against-him/.

7    "S.J. Res. 29. Approval of Resolution Banning the Poll Tax as Prerequisite for Voting in Federal Elections," Govtrack, March 27, 1962, https://www.govtrack.us/congress/votes/87-1962/s226.

8    "HR. 7152. Passage," Govtrack, June 19, 1964, https://www.govtrack.us/congress/votes/88-1964/s409.

Rights Act of 1965,[9] and even the confirmation of progressive Thurgood Marshall (the first black person nominated to the U.S. Supreme Court).[10]

Biden won.

In 1977, heading into his re-election campaign, Biden decided that opposing school desegregation was going to be his big legislative issue. However, instead of laying out practical and legal problems associated with forced busing, he preferred to racialize it, explaining that mandatory busing would cause his children to "grow up in a racial jungle."[11]

In order to "save" his children from growing up in a "racial jungle," Biden worked with open and notorious segregationists in the Senate to push his bill.[12] Today, when asked about his past efforts working with these bigots, he explains, "You got to deal with what's in front of you and what was in front of you was a bunch of racists and we had to defeat them."[13] Apparently, you defeat racists by recruiting them to join your anti-desegregation efforts. Or, in Joe Biden's words, "at least there was some civility" in the Senate.

Ah, yes, civility.

---

9    "To Pass S. 1564, The Voting Rights Act Of 1965," Govtrack, May 26, 1965, https://www.govtrack.us/congress/votes/89-1965/s78.

10   "Confirmation of Nomination of Thurgood Marshall, The First Negro Appointed to the Supreme Court," Govtrack, August 30, 1967, https://www.govtrack.us/congress/votes/90-1967/s176.

11   Grace Panetta, "Joe Biden Worried in 1977 That Certain De-Segregation Policies Would Cause His Children to Grow Up 'in A Racial Jungle'," *Business Insider*, July 15, 2019, https://www.yahoo.com/entertainment/joe-biden-worried-1977-certain-182631643.html.

12   Bradner, "Joe Biden Recalls."

13   Janell Ross, "Joe Biden Didn't Just Compromise With Segregationists. He Fought For Their Cause In Schools, Experts Say," *NBC News*, June 25, 2019, https://www.nbcnews.com/news/nbcblk/joe-biden-didn-t-just-compromise-segregationists-he-fought-their-n1021626.

By his third term, Senator Biden had received a leadership award from segregationist Democrat George Wallace. He traveled to Alabama to personally accept the award and gave a speech where he bragged that "we [Delawareans] were on the South's side in the Civil War."[14] And when given a chance to vote for Clarence Thomas, the second black person to be named to the Supreme Court, Biden voted no.[15]

In 2005, when he once again decided that he was ready to run for the White House, Biden went on Fox News. When asked a straightforward question about whether the country would elect an East Coast Democrat, Joe Biden took pains to assure America that he was no northeastern liberal. He explained, "My state was a slave state. My state is a border state. My state has the eighth-largest black population in the country."[16]

Later in 2006, while in the early stages of that presidential campaign, Biden reminded a South Carolina audience that Delaware had been a "slave state."[17] This history lesson was only presented to encourage those to support him who might otherwise think that he was a progressive on race relations. That was only a few months before his backhanded compliment to Senate colleague and 2008 primary competitor Barack Obama: "I mean,

14    Andy Kroll and Jamil Smith, "Joe Biden in 1987: 'We (Delawareans) Were on the South's Side in the Civil War'," *Rolling Stone*, July 19, 2019, https://www.rollingstone.com/politics/politics-news/joe-biden-delaware-civil-war-860886/.

15    Roll Call Vote 102nd Congress, 1st Session, On the Nomination of Clarence Thomas, October 15, 1991, https://www.senate.gov/legislative/LIS/roll_call_votes/vote1021/vote_102_1_00220.htm.

16    Vaughn Ververs, "Explain to Me Why This Isn't a Scandal," *CBS News*, December 5, 2006, https://www.cbsnews.com/news/explain-to-me-why-this-isnt-a-scandal/.

17    Kathleen Parker, "Joe Biden Releases His Inner Bubba," *Baltimore Sun*, December 8, 2006, https://www.baltimoresun.com/news/bs-xpm-2006-12-08-0612080143-story.html.

you got the first mainstream African-American who is articulate and bright and clean and a nice-looking guy."

Even while running in his successful presidential campaign in 2020, Biden didn't stop racializing the conversation. At a gathering of minority journalists, Biden offered that "unlike the African American community, with notable exceptions, the Latino community is an incredibly diverse community with incredibly different attitudes about different things."[18] Later, during the 2020 campaign, Biden went on Charlamagne Tha God's radio show to tell blacks who were unsure of whether to vote for him or Trump, "If you have a problem figuring out whether you're for me or Trump, then you ain't black!"[19]

To sum up, President Biden claims to be a champion for blacks. In fact, blacks are just a stepping stool for him to reach whatever high office he is pursuing. If it helps to be "pro-black," he is. But if being pro-black gets in the way, he'll just as easily go the other direction.

There is a big difference between helping blacks and exploiting racial tensions. Biden's record shows that he embraces the latter. In fact, with the record he has, it's surprising that he's so public with his embrace of blacks. The benefits of exploiting racial tensions seem to be the best explanation for his actions.

But the tide is turning. White women, the working class, and even Hispanics have abandoned Democrats, leaving blacks as their single largest bloc of supporters, but as more and more

18    Matthew Choi, "Biden: Latino Community is Diverse, 'Unlike the African American Community'," *Politico*, August 6, 2020, https://www.politico.com/news/2020/08/06/joe-biden-latino-african-american-remark-392354.

19    Eric Bradner, Sarah Mucha, and Arlette Saenz, "Biden: 'If You Have a Problem Figuring Out Whether You're for Me or Trump, Then You Ain't Black'," *CNN*, May 22, 2020, https://www.cnn.com/2020/05/22/politics/biden-charlamagne-tha-god-you-aint-black/index.html.

blacks see the actual record of the Left due to the policies that they have promoted, skepticism grows.

Conveniently, the White House has embraced a new tool to keep blacks in line: critical race theory.

## CRITICAL RACE THEORY HAS EXPLODED UNDER BIDEN'S WATCH

A once-obscure academic doctrine, Critical Race Theory (CRT) has swept the nation, starting after the death of George Floyd at the hands of Minneapolis police officers in 2020, and has been expanded dramatically by the Biden Administration. Developed by the Frankfurt School, CRT was promoted by Marxist academics affiliated with the Institute for Social Research at the Goethe University in Frankfurt, Germany. The think tank relocated to New York in 1934 to escape the Third Reich,[20] gaining a substantially wider audience for its most prominent figures, including Max Horkheimer, Theodor Adorno and Herbert Marcuse.

Most of the Frankfurt School returned to Germany after World War II,[21] but Marcuse—who held teaching positions at Columbia, Harvard, and the University of California at San Diego from 1952 to 1970—rose to prominence and is popularly known as the "Father of the New Left."[22]

Marcuse's vision of CRT tears at the very cultural fabric holding our diverse nation together, affecting classrooms, workplaces,

---

20　The Editors of Encyclopaedia Britannica, "Frankfurt School—German Research Group," *Encyclopaedia Britannica Online*, last updated September 5, 2022, https://www.britannica.com/topic/Frankfurt-School.

21　Nicki Lisa Cole, Ph.D., "The Frankfurt School of Critical Theory," ThoughtCo, updated on October 15, 2019, https://www.thoughtco.com/frankfurt-school-3026079#.

22　"The Many Dimensions of Herbert Marcuse," Brandeis University, accessed October 31, 2022, https://www.brandeis.edu/marcuse2014/about.html.

the U.S. Armed Forces, and every other institution in the country. And while CRT is certainly a bad idea for America as a whole, it is especially hurtful for black America.

The Marxist framework of CRS divides American society between oppressors and oppressed. However, it replaces alleged class or income oppression with alleged racial oppression. True to its Marxist origins, CRT is revolutionary in nature—seeking nothing less than the complete transformation of society, using race as the vehicle to bring about change.

CRT starts with the assumption that the United States is irredeemably racist, with privileged white males exercising dominance over everyone else, particularly working to ensure that people of color are kept in check.

## RACISM WITHOUT RACISTS

In CRT's analysis, race is an all-encompassing, monocausal explanation for any and all disparities in American society. CRT is thus able to magically explain how you can have racism without racists. CRT asserts that bigotry is systemic. That is, they say that acts of bigotry are inherent in the American system and that these actions are so subtle they are able to cause differences among racial groups—without any need for intervention by any individual actors, which can be identified.

This approach completely reverses our criminal justice system and that of most of the West.

Our system requires the identification of a victim and a victimizer. CRT ignores this requirement.

If I go out in the parking lot and discover my window is shattered, CRT implies that I should receive recompense from the broader society regardless of whether I identify the person who shattered my window. CRT doesn't care who broke the window— even if I broke the window myself.

Our justice system rightly requires a person to be accused when violations are alleged before compensation occurs to, among other things, prevent compensation to people who created their problem and also to prevent people who had nothing to do with the problem from being forced to contribute.

Purportedly, CRT claims racism is deeply embedded within every aspect of our society, a reflection of what it calls "white privilege," the jargon for the phenomenon that explains how the unjust American system works. No doubt the Wizard of Oz would envy the ability of American society to automatically and consistently achieve racist outcomes without the need for special intervention from human actors.

Like Dorothy in *The Wizard of Oz*, Americans can't get back home until they kill the Wicked Witch of systemic racism.

Is there actually a menacing force behind the curtain manipulating outcomes, or is it more likely that outcomes are random? In all other discussions, the use of logic, reason, and debate help to define the contours of a concept. CRT attempts to exempt itself from criticism by adopting its own vocabulary and suggesting that merely questioning its tenets is ipso facto proof of systemic racism. This is in fact a key failing of CRT—you're expected to accept its thesis on faith rather than rely on evidence.

## EQUITY ≠ EQUALITY

Also gone is equality of opportunity. CRT dispenses with MLK and his dream that his children would "one day live in a nation where they will not be judged by the color of their skin, but by the content of their character."[23] It is instead replaced by "equity," an

---

23    The Associated Press, "Martin Luther King Jr. 'Content of Character' Quote Inspires Debate," Masslive Media, January 21, 2013, https://www.masslive.com/news/2013/01/martin_luther_king_jr_content.html.

idea that differences among individuals require that each individual is allocated the resources necessary to reach an equal outcome. In contrast, equality means each individual is provided the same resources or opportunities without regard to the outcome.

Equality of opportunity doesn't happen naturally. It requires a commitment by society. But it can operate within broad contours like limiting special privileges for some or ensuring that others aren't disfavored. It can largely occur through private voluntary action, with the government operating as a back stop.

Consider this: presently, it is illegal to refuse to hire someone because of their race. But overwhelmingly, hiring decisions happen today in which no discrimination occurs. This is not the result of the Civil Rights Act, but it is the consequence of the broad acceptance by the American population of the non-discrimination principle.

On the other hand, equity requires a herculean effort and is all encompassing. Government must work to determine which groups have been disadvantaged and then restore them. It must determine how restoration is measured and calculate the appropriate amount. Are all blacks equally disadvantaged? Are Michael Jackson, Reggie Jackson, or Jesse Jackson all deprived to the same degree? How is that decision made? What of their children? Are the challenges and difficulties of the white working class ignored? Are Asians in need of equity? Within the community of blacks, are women and men to be treated similarly, or should the effort of restoration be modified on the basis of gender? These questions aren't easy, so getting answers will require a hugely broad bureaucracy. Note that this wouldn't be a one-time effort; it would require an ongoing operation. Is the requirement worth a commitment of 10 percent of America's GDP, or might it be 50 percent?

At present, practically every large employer and many medium-sized ones have an Equal Employment Opportunities office, as do colleges and universities. They also operate broadly within the public sector. Additionally, local governments have ordinances that impose similar requirements on small business.

Since CRT claims that the present existence of EEO compliance offices and rules are insufficient to overcome inequity, what type of compliance would be necessary? Would the equity force operate like the IRS, auditing people and companies? Might the IRS rule that "Americans are guilty until proven innocent" also applies to equity audits?

What areas of government would be exempt from equity requirements? Would new bridge construction or national security be exempt from equity? What percentage of the government bureaucracy would need to be devoted to achieving equity? Because inequity is systemic, according to CRT, rooting it out won't be easy. It doesn't simply disappear. Society must be eternally vigilant.

While these types of questions demonstrate the scope of the implications of equity versus equality, advocates often speak about it as a simple endeavor.

> *"We have to address this in a way that is about giving resources based on equity, understanding that we fight for equality, but we also need to fight for equity."*
>
> — VICE PRESIDENT KAMALA HARRIS[24]

In late September 2022, after Hurricane Ian tore through Florida, Vice President Harris suggested that assistance to those whose homes and livelihoods were destroyed should be distributed based on equity. Not only would such an approach dramati-

---

24    Ribhu Singh, "'Real People Shouldn't Talk Like This': Kamala Harris Slammed For Controversial Statement On Hurricane Ian Relief," *OK!*, October 4 2022, https://okmagazine.com/p/kamala-harris-slammed-equity-statement-hurricane-ian-relief/.

cally reduce the timeliness of assistance, but it would also be illegal under the present law. On the other hand, more than 75 percent of the residents of Lee County, Florida—where Ian hit directly— were still without power as of one week after the storm.[25] Under the auspices of CRT, assisting some Lee County residents to get power back on before others could indeed dramatically balance existing inequities. But at what cost?

CRT doesn't attempt to answer these questions or concerns. It pushes blithely for a rejection of all things American. Even the Declaration of Independence must be set aside. Its claim that all men are created equal contradicts CRT's claim that government must make people equal regardless of circumstance. Instead of avoiding quotas, CRT makes them vital, as they may provide the sole measure of success.

And CRT comes with a whole new vocabulary.

At least one CRT theorist, Columbia University Law Professor Kimberle Crenshaw[26], explains that systemic racism continues as a consequence of "intersectionality"[27]: the notion that there are interlocking systems of oppression in which race, gender, class, and other characteristics "intersect" and overlap.

Marcuse advocated censorship in the name of free-speech. Not unlike the claim in George Orwell's *Animal Farm*—"All ani-

---

25    "Governor Presses County Electric Cooperative to Expedite Restoration," *Fox4 WFTX,* October 2, 2022, https://www.fox4now.com/news/local-news/ governor-presses-county-electric-cooperative-to-expedite-restoration.

26    "Kimberlé Crenshaw on Intersectionality, More than Two Decades Later," African American Policy Forum, Columbia Law School, June 8, 2017, https://www.law.columbia.edu/news/archive/kimberle-crenshaw- intersectionality-more-two-decades-later.

27    Definition of intersectionality: "The complex, cumulative way in which the effects of multiple forms of discrimination (such as racism, sexism, and classism) combine, overlap, or intersect especially in the experiences of marginalized individuals or groups," *Merriam-Webster Dictionary Online,* https://www.merriam-webster.com/dictionary/intersectionality.

mals are equal, but some animals are more equal than other,"[28] Marcuse claimed some type of speech is worse than others. He advocated the "withdrawal of toleration of speech and assembly from groups and movements that promote aggressive policies, armaments, chauvinism, discrimination on the grounds of race and religion, or that oppose the extension of public services, social security, medical care, etc."[29]

If this sounds remarkably like today's claims by leftists that if you don't support a large welfare state, quotas, or giving leniency to violent criminals, you're a racist—welcome to the CRT world envisioned by Marcuse.

Before his death in 2018, Rev. Dr. Wyatt Tee Walker—executive director of the Southern Christian Leadership Council from 1960 through 1964, co-founder of the Congress of Racial Equality (CORE) and also Martin Luther King's "field general" against notorious Birmingham Commissioner of Public Safety Theophilus Eugene "Bull" Conner—made it clear that he believed King would oppose CRT if he were alive today. Walker said that CRT is "taking us in the wrong direction: separating even elementary school children into explicit racial groups and emphasizing differences instead of similarities" and that CRT embraces a "post-Marxist/postmodern approach that analyzes institutional group power structures rather than on a spiritual or one-to-one human level."[30]

---

28  "George Orwell, *Animal Farm*," Goodreads, accessed December 14, 2022, https://www.goodreads.com/quotes/6466-all-animals-are-equal-but-some-animals-are-more-equal.

29  "Repressive Tolerance" (full text), Robert Paul Wolff, Barrington Moore, Jr., and Herbert Marcuse, *A Critique of Pure Tolerance* (Boston: Beacon Press, 1969), pp. 95-137, https://www.marcuse.org/herbert/publications/1960s/1965-repressive-tolerance-fulltext.html.

30  Wyatt Tee Walker and Steve Klinsky, "A Light Shines in Harlem," *Real Clear Politics*, September 24, 2015, https://www.realclearpolitics.com/articles/2015/09/24/a_light_shines_in_a_harlem_charter_school_128189.html.

Anytime you see a policy that seeks to divide American society between oppressors and oppressed, with race as the measure of status, you've stumbled across racism.

On his first day in office, President Biden issued Executive Order 13895.[31] Purportedly, the order advances racial equity and supports underserved communities. In reality, it divides blacks and whites and limits economic opportunity for both, and as it is implemented, it is part of a long-term effort on the part of Biden and progressives to use racial wedges in the US for political advantage.

## BIDEN'S PUSH FOR CRT CRIPPLES BLACK AMERICA

### *CRT Programs Promote Segregation on College Campus*

CRT-inspired curricula encourage students to self-segregate into distinct racial groups. One CRT tool that has arisen on campus has been the adoption of "affinity spaces," which separate students and even staff on the basis of race, purportedly to make learning easier and to minimize misunderstandings. While this option doesn't promote learning or tolerance, it does normalize segregation.[32]

In 2021, Anderson University, a private college in Indiana, created a Racial Equity Task Force.[33] One of its actions was to cre-

---

31    President Joseph Biden, Exec. Order 13985 of January 20, 2021, 86 FR 7009, "Advancing Racial Equity and Support for Underserved Communities Through the Federal Government," https://www.federalregister.gov/documents/2021/01/25/2021-01753/advancing-racial-equity-and-support-for-underserved-communities-through-the-federal-government.

32    Rick Hess, "No, the Evidence Does Not Support Racial 'Affinity Spaces' in Schools," *Education Week*, September 1, 2021, https://www.edweek.org/teaching-learning/opinion-no-the-evidence-does-not-support-racial-affinity-spaces-in-schools/2021/09.

33    John S. Pistole, "Anderson University Statement on Racial Equity Task Force Listening Groups," *Anderson University Blog*, April 8, 2022, https://anderson.edu/blog/anderson-university-statement-on-racial-equity-task-force-listening-groups/.

ate so-called "listening sessions" on campus, where students were separated by race. There's little to no evidence that these aid student learning and clear evidence that they violate federal law: Title VI of the Civil Rights act specifically bans this behavior.[34] Per the statute, "No person in the United States shall, on the ground of race, color, or national origin, be excluded from participation in, be denied the benefits of, or be subjected to discrimination under any program or activity receiving Federal financial assistance." When schools or other institutions engage in this behavior, they violate the law and harm the idea of a color-blind society.

The President often refers to what he calls Jim Crow 2.0. CRT policies like affinity groups are Jim Crow 1.0, a terrible throwback to the nineteenth and early twentieth century. Back then, segregation supporters said that separation was a net positive for America, claiming it was good for blacks and whites. This sounds eerily similar to the arguments made by CRT advocates today.

Segregation, while especially bad for blacks, wasn't good for Americans, black or white,—it was only good for the elites who promoted segregation. Blacks suffered from having limits placed on their ability to eat out, dress, or get auto service, but the truth is every working-class American was hurt, too. White restaurant operators, dress shops, and auto repairmen suffered when they couldn't offer their services to any interested parties regardless of race. Overall, that meant fewer meals sold, dresses made, or cars serviced. When both blacks and whites realized that they would be happier and more prosperous if they could live, shop, and interact with whomever they wanted without government interference, the civil rights movement exploded.

---

34   "Education and Title Vi of the Civil Rights Act of 1964," Office of Civil Rights, U.S. Department of Education, https://www2.ed.gov/about/offices/list/ocr/docs/hq43e4.html.

Today, both the tuition-paying parents and the students themselves reject the idea that separating students along racial lines promotes equality. If parents are having difficulty understanding how segregating children by race can advance equality and reduce racial division, imagine how difficult it must be for the children.

The claim that "we must segregate schools in order to desegregate them" is reminiscent of the Vietnam cry that "we must burn the village in order to save it." It is likely to be just as effective.

Focusing on racial differences and forcing friends apart and into their racial "affinity groups" will create higher levels of racial animus, not reduce it.

## CRT Stymies Success

CRT presupposes that blacks (merely because of their race) have no control over their future. When they are convinced that nothing they do can improve their situation, many people quit trying. Such a thesis is especially corrosive in the black community, because in a community that needs to focus on playing catch up, both economically and socially, an entire generation can fail to take action out of fear of failure, and the economic and social gap will continue into the next generation.

The second way that success is stymied in the black community is that CRT insists on preferential, raced-based admissions to colleges and universities. Even if you agree with the goals of CRT, waiting for college to remedy past inequity doesn't work. Lower standards for minority admissions result in more students failing. If they are academically capable, but not at the top of their classes, the mismatch of minority students' skills with their non-minority counterparts (mostly enrolled through merit) at top tier schools results in contrast of grades and graduation rates.

Lower standards also advance the falsehood that black students are less intelligent or less capable than their peers. Tragically, this message is presented to blacks as well as whites.

The sad story is that when black kids fail in college, they may conclude that they are not college material. But in fact, if colleges use traditional admission standards, these young black students might find a different college where they would likely graduate and even thrive. Teaching black kids that they aren't college material is corrosive to their true abilities.

Notably, when mismatched minority students are enrolled in college and fail or drop out, another terrible lesson is learned: their counterparts may conclude that race and academic achievement correlate. Teaching young bright non-black students that blacks can't complete academically may leave the next generation of leaders in America with a false impression for the rest of their lives. That false perception is detrimental to blacks.

Furthermore, Americans do not agree with separate admission standards based on race. In fact, large percentages of whites and non-whites alike oppose these policies. A recent poll by Grinnell College revealed a two-to-one ratio of opposition by both whites and non-whites to affirmative action admissions.[35]

## CRT Requirements for Big Government Hurt Blacks

Part and parcel of CRT's agenda is the creation of a significantly larger role for Washington, D.C. Such an expansion poses a significant threat to black America.

When the country was established, America's Founding Fathers envisioned a thriving commercial republic where the government

---

35    National Poll, "A Majority of Americans Thinks Public Schools are on the Wrong Track, Fueled by How Racism is Addressed in the Classroom," Grinnell College, March 23, 2022, https://www.grinnell.edu/news/grinnell-poll-education-march-22.

had limited powers and Americans could be free to achieve "life, liberty and the pursuit of happiness."[36] They understood that the larger a government becomes, the greater the risk it will become oppressive—especially for political minorities. Consequently, one of the most important features of the American system is that it distributes power among three branches of government as well as to the states and operates with checks and balances.

> *I am not a friend to a very energetic government.*
> *It is always oppressive.*[37]

— THOMAS JEFFERSON to James Madison December 1787

A government of limited powers has been and will always be the friend of all minorities. Big government, on the other hand, always tramples liberty and hurts everyone. In fact, blacks have paid an enormous price whenever America has failed to heed Jefferson's warning. Despite this history, progressives continue to press for more and greater responsibilities—and authority—for government at both the state and federal level.

Starting shortly after the end of the Civil War, vicious and destructive laws were adopted in many parts of the country that placed severe restrictions on the life, liberty, and the pursuit of happiness of blacks.[38] Historians refer to these as Jim Crow laws,

---

36    "Declaration of Independence: A Transcription." America's Founding Documents, U.S. National Archives and Records Administration, last modified June 8, 2022, https://www.archives.gov/founding-docs/declaration-transcript.

37    Thomas Jefferson to James Madison, December 20, 1787, Founders Online, National Archives, https://founders.archives.gov/documents/Jefferson/01-12-02-0454.

38    Melvin I. Urofsky, "Jim Crow Law, United States [1877-1954]," *Encyclopaedia Britannica Online*, September 9, 2022, https://www.britannica.com/event/Jim-Crow-law.

named for "Jump Jim Crow," a minstrel routine (whose earliest performance was in 1828 by Thomas Dartmouth Rice).[39]

Jim Crow laws limited voting and property ownership for blacks, and generally made their lives harder. Initially, blacks could at least re-locate to other parts of the country that weren't as oppressive.

> *The Caucasians…are not going to let their standard of living be destroyed by negroes, Chinamen, Japs or any others.*
>
> — SAMUEL GOMPERS, founder of the
> American Federation of Labor, 1905

Perhaps feeling somewhat left out, Congress in the 1930s enacted a series of workplace laws that were specifically designed to harm the ability of blacks to compete in the labor market. This effort undid a remarkable phenomenon: until then, blacks had been employed at higher rates than whites.[40]

One of these anti-black federal laws was the 1931 Davis-Bacon Act that requires contractors to pay "prevailing wages" for all federally-funded construction projects over $2,000. "Prevailing Wages" were pay rates set by unions for union members. Unions limited blacks from membership as a means of artificially boosting the earnings power of their members. Blacks often worked for lower hourly rates than whites, which lowered market rates for "skilled labor" jobs.

During the Great Depression, private sector construction was all but halted, leaving public works projects as the only employment

---

39    The Editors of Encyclopaedia Britannica, "Thomas Dartmouth Rice," *Encyclopaedia Britannica Online,* last updated September 15, 2022, https://www.britannica.com/art/Jim-Crow-minstrel-routine-by-Rice.

40    Robert W. Fairlie and William A. Sundstrom, "The Emergence, Persistence, and Recent Widening of the Racial Unemployment Gap," *Compensation and Working Conditions* 52, no. 2 (2001): 252-270, doi: 10.2307/2525165.

option. Before enactment of Davis-Bacon blacks were over-represented in the construction industry all across America.[41] After Davis-Bacon blacks were all but banished from work in federal and state funded construction projects since they couldn't be members of the local union—a requirement of Davis-Bacon.

## ENGINEERING MARVEL OR RACIST RELIC?

The Hoover Dam is one of the wonders of the engineering world along with the Golden Gate Bridge and the International Space Station.[42] Today, the Hoover Dam uses some seventeen turbines to generate electricity for over a million homes and is critical to flood prevention along the Colorado River.[43] Work started on the project in 1931, and more than 21,000 men were hired to work on the project until it finished in 1936,[44] yet only twenty-four of them were black.[45] This isn't a unique situation. The Davis-Bacon Act did then exactly as it was designed to do: employers stopped hiring blacks and replaced them with whites.

Blacks ended up unemployed at significantly higher rates than their white counterparts.[46] While you might think that, during a

41    Jessica Looman, "Five Facts About Davis-Bacon and Related Acts," *U.S. Department of Labor Blog*, April 6, 2022, https://blog.dol.gov/2022/04/6/five-facts-about-davis-bacon-and-related-acts.

42    M. L. Stein, "The Mighty Hoover Dam Is a Modern Wonder," *Los Angeles Times*, April 20, 1986, https://www.latimes.com/archives/la-xpm-1986-04-20-tr-875-story.html.

43    Jessica Beasley, "The 7 Wonders of the Engineering World," *ICE Community Blog*, Institution of Civil Engineers, August 11, 2021, https://www.ice.org.uk/news-and-insight/ice-community-blog/august-2021/wonders-of-engineering-world.

44    "The Diversity of the Hoover Dam," National Park Service, February 12, 2019, https://www.nps.gov/lake/learn/news/the-diversity-of-the-hoover-dam.htm.

45    "Hiring African Americans," PBS, accessed December 14, 2022, https://www.pbs.org/wgbh/americanexperience/features/hoover-african-americans/.

46    Christopher Klein, "Last Hired, First Fired: How the Great Depression Affected African Americans," History Channel, August 31, 2018, https://www.history.com/news/last-hired-first-fired-how-the-great-depression-affected-african-americans.

serious economic downturn, employers would be even more willing than ever to accept the labor of blacks at lower cost—as they had been doing since the 1880s—the FLSA and Davis-Bacon made that unlawful.

Sadly, even when America was most vulnerable—during the Great Depression when jobs were scarce—Washington pushed its Big Government jobs-preference plan, which operated on the basis of race. Though Washington cloaked this racist agenda in the language of "prevailing wages," the ruse worked. Soon black unemployment was triple that of whites.[47]

Today, as in the early twentieth century, minority-owned firms tend to be small and unable to pay union wages. Davis-Bacon limits their ability to get federal construction projects today as it did when it was first passed. All Americans (including blacks) pay for federally funded construction projects today, yet Davis-Bacon means fewer black taxpayers disproportionately participate in those contracts because nearly half of all black union members work in the public sector.[48] Almost no federally funded construction is done directly by the federal government, which means that blacks are locked out of these projects, since even today they aren't admitted to construction unions.[49]

Repealing Davis-Bacon would create nearly 50,000 new jobs, and most of these would go to minorities. Today only 7.5 per-

47    "African American Life During the Great Depression and the New Deal,"
      Encyclopaedia Britannica Online, last updated December 2, 2022,
      https://www.britannica.com/topic/African-American/African-American-
      life-during-the-Great-Depression-and-the-New-Deal.

48    Cherrie Bucknor, *Black Workers, Unions, and Inequality* (Washington:
      Center for Economic and Policy Research, August 2016,) https://cepr.
      net/images/stories/reports/black-workers-unions-2016-08.pdf?v=2.

49    Travis Watson, "Union Construction's Racial Equity and Inclusion Charade,"
      *Stanford Social Innovation Review (SSIR)*, June 14, 2021, https://ssir.org/
      articles/entry/union_constructions_racial_equity_and_inclusion_charade.

cent of the construction workforce is black—a legacy of Davis-Bacon.[50]

## A KLANSMAN LEADS THE NEW DEAL

Another statute, the Fair Labor Standards Act, was even more deadly for black job creation, because it wasn't tied to federal appropriations. And its Klansman sponsor ended up getting appointed to the Supreme Court.

Democratic Senator Hugo Black from Alabama is the father of the forty-hour work week. He was also a member of the Ku Klux Klan. First elected in 1927, Hugo Black had joined the KKK a few years earlier in anticipation of a career in the United States Senate.[51] Although he would later claim that he had made a mistake in joining, the Klan had publicly backed his successful campaign.[52]

In 1933, he originally introduced a thirty-hour work-week bill, which was amended, and in 1938 became the Fair Labor Standards Act.[53]

While most Americans assume that the federal minimum wage law and the forty-hour work week were created to protect unskilled workers, the truth is more sinister. These laws were part of the racist effort in the early twentieth century to give white workers an advantage over black ones.[54]

---

50   *Construction Laborers*, Data USA (New York: Deloitte), accessed December 14, 2022, https://datausa.io/profile/soc/construction-laborers.

51   Hugo L. Black, Arlington Cemetery, Section 30, Grave 649-LH, https://www.arlingtoncemetery.mil/Explore/Notable-Graves/Supreme-Court/Hugo-Black.

52   Virginia Van Der Veer, "Hugo Black and the K.K.K.," *American Heritage* 19, no. 3 (1968), https://www.americanheritage.com/hugo-black-and-kkk.

53   "Hugo Black, 1937-1971," Supreme Court Historical Society, accessed December 14, 2022, https://supremecourthistory.org/associate-justices/hugo-black-1937-1971/.

54   Cooper, "Untold, Racist Origins."

In truth, much of the "New Deal" was racist.[55]

For instance, the NAACP opposed the National Industrial Recovery Act (NIRA) and the Social Security Act (SSA) of 1935.[56] The NIRA was derided by blacks as the "negro removal act."[57] Once enacted, the SSA's limits resulted in two-thirds of blacks throughout the country being ineligible for the program and significantly expanded the black-white income gap.[58] And when the Supreme Court struck down the NIRA in 1935, blacks cheered louder than the NIRA's big business opponents.[59]

For men of ambition, the New Deal created significant opportunities, regardless of its impact on blacks. Hugo Black was a great soldier for the New Deal who took advantage of those opportunities for advancement. As a result, FDR nominated Black to replace retiring Justice Willis Van Devanter on the Supreme Court. Black had acknowledged to several of his Senate colleagues that he had joined the Klan, but his official line was that he had resigned his membership. Later, the Roosevelt White House would deny any knowledge of his Klan membership.

---

55  Most historians agree that the exclusion of agricultural and domestic employees in the National Labor Relations Act should be understood as part of the pattern of racist exclusions enacted in the major New Deal Era statutes. See, e.g., Paul Frymer, *Black and Blue: African Americans, the Labor Movement, and the Decline of the Democratic Party* (Princeton: Princeton University Press: December 9, 2007), 27-28.

56  James Gilbert Cassedy, "African Americans and the American Labor Movement," *Prologue* 29, no. 2 (Summer, 1997), Federal Records and African American History, National Archives, https://www.archives.gov/publications/prologue/1997/summer/american-labor-movement.html.

57  Ken I. Kersch, "Blacks and Labor—the Untold Story," *National Affairs, Inc.*, American Enterprise Institute, Summer 2002, https://www.nationalaffairs.com/public_interest/detail/blacks-and-laborthe-untold-story.

58  Derrick Johnson, "Viewing Social Security Through The Civil Rights Lens," *The Crisis*, August 14, 2020, https://naacp.org/articles/viewing-social-security-through-civil-rights-lens.

59  Kersch, "Blacks and Labor."

Reporter Ray Sprigle of the *Pittsburgh News Gazette* won a Pulitzer for his series exposing Black's racist past, including that he had been awarded a KKK "Golden Passport" as well as holding a life-time membership in the Klan.[60] Sadly, the expose didn't stop Black's confirmation or force him to resign.

The Davis-Bacon Act still exists, and its effects that hurt blacks in the workforce persist to this day.[61] .Today, commentators see the unemployment gap between black and white Americans and wonder how it persists—and the answer is that progressive regulations do what they were designed to do.

The alliance between blacks and Big Government advocates has been a one-way relationship since it began. Radicals and progressives who worship at the altar of an ever bigger and more encompassing government have rallied the votes of blacks to create a behemoth that taxes, regulates, and even strangles Americans' economic success in a way that the nation's Founders never could have imagined. Meanwhile, the progressives pursue their own goals while the interests of blacks become further and further removed from a central place in American society. Ultimately, the New Deal is a raw deal.

> *What is freedom? It is the right to choose one's own employment.*
>
> — FREDERICK DOUGLASS, Massachusetts Anti-Slavery Society Boston Speech, 1865[62]

---

60   "Raymond Sprigle of *Pittsburgh Post-Gazette*," The Pulitzer Prizes, accessed December 14, 2022, https://www.pulitzer.org/winners/raymond-sprigle.

61   *Project 21: Blueprint for a Better Deal for Black America* (Washington: National Center for Public Policy Research, April 2018), https://nationalcenter. org/project-21-blueprint-for-a-better-deal-for-black-america/.

62   Frederick Douglass, "What the Black Man Wants" (Boston Massachusetts Anti-Slavery Society, Boston, MA, April 1865), https://historynewsnetwork.org/article/179721.

## CRT IS REVERSE RACISM

If the anti-black bigotry of their past isn't enough, Democrats' newest effort, anti-white bigotry, is just as bad. Calling for what they call "restorative justice," CRT seeks to use Washington to squash whites to aid blacks. The justified backlash has and will foment anti-black racial division. The new term is "anti-racism." CRT advocate Ibram X. Kendi explains, "The only remedy to past discrimination is present discrimination."[63] In other words, anti-racism is just racism with a new target: whites. Kendi's solution is completely unbounded from cause and effect. Instead of holding actual bigots responsible for their bad behavior and forcing them to restore to their victims the value of the property or income taken from them, "anti-racism" proposes Jim Crow twenty-first-century style.

It is true that finding living bigots and their living victims is difficult. But justice involves punishing or penalizing *perpetrators*, not the richest or the nearest white person. When a bank is robbed, police don't arrest any random person just to close the case. Law enforcement has to do the hard work of finding the bank robber.

CRT supporters think that race alone is a proxy for guilt and any refusal to accept this standard is proof of racial animus. Actually, refusing to use race alone is proof of a willingness to seek justice.

Under the CRT standard, even the Civil Rights Act of 1964 would fail. Title II of the Civil Rights Act prevents a restaurant or store from denying an individual access on the basis of his or her race, color, religion or national origin. It requires anyone who

---

63    Ibram X. Kendi, "Ibram X. Kendi Defines What it Means to be An Anti-Racist," Penguin Extracts, June 9, 2020, https://www.penguin.co.uk/articles/2020/june/ibram-x-kendi-definition-of-antiracist.html.

claims racial mistreatment to provide the name of the place, the time and date, and the circumstances of the discrimination. Thus, Title II doesn't allow aggrieved parties to sue Walmart or Home Depot for discrimination in the past. Notably, these two companies didn't even exist before the civil rights era.

CRT urges its followers to go where even civil rights statutes fear to tread. Pursuing what they call "restorative justice," CRT divides America between the racial haves and the racial have nots. The haves get benefits and advantages on the basis of their race. The have nots face penalties and obstacles on the basis of their race. In practice, there is no difference between the Jim Crow of the past and the Jim Crow of our time. In the twentieth century, black Americans rightly chose the American legal and political system to rectify wrongs. Today's activists avoid the legal and political system to accomplish their ends.

Make no mistake: penalizing Americans (some of whom don't even have ancestors in America), who are far removed from the codes of the Jim Crow era, only creates new unfairness and discrimination.

## CRT WILL CAUSE HOSTILITY TOWARD BLACKS

Tribalism doesn't work for a minority. If CRT advocates have their way, Americans will break down within ethnic groups, ultimately allowing the smaller groups to be overrun by the larger groups. The last thing blacks or any minority group should want is policy based on ethnicity. Minorities thrive when the rules in the public square apply to individuals rather than to groups. Instead of separatism, minorities rightly pursue, *and the Civil Rights Act affirms*, policies that protect all Americans, not just particular groups. Contrary to the CRT mantra, racist government policy is exactly the wrong way to address concerns for minorities. As U.S.

Supreme Court Chief Justice John Robert wrote in the 2007 case *Parents Involved in Community Schools v. Seattle School District No. 1*, "the way to stop discrimination on the basis of race is to stop discriminating on the basis of race."[64]

Transforming the United States into a radical leftwing country with no protections for individuals wouldn't reduce racial discrimination but increase it. The history of autocratic regimes reveals that minority rights are regularly trampled.[65]

Moreover, restoring a Jim Crow rule that allows race as the basis for privilege and punishment isn't just a bad idea. But if normalized it will ultimately harm blacks. For instance, what will blacks—a minority or any other racial minority—do if the political tide shifts and instead of policies *favoring* blacks, society decides to formally marginalize minority groups on the basis of race claiming that the pro-black policies of CRT need to be corrected for. Laws based on protections of all individuals makes that less likely. Laws based on preferential advantage for groups on the basis of race threaten all individuals—especially minorities.

Joe Biden and much of his party have come full circle on the issue of race. Instead of disregarding race and recognizing that it is a poison that should be avoided at all cost, he has embraced the use of race as a policy tool.

According to President Biden and his party, America is more racist today than it once was. Twenty-first-century racism is more insidious because it is a bigotry that dare not speak its name. Instead, it allegedly hides in shadows, and its adherents refuse to acknowledge their support.

---

64    Parents Involved in Community Schools v. Seattle School Dist. No. 1, 551 U.S. 701 (2007) (June 28, 2007), Justia, accessed November 1, 2021, https://supreme.justia.com/cases/federal/us/551/701/.

65    See Cuba, Germany, the former Soviet Union generally.

Biden and his allies have created a far more sinister form of racism. It doesn't wear hoods; it doesn't burn crosses; it does not physically intimidate. Pretending to be part of the effort to stop bigotry against minorities, "anti-racism" adopts almost all of the tools of the Jim Crow era to achieve its aims. Committed to rooting out this new bigotry, President Biden puts on the armor of Don Quixote and, in the process, tramples the rights and freedoms of innocent men and women.

This time, any white person is suspect. Separate treatment, housing, and even dining is demanded. Employees are to be divided by race and evaluated accordingly. Schools are encouraged to have separate dwellings, and admissions policies effectively block many Asians and whites from attending elite schools.

Biden and his army of "anti-racists" have transmogrified bigotry to mean "mere advocacy of deregulation, free-markets, and equal justice before the law." If you don't buy into their efforts, you, too, are categorized as a racist.

For example, the White House forced the Department of Defense to hold an all-Services one-day stand-down to address "extremism" within the nation's Armed Forces.[66] In the midst of recruitment struggles, this was exactly the wrong directive, and it certainly wasn't needed. A 2019 Pew Research Center report describes the nation's military now as "more racially and ethnically diverse than in previous generations."[67] In fact, significant

---

66  Secretary of Defense Lloyd Austin memorandum for Senior Pentagon Leadership, Defense Agency and DOD Field Activity Directors, "Stand-Down to Address Extremism in the Ranks," February 5, 2021, https://media.defense.gov/2021/Feb/05/2002577485/-1/-1/0/STAND-DOWN-TO-ADDRESS-EXTREMISM-IN-THE-RANKS.PDF.

67  Amanda Barroso, *The Changing Profile of the U.S. Military: Smaller in Size, More Diverse, More Women in Leadership* (Washington: Pew Research Center, September, 2019), https://www.pewresearch.org/fact-tank/2019/09/10/the-changing-profile-of-the-u-s-military/.

racial progress has been made in the military. According to the Defense Department's 2017 Annual Demographics Report, 57 percent of U.S. Service members today are white, a significant change from 64 percent in 2004.[68] The report also shows there are "more women serving in the military, and as ranking officers, in 2017 than ever before."[69]

### Demographic shifts in today's military show growing representation of racial and ethnic minorities

*% of active duty forces that are ...*

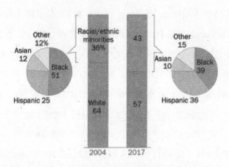

Note: Includes only the four military branches of the Department of Defense. "Other" includes American Indian, Native Hawaiian or Pacific Islander, multiracial, and other/unknown. The army does not report "multiracial." White, black, Asian and "other" include those who are non-Hispanic. Hispanics are of any race.
Source: U.S. Department of Defense 2004 and 2017 annual Demographics Reports.

**PEW RESEARCH CENTER**

Blacks have willingly served and died in every single one of the country's wars all the way back to the Revolutionary War.

---

68  *Profile Of The Military Community*, Office of the Deputy Assistant Secretary of Defense for Military Community and Family Policy (ODASD (MC&FP)) (Washington: Department of Defense, 2017), https://download. militaryonesource.mil/12038/MOS/Reports/2017-demographics-report.pdf.

69  Barroso, *Changing Profile*.

Today, black men make up 17 percent of all Service members—nearly two and a half times their population percentage.[70] Far from being hostile to blacks, the U.S. military in the twenty-first century is a place for acquiring leadership and training skills, and blacks, especially men, agree.

On the other hand, the President's order promotes an inferiority doctrine that Frederick Douglass warned about at the conclusion of the Civil War: "If the Negro cannot stand on his own legs, let him fall also. All I ask is, give him a chance to stand on his own legs! Let him alone! If you see him on his way to school, let him alone, don't disturb him!"[71]

CRT and the White House have taken the black inferiority doctrine to new heights. In fact, racism has lost all meaning under President Biden's watch. No longer must a racist skulk around wearing hoods at night, spilling ballot boxes, or engaging in acts of intimidation against a fellow American on the basis of race. Today, mere advocacy of deregulation, free-markets, and equal justice before the law can get anyone tagged as a bigot.

Today, one in six newlyweds is married to someone of a different race. This means that more than 11 million people are intermarried.[72] The most dramatic increases in intermarriage have occurred among black newlyweds.[73]

---

70    Cooper, *Making Black America Great Again*, p. 137.

71    Douglass, "What the Black Man Wants."

72    Gretchen Livingston And Anna Brown, "Intermarriage in the U.S. 50 Years After Loving v. Virginia," Pew Research Center, May 18 2017, https://www.pewresearch.org/social-trends/2017/05/18/intermarriage-in-the-u-s-50-years-after-loving-v-virginia/.

73    Livingston and Brown, *Intermarriage*.

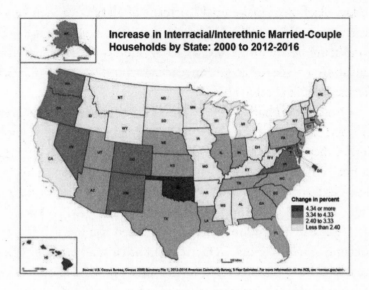

US Census Bureau.[74]

Consider workplace discrimination claims. According to the most recent data, for the last five years, the number of Equal Employment Opportunity Commission claims of racial discrimination have steadily declined.[75]

---

74   Lydia Anderson, Rose M. Kreider, and Brittany Rico, "Growth in Interracial and Interethnic Married-Couple Households," U.S. Census Bureau, July 9, 2018, https://www.census.gov/library/stories/2018/07/interracial-marriages.html.

75   Press Release, "EEOC Releases Fiscal Year 2015 Enforcement and Litigation Data," U.S. Equal Employment Opportunity Commission (EEOC), February 11, 2016, https://www.eeoc.gov/newsroom/eeoc-releases-fiscal-year-2015-enforcement-and-litigation-data.

US Equal Employment Opportunity Commission.

| Enforcement and Litigation Case Report | |
|---|---|
| 2020 | 22,064 |
| 2019 | 23,976 |
| 2018 | 24,600 |
| 2017 | 28,528 |
| 2016 | 31,027 |

Even the gap between whites and blacks in prisons has narrowed dramatically. According to U.S. Bureau of Prisons, the number of blacks sentenced to prison dropped by 31 percent from 2007 to 2017, substantially shrinking the gap with whites.[76]

76    Jennifer Bronson, Ph.D., and E. Ann Carson, Ph.D., *Prisoners in 2017,* Office of Justice Programs, Bureau of Justice Statistics (Washington: U.S. Department of Justice, April 2019), https://bjs.ojp.gov/content/pub/pdf/p17.pdf.

## Racial and ethnic gaps shrink in U.S. prison population

*Sentenced federal and state prisoners by race and Hispanic origin, 2007-2017*

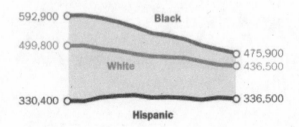

Note: Whites and blacks include those who report being only one race and are non-Hispanic. Hispanics are of any race. Prison population is defined as inmates sentenced to more than a year in federal or state prison.
Source: Bureau of Justice Statistics.

**PEW RESEARCH CENTER**

US Bureau of Prisons.

Prior to the onset of the pandemic, employment for blacks in America had exploded. Through 2019, black unemployment stood at the lowest levels recorded since the onset of the Great Society.[77]

---

77    Cooper, *Making Black America Great Again*, p. 26.

## U.S. and African American unemployment rates since 197

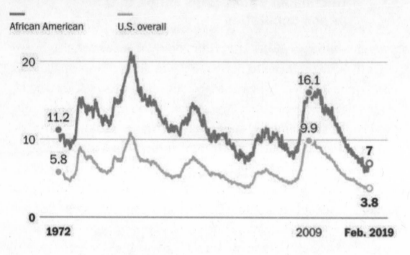

African American    U.S. overall

US Bureau of Labor Statistics.

Far from America being a place where blacks are stymied because of their race, the measures of integration continue to show the great strides that America has made. Whether remaining anti-black discrimination is overt, or covert—as CRT supporters claim—the evidence shows that using government to protect blacks is, as history has shown, harmful for blacks and the rest of the country.

For Joe Biden and his supporters, these facts are inconvenient. They are seeking out the "racism" that Americans simply aren't committing, and this quest creates a challenge to their very rationale: if blacks don't need progressives to succeed, the modern Left's entire house of cards collapses. The better America becomes, the louder they condemn, calling into question whether they were ever committed to racial equality, or—like Democrats of the nineteenth and twentieth centuries—used race solely as a means of gaining votes.

The country's founding is predicated on the notion of self-government, which requires the willingness and effort of citizens to enter the public square to persuade their fellow countrymen. This task is much harder when the policies of progressives attack the center-right principles that Americans live by day in and day out. President Biden and his supporters resort to the use of unfair claims of racism to bolster their poor ability to make their case.

Whether they are called quotas, preferences, or anti-racism, policies that single out Americans of any race for either an advantage or disadvantage are dangerous, and they contravene MLK's dream. President Biden and his party's opposition to colorblind policies in the allocation of public goods and services is reminiscent of the segregation policies of the early twentieth century. Under President Biden, America is divided, and Americans (black, white, or brown) all suffer and are deprived. By resorting to race-baiting and racial separatism, Biden undermines the real interests of blacks: to live in a society where racial bigotry recedes into the background and people of every race, from every background, can prosper.

## EPILOGUE

Joe Biden's record of mistreatment has gotten little to no attention from the mainstream media. Yet Black Americans have lost ground in so many areas, in so little time—primarily as a consequence of the policies of Joe Biden and progressives—that it should be front page news.

Whether motivated by malign intent or ignorance, Biden's polices—and decades of progressive approaches—have shackled black Americans, robbing them of their potential.

Macroeconomic policies—that encourage growth and allow people to tap into their potential—matter to all Americans, but they are particularly important to blacks, who need to catch up with the rest of the country. America needs to embrace a growth strategy that focuses on increasing the size of the pie, rather than one that attempts to divide its existing assets by taking from some and giving to another. This strategy of division has crippled blacks and other struggling groups, including the white working class.

In its efforts to cheer on greater government intervention, the mainstream media has failed to document the amazing improvements that have occurred in the lives of blacks during boomtimes. Whether under Reagan, Clinton, or Trump, blacks prospered when the economy grew. In fact, under the previous president, blacks became more prosperous and at faster rates than the general population.

The same is true with bust times. The media has failed to discuss the travails of blacks during the Carter, Bush 43, Obama, and Biden economic busts. Yet it was during these periods that blacks lost more ground than the rest of the population.

Our founders intended the First Amendment's protections of the news media to insure that all Americans have the information they need to keep government accountable for its actions.

The narrative pushed by progressives today—that the prosperity gap between blacks and the rest of America is due to "systemic racism"—has no basis in data. This narrative overwhelmingly fails to explain why blacks gained so much and so fast in prosperity during the Reagan and Trump years, relative to the rest of nation.

Philosopher George Santayana said, "Those who cannot remember the past are condemned to repeat it."[78] America has

---

78    George Santayana, The Life of Reason, 1905. From the series Great Ideas of Western Man.

already experienced a period of racial separation and its correlated economic deprivation once. As we are twenty years into the twenty-first century, now is a good time that all Americans should resolve to ensure that the 21st century will not be a period of racial separation and economic deprivation.

In the twentieth century, the leftist party, the Democrats, had to be dragged kicking and screaming to embrace racial equality, only coming together after the rest of the country together to reject their separatism. Now, as the twenty-first century starts, progressives, including President Biden, are once again rejecting the idea of individuals being equal before the law.

Then, some of their supporters were genuinely racists, but most were merely politically opportunistic. Today, the same is true. There are some Democrats today who are true separatists, but most, including President Biden, are simply politically opportunistic. Tragically, the damage is the same.

## A RACIAL ANTINOMIAN HERESY

Separating America into the racial haves and the racial have-nots undermines a bedrock principle of America: equality under the law for everyone. And it does something more: it leads to the adoption of a "racial antinomian heresy." "Antinomianism" literally translates from ancient Greek as "against law"—it rejects the idea that rules or laws should be adhered to by its creators, positing that they are somehow above the law they make.

The Apostle Paul was confronted with this issue within the early Christian church. He explains in the New Testament that the followers of Christ may not break God's laws, merely because they will be forgiven if they do. He says that the laws of God are just and holy and that everyone should strive to adhere to them. But if and when we fail while trying to adhere to them, we receive forgiveness given as part of God's purpose and design.[79] If we actively work to break God's law, under the idea that we can do whatever we want, we actually will not receive grace and "cannot inherit the kingdom of God."[80]

The same principle is true with "racial antinomian heresy," which promotes a theory that almost any injustice is warranted in the effort to end anti-black bigotry. This approach is wrong-headed. But the idea that blacks have been mistreated in the past does not justify ignoring bad behavior by blacks today. Mistreating poor whites or Asians to compensate for past mistreatment is unjust. There should be no special group that is exempt from the laws and codes of conduct in America. All groups—black, white, brown, and other—occasionally break the law, and anyone who does should face the consequences.

Remember, the sin against Rosa Parks wasn't denying her a place on the bus because of her race. It was denying her a place on the very bus that she as a citizen had already paid for with her tax dollars. Rosa Parks isn't aided by punishing nonblack Americans who also have paid to ride the bus.

In the spring of 2021, a black man injured twenty-nine people in a mass attack in a New York City subway station. Disguised as a construction worker, he took out "a 9mm semiautomatic Glock and fired 33 rounds at commuters, hitting 10 victims and leaving at least 19 others wounded."[81] In what investigators described as

---

79   Romans 3:25–26 NIV "…in His forbearance God had passed over the sins that were previously committed, to demonstrate at the present time His righteousness, that He might be just and the justifier of the one who has faith in Jesus…"

80   I Corinthians 6:9 NIV.

81   Joe Marino et al. "At Least 29 Injured in Brooklyn Subway Shooting, Undetonated Devices Found," *New York Post*, April 12, 2022, https://nypost.com/2022/04/12/nypd-investigating-possible-explosion-in-brooklyn-subway-station/.

a "miracle," none of the explosives went off, and the handgun he was carrying jammed.

Did President Biden speak out about the incident? Did the media seek to assess what the racial implications were of this event? Was the attack discussed on Twitter as an example of race relations in America? No. But can you imagine what would have happened if the attacker had been white?

The "racial antinomian heresy" excuses bad behavior by blacks while seeking out special opprobrium for criminal acts by whites. This is dangerous. If it is not stopped, it will mean more violent behavior by black criminals and greater enmity against blacks by whites and every other racial group. The "racial antinomian heresy" will lead America to hell. Tragically, the broad move by Biden and the progressives to decriminalize some violent behavior, in order to protect blacks, is seen as a green light by some within the black community to carry out an anti-white racial animus. This is no exaggeration. Anti-white bigotry is growing in America, and it is just as insidious as anti-black bigotry. American leaders, not just the elected ones, must reject the idea that some racially motivated bad acts are excusable. Both Washington and news media must be united in condemning this trend. President Biden should lead the effort.

The fixation on the phony charge that "white supremacy" is a growing danger has also limited America's ability to focus on all types of racial animus regardless of the perpetrator. Ultimately fighting bigotry, regardless of who the victims are, is made harder for progressives, including President Biden, because the notion that incidents of racial unfairness travel in only one direction buttresses their political power. They all but ignore racial injustice to whites. If progressives set a standard and example of equality for all, they believe they risk losing their hold on black America

But America, the exemplar of self-government in the world, cannot succeed if Americans allow these new ethnic divisions to continue. Instead of greater interference in the freedom of Americans to interact, they need less. Instead of society attempting to impose organizational arrangements using race, people must make their own choices as individuals.

Black Americans will be on the path to prosperity when all Americans embrace principles that are uniquely American: unfettered capitalism, freedom of conscience, and an embrace of traditional concepts of faith that were critical to America's success. Restoring the primacy of these principles will bring the kind of opportunity and achievement for blacks that almost all Americans seek. The outlook need not be bleak: recent experience shows the way, and we know what works and what doesn't.

The eight years of the Obama Administration resulted in a terrible trend for blacks, in contrast to the four years of the Trump Administration that saw fantastic achievements for blacks. Every year from 2010 to 2016, the homeownership rate for blacks declined.[82] Every year of the Trump Administration, the homeownership rate for blacks increased.[83] The white-black employment gap expanded under Obama and shrank under Trump.[84] In absolute terms, the number of blacks in poverty was substan-

---

82  *Snapshot of Race and Home Buying in America*, National Association of REALTORS® Research Group (Washington: National Association of Realtors, February, 2022), https://cdn.nar.realtor/sites/default/files/documents/2022-snapshot-of-race-and-home-buying-in-the-us-04-26-2022.pdf.

83  NAR, *Snapshot of Race.*

84  Andre M. Perry, "Black workers are being left behind by full employment," Brookings Institution, June 26, 2019, https://www.brookings.edu/blog/the-avenue/2019/06/26/black-workers-are-being-left-behind-by-full-employment/.

tially lower under the Trump Administration[85] than during the Obama years.[86]

President Biden could be a historic figure if he put down the woke sword and embraced the shield of American exceptionalism. Instead of his redistributionist sympathies, he could genuinely seek the success of all sectors of America. Imagine an America where blacks and whites regularly achieve employment gains and where blacks buy homes and cars at the same levels as whites.

Not only is that world possible, but it once existed. Prior to the Great Depression, more blacks were likely to be born in two-parent households than Americans as a whole. Blacks were least likely to be in federal prison and more likely to be hired than any other ethnicity. A hundred years ago, the policies of Warren G. Harding and Calvin Coolidge made this possible.

Today, blacks as a political force made Biden's presidency possible, but blacks must close the door on his re-election—for America's sake and for their own. The wealth gap, underemployment, and other ailments in the black community can only be reversed by recognizing that these are in fact a "feature, not a bug" of progressive policies. These harmful woke policies have caused suffering and pain for the whole country, particularly for black Americans.

President Biden and the progressives have cynically exploited race to achieve their goals to reinvent the economy and, indeed, America. Blacks are merely a stepping stool to those goals.

---

85    Cooper, *Making Black America Great Again*, p. 43.

86    Zane Mokhiber and Jessica Schieder, *By the Numbers: Income and Poverty, 2017, Working Economics Blog* (Washington: Economic Policy Institute, September 12, 2018), https://www.epi.org/blog/by-the-numbers-income-and-poverty-2017/.

Woke policies chain black America. They stifle hopes and dreams. Core strategies of faith, family, and commerce are the solution to being unshackled.

If the progressives can't be trusted to end their pernicious efforts, blacks must and should reject them. Black Americans must embrace the ideas of Frederick Douglass and today's Thomas Sowell. Instead of accepting carve-outs and special subsidies cynically offered by Biden Administration and the wokes, blacks must tap into the economic opportunities that exist all across America. To become "unchained," black America must loosen Biden's grip on black America.

American blacks need to head in a new direction.

In the process, black America—and all of America—can thrive and prosper.